# Politics, Language, and Culture

**Recent Titles in**
**Series in Language and Ideology**

# Politics, Language, and Culture

*A Critical Look at Urban School Reform*

JOSEPH W. CHECK

Series in Language and Ideology
*Edited by Donaldo Macedo*

PRAEGER

**Westport, Connecticut
London**

Library of Congress Cataloging-in-Publication Data

Check, Joseph W., 1947–
    Politics, language, and culture : a critical look at urban school reform / Joseph W. Check.
      p.  cm.—(Series in language and ideology, ISSN 1069–6806)
    Includes bibliographical references and index.
    ISBN 0–89789–647–5 (alk. paper)
    1. Education, Urban—Political aspects—United States—Case studies.  2. Educational
change—United States—Case studies.  3. Multicultural education—United States—Case
studies.  I. Title.  II. Series.
    LC5131.C45  2002
    370′.9173′2—dc21     2002021576

British Library Cataloguing in Publication Data is available.

Library of Congress Catalog Card Number: 2002021576
ISBN: 0–89789–647–5
ISSN: 1069–6806

First published in 2002

Praeger Publishers, 88 Post Road West, Westport, CT 06881
An imprint of Greenwood Publishing Group, Inc.
www.praeger.com

Printed in the United States of America

The paper used in this book complies with the
Permanent Paper Standard issued by the National
Information Standards Organization (Z39.48–1984).

10 9 8 7 6 5 4 3 2 1

# Contents

# Acknowledgments

I can mention only a few of the many people who helped and encouraged me in the writing of this book. Donaldo Macedo offered me the opportunity to turn a fuzzy set of ideas into a full-blown treatment of urban reform. Olga Frechon, Donna Muncey, and Ellie Kutz served as responsive readers and wise critics at crucial stages. Carol Tateishi helped me understand the complicated workings of the San Francisco and Oakland school systems, and arranged focus groups with Bay Area practitioners. Linda Eisenmann offered important insights about the history of urban education.

I am particularly grateful to the many practitioners, both named and unnamed, who allowed me to learn from them, both on and off the record. My colleagues in the Boston Writing Project and throughout the National Writing Project network were unfailingly generous with their time, acting as a supportive yet critical audience for concepts still in the formative stage. *The Quarterly* of the National Writing Project printed an earlier version of Chapter 4.

Teachers and administrators in many parts of the country gave me insider insights into the workings of their urban schools and classrooms. These include many of my students in the Leadership in Urban Schools Doctoral Program at the University of Massachusetts Boston.

Last but far from least, my wife Angela and my children Joe and Pietra gave me continuous support and encouragement throughout the entire project.

## Part I

# Context, History, and a Composite Case

## INTRODUCTION

Since the publication of *A Nation at Risk*[1] in 1983, attempts to reform our K-12 educational system have steadily mounted in scope, complexity, and cost.

Within the reform debate powerful voices have promoted a "calamitist" view of public schools. Calamitists argue that American schools are in an unprecedented state of academic and moral decline, that immediate and drastic steps must be taken to reverse this decline, and that the most promising solutions are those that undo much of the recent history of public education. These solutions include mandating curriculum; linking promotion and graduation to statewide, standardized tests; retreating from past commitments to affirmative action, bilingual education, and special needs; undermining teachers' autonomy and seniority; and providing public funding for alternatives such as vouchers and privatization.

The calamitist view is found in particularly virulent form in cities, where parents, voters, mayors, and state legislators have lost both faith in and patience with the failing status quo. In the most celebrated case the Illinois legislature dismantled the central office of the Chicago Public Schools, transferring control of a multimillion dollar budget to individual school councils and granting them unprecedented autonomy. In a second phase, the legislature placed control of the school system in the hands of the mayor, who appointed his budget manager, a fiscal expert with no experience in education, as Superintendent of Schools.

The closely watched Chicago experiment has had a national ripple effect. By June, 2000 at least five major school systems, including America's three largest, had turned to non-educators to fill the superintendent's chair.

The new superintendents were most often white, male, and experienced in finance, law, or politics. In addition to Chicago's former city budget director, New York's top educator was a former corporate lawyer, San Diego's the former chief federal law officer for Southern California, Seattle's a former investment banker, and Los Angeles' the high-profile former governor of Colorado. Since superintendents typically rise through the ranks as teachers and principals, the new appointments were evidence of widespread lack of faith in traditional educational leadership and management practices and of a conviction on the part of those in power that corporate thinking can "turn around" troubled urban systems. Seattle Superintendent Joseph Olschefske, for example, listed among his accomplishments "a key leadership role in the transformation of the District into a market-based school system" and restoring "the District's credibility as a steward of public funds" by cutting the budget 10 percent.[2]

It is too early to know whether corporate managers will prove more effective than traditional superintendents, or more adept at escaping the revolving door that has plagued the superintendency in highly politicized urban systems. As one commentator remarked, "It takes three to five years to make real change. The problem is that large districts are so unmanageable and unstable that the average superintendent only lasts 2 1/2 years."[3] Drastic change is now the norm because no one can defend the constant failure perceived to be the current state of urban schooling: low test scores marked by a persistent "achievement gap" between white students and students of color; intermittent attendance; high dropout rates, particularly for Latino students; deteriorating physical plants; students who are unmotivated and often unruly; and lackluster teaching.

Proponents of systemic urban reform have set for themselves a lofty goal: high academic achievement for all. But in any corporate or public turnaround identifying problems, assigning blame, and changing the Chief Executive Officer (CEO) is notoriously easier than implementing successful solutions.

One can agree that urgent change is needed without agreeing to wholesale condemnation of all that currently exists and without accepting uncritically the solutions that arise from such condemnation. In fact, when judged by its own yardstick of academic achievement for all, systemic reform appears to be having limited effect. Despite widely publicized portraits of successful individual teachers and programs, there is scant evidence of lasting progress on a large scale. In 1999 the Carnegie Corporation, a private funder keenly interested in urban reform, assessed the situation this way: "Over the last decade, hundreds of urban schools have been involved in school reform efforts, resulting in encouraging improvements in academic achievement. However, student achievement in urban schools continues to be well below the standards needed for a productive, more equitable society. While there are many excellent schools, there are few, if any, urban districts where all schools are improving."[4] Another recent survey offered this judgment: "Optimistic visions of remaking America's schools have given way to the sober recognition that systemic reform—changing what goes on in classrooms across districts, states, and the country as a whole—is much harder than anyone imagined it would be."[5] Despite the investment of years of labor and hundreds of millions of dollars, success remains elusive.

Politically, reform has been characterized by increasing state intervention in what has traditionally been an area of local autonomy. State reforms have mandated sweeping changes in curriculum, instructional methods, assessment, and funding. At the same time, private and university-based reform initiatives such as the League for Democratic Schools, Accelerated Schools, the ATLAS Project, Success for All, the Annenberg Challenge, Comer Schools, Jobs for the Future, and the Coalition of Essential Schools have pursued reform through voluntary national affiliations. Mandated public and voluntary private initiatives together provide much of the available pool of ideas, strategies, and personnel for systemic urban reform. Their ranks support what amounts to a national consultancy of outside experts, nationally known authors, and purveyors of "exemplary programs." Moreover, urban school systems have access to targeted public and private money to fund the reform strategies favored by this national consultancy. Under the Comprehensive School Reform Demonstration Act (CSRD) cities choose exemplary programs from a short list identified by the state, then use federal money to adopt them. The $500 million Annenberg Challenge, active in at least nine major metropolitan areas, is attempting to achieve similar goals by concentrating previously separate private and corporate funding sources under a single umbrella.

Cash-strapped local authorities turn to outsiders because they often have little faith in their school system's ability to reform itself. CSRD, The Annenberg Challenge, state reforms, and similar, smaller programs give them access to outside expertise supported by outside dollars. This pumps additional money and new ideas into underfunded urban systems, jump-starting changes that might otherwise be impossible. But before reformers even enter schools they are entangled in contradictions. They are change-oriented outsiders in local environments run by insiders who often resist change; their mission is to transform core structures and methods of teaching, yet they have little influence over local decisions; and though they preach fundamental change, they are supported by the type of funding that has traditionally been used for "add-on," enrichment, and compensatory programs.

So far, reliance on top-down reform, outside experts and exemplary programs has not achieved widespread, lasting change in urban schools. But the goal has been so worthy, the intentions so good, the amounts of money so large, and the limited successes so effectively publicized that few have dared to raise a critical voice. If reform is to succeed, this critical "free ride" must end. Reform has become the new status quo of urban schooling, and unless its proposals and performance are subject to the same scrutiny that reformers routinely give to the old status quo, the urban reform movement will never come near to realizing its lofty ambitions.

Happily, individual aspects of reform have begun to receive such scrutiny. The use of mandated, high-stakes tests as the sole criterion for student achievement is drawing increasing criticism. Documentation of the success of reform programs that is conducted solely by the promoters of those programs, a common practice, also has been challenged.[6] But three other essential avenues for critique have been virtually ignored: learning from our long history of previous attempts at reform, listening seriously to the voices of urban practitioners, and going beyond "best practices" in pedagogy and school organization to view reform in the larger, more controversial urban contexts of politics, language, and culture. In this book I will present a critique of urban school reform that emerges from an exploration of these three avenues.

## THE CURRENT SITUATION

In 1995–96, America's 100 largest districts represented less than 1 percent of the districts in the nation, but educated 23 percent of all public school students and employed 21 percent of the nation's teachers.[7] With urban dropout rates hovering between 30 percent and 40 percent and test scores well below national averages, it is clear that we desperately need to get better at educating urban students. Current reform designs are well-intentioned attempts to make a difference, and progress is undeniably being made. But a one hundred year history of previous attempts at reform suggests that schools change reforms as much as reforms change schools, and that mandating change at the top of the hierarchy and achieving change at the bottom are often two entirely different things. We possess instructional and management strategies for change as well as a host of school-change models, but on the level of implementation—making exemplary programs or "best practice" strategies take hold in chaotic urban environments—these strategies are often employed in vain. In the pages that follow I will ask, in a systematic way, why this is so.

My greatest fear is that the pervasiveness of simplistic thinking about urban reform will result in a widespread perception of failure, and that the bill for this failure will be paid by those who least deserve to pay it—urban students and their parents, and the many urban teachers and administrators who are working hard every day to make things better.

My hope is that the perspectives, tools, and examples presented in this book—the "critical look" of the title—will help readers, whether they be students, educators, policymakers, or parents, to think deeply and carefully about the complex and difficult enterprise of improving urban schools. I further hope that by using these critical viewpoints to see their own experience they will be better equipped to participate in the exciting and nationally crucial struggle for educational equality and excellence that authentic urban reform represents.

My critical examination is based on the following beliefs about the current situation:

- Legislators, policymakers, and voters have lost faith in both the methods and the people who make up our urban educational system. As a result, they have turned to a host of outside experts, national consultants, and "exemplary programs" for answers to the improvement of urban education. Unfortunately, current experience and the historical record suggest strongly that outside experts and exemplary programs will not create lasting positive change in urban schools.

- The alarmist notion that we are in an unprecedented crisis that represents a complete break with the past is deceptive and false. What is happening today, including efforts at reform, is connected to what has gone before. Study of past efforts at reform can inform present efforts in important ways, because many of today's problems and solutions are recurrences of traditional tensions in American education.

- Current reform efforts concentrate on improving student outcomes by changing school structures, curriculum, and pedagogy. But these are not the only, or perhaps even the primary, causes of urban school failure. Systemic reformers have been reluctant to address three major obstacles to better student achievement and better management of urban schools: the effects of politics, language, and culture, including race. Significant advances in research and practice are taking place in these areas, but there is a disjunction between these initiatives and the school reform community. The highly active communities in multicultural education, anti-racism education, second-language learning, and cultural studies, for example, spin in orbits that are almost completely separate from the orbits of systemic reform. This separation is reflected at the school and district levels where, for instance, bilingual teachers and teachers of English Language Learners (ELL) are often out of the planning and decision-making loop, even though their students form large percentages of the population of schools under reform.

- Reform's failures do not stem from a lack of ideas. We have a plethora of instructional and management strategies and a host of whole school change models. What we lack is careful attention to issues of implementation—making exemplary programs or "best practice" strategies actually work as change forces. This lack is related to the absence of voices, in the reform conversation, of people at the implementation level—teachers, administrators, and "bridge professionals," who have one foot in the schools and the other in an agency, university, or similar outside entity. Bridge professionals work in schools wearing a reform hat, but typically are not full-time employees of the school system. Their ranks include coaches, consultants, specialists, facilitators, coordinators, and professional development school faculty. Teachers and principals in particular, since they are the primary implementers of reform strategies, need to be actively involved in both the planning for and modification of change strategies at the school level.

Instead, changes too often are imposed from outside or above with little authentic
input from the local site.

- In seeking solutions to this dilemma, we should not abandon our current efforts,
  but recognize their limitations and use them as a base for a conceptually wider
  approach which involves individual schools much more actively in the reform
  process. The goal should be, not to implement "exemplary programs" in cookie-
  cutter fashion as "magic bullets" to save schools that are deemed incapable of
  saving themselves, but to use outside resources to help schools turn themselves
  into unique, "exemplary contexts" that meet system goals and student needs in
  a synthesis of old and new, outside and inside knowledge, that is fashioned primarily by the school itself.

## THE PLAN OF THE BOOK

Part I explores these propositions by examining three important areas:
the urban context; current conceptualizations of reform; and the historical
context for reform, particularly as it relates to the education of immigrant
and minority students. Part II describes historical, political, linguistic, and
cultural influences on reform in three urban centers: Chicago, San Francisco and Oakland, CA, and Boston. Throughout, the narrative draws on
the insights of teachers, principals, and "bridge professionals" with extensive experience in the implementation of change.

In Chapter One I pose two questions: What do we mean by urban? and
What counts as reform? To answer the first I examine definitions, public
images, statistics, and basic beliefs to construct a working definition of
"urban" in the contemporary educational context. To answer the second I
survey reform networks and individual reform programs and briefly explore
the legislative history of the principal federal effort to support urban systemic reform, the Comprehensive School Reform Demonstration Act of
1998.

Chapter Two begins by answering the question "What does it mean to
take a critical look?" This is followed by two critiques of the current reform movement: one based on the language of reform, and one examining
reform as a kind of blame.

Chapter Three uses two kinds of history to deepen our understanding of
current reforms: the history of previous efforts at change, and the educational histories of the African, Asian, and Hispanic American communities
from which most of today's urban students are drawn.

Chapter Four looks closely at implementation issues by profiling a composite urban school, East Elementary, that has adopted an exemplary reading program as a vehicle for whole school change.

In Part II, Chapters Five, Six, and Seven each look at one of the book's
three key concepts—politics, language, and culture—through the lens of a
city school system undergoing change. Chapter Five looks at reform politics
through the history of reform in Chicago and the eyes of Chicago teachers.

Chapter Six uses San Francisco and Oakland to take a similar look at language issues. Chapter Seven uses Boston to examine issues of culture and race. Each of these chapters begins with a brief multicultural history of the school system in question and then tells the story of reform in that city largely through the voices of local practitioners.

## NOTES

1. National Commission on Excellence in Education, *A Nation at Risk: The Imperatives for Educational Reform* (Washington, DC: U.S. Department of Education, 1983).

2. Seattle Public Schools Website, "Superintendent profile," <*http://www.seattle schools.org/district/leadership/supbio*> (2 June 2000).

3. Tamar Lewin, "Educators Are Bypassed as School System Leaders," *The New York Times,* 8 June 2000, A1, A20.

4. Carnegie Corporation, *The New York Times,* 3 January 1999, classified advertisement.

5. Edward Miller, "Idealists and Cynics: The Micropolitics of Systemic School Reform," *The Harvard Education Letter* XII, 4 (1996): 1–3.

6. Stanely Pogrow, "What Is an Exemplary Program, and Why Should Anyone Care?," *Educational Researcher* 27, 2 (1998): 22–28.

7. B. A. Young, *Characteristics of the 100 Largest Public Elementary and Secondary School Districts in the United States: 1995–96,* NCES 98–124 (Washington, DC: National Center for Education Statistics, 1998).

*Chapter 1*

# What Do We Mean by Urban?
# What Counts as Reform?

## DEFINING ASPECTS OF THE URBAN CONTEXT

A subject like urban school reform tempts one to leap immediately into cases and strategies, problems and solutions. It is fortifying to recall James Joyce's counsel that "The longest way around is the shortest way home." In any critical discussion it is dangerous to leave unexamined the bedrock terms, the words so common we barely know they are there. The danger is that we may proceed as if we all understand the same thing when we hear or read such terms when, in fact, our understandings may be quite different. *Urban* is such a word.

To clarify the concept, I will explore four defining aspects of *urban-ness* in public education: definitions, images and perceptions, statistical and demographic profiles, and beliefs, including the belief that urban schools are connected to the larger, mainstream story of American education.

### Definitions

The dictionary on my desk, almost thirty years old, provides some idea of how much our conceptions of urban have changed from the 1970s to the present. Two definitions of *urban* it gives are: "characteristic of the city as distinguished from the country" and "in U. S. census use, designating or of an incorporated or unincorporated place with at least 2,500 inhabitants."[1]

Most people today would consider a community with 2,500 inhabitants a small town. More importantly, city versus country is an opposition that grows less useful as traditional rural life in the United States becomes more and more threatened. The urban/rural dichotomy that characterized the first half of the twentieth century increasingly gave way, in the post-war decades, to an urban/suburban one. In certain ways—high levels of poverty among students and their families, buildings in poor repair, a shrinking resource base, the continual struggle to attract and hold qualified teachers—urban and rural schools now have more in common with each other than either does with schools in affluent suburbs.

The urban/suburban dichotomy is itself being replaced by a third concept, that of mega-metropolitan areas which encompass urban, suburban, and even rural sectors within a sprawling zone of population density. Many Americans now live in one community, work in a second, and shop in a third. The life of cities thus affects the economic fortunes and social attitudes of a much wider public than just those who live within city borders. These effects range from the enormous influence of rap music and hip-hop fashion to the concentration, in downtown areas of major cities, of world-class museums, universities, and hospitals.

### Images and Perceptions

Responses evoked by the word *urban* go far deeper than dictionary meanings, for they are products of emotion and imagination as well as reason. Consider asking these questions, for example, in a room full of proponents of school reform: Are cities places of opportunity or places of blight? Is it safe to walk down the street in a city? Would you send your child to a city public school? Such questions call forth conflicting emotions and powerful images involving fear, hope, resignation, excitement, anxiety, and deeply held convictions about safety, diversity and community. How people answer them often depends on unique circumstances having to do with an individual's background, education, hopes, and experiences.

From colonial times until the present, conflicting images of cities have colored American civic dialogues. One tradition identifies the city with a paradise or holy land where dreams of social harmony find fulfillment. Philadelphia is the "city of brotherly love." Los Angeles is literally "the city of angels" and metaphorically, as home of Hollywood, the "city of dreams." Pilgrim leader John Winthrop, Massachusetts' first governor, famously envisioned the Puritan commonwealth as a godly society, a perfected "city on a hill." Today Boston boasts a *City on a Hill* charter school, living testimony to the continuing power of Winthrop's image.

A contrasting tradition identifies cities with negative images: "mean streets," the "urban jungle." These images paint cities as dark and dangerous places, morally and physically threatening locales of chaos, crime, and congestion. This negative image of cities has traditionally been contrasted with an idealized version of small town America and, more recently, of virtuous, hardworking suburbs.

Powerful media images have given a new dimension to this second tradition, serving as a kind of visual shorthand for the perception of cities as centers of violence and racial strife. These include, from Los Angeles alone, the video of white police officers beating Rodney King, the nationally televised chase of O. J. Simpson in the white Bronco, and a crowd of young black men pulling Reginald Denny from his truck in South Central and severely beating him.

Where urban education is concerned, images are particularly important, because many groups involved in school reform—policymakers, university "experts," business leaders, many of the taxpayers who foot the bill for reform—have little first-hand experience with urban schools. Often in the popular imagination cities have been demonized and politicized as places of crime, drugs, poverty, immigrants, over-crowding, and political malfeasance. Urban education has been tarred with this same brush as a corrupt, inefficient, and failing enterprise serving a largely alienated and academically substandard clientele. The former federal attorney who now heads the San Diego Public Schools, attempting to put a positive spin on this kind of attitude, has called working in urban education today "the equivalent of the Peace Corps of the 60s or the civil rights movement of the 50s."[2]

In much the same vein, public storytelling about urban educators has often featured single, heroic souls battling insurmountable odds. Best sellers like Samuel Freedman's *Small Victories* (New York City) and Tracy Kidder's *Among Schoolchildren* (Holyoke, MA), focus on "a year in the life of" an urban teacher.[3] The stories of East Los Angeles calculus teacher Jaime Escalante and baseball bat-wielding New Jersey principal Joe Clark have reached the public not just in print form but also as movies (*Stand and Deliver*, 1987; *Lean on Me*, 1989).

These media portraits evoke mixed feelings in many urban teachers and principals. They are glad that someone has taken the trouble to highlight what goes on in urban schools and present it dramatically. At the same time, they are troubled by the implication that urban students are mostly dangerous delinquents or gang members and that urban educators must be militaristic, superhuman, or saintly to succeed. They know that for the most part successful urban teaching, like successful teaching anywhere, is neither confrontational nor, in its outward manifestations, spectacular. Instead it is built on dailyness, on teacher-student relationships nurtured through mundane, regular contact, a deep level of craft, and caring. From this perspective, gripping tales of heroic individuals may attract readers and viewing audiences, but they present a distorted picture of both the challenges and the successes of urban education.

If we are to gain an understanding of urban school reform as a national issue, not just an individual, heroic saga, we need to build a much fuller, more reality-based picture. One way to begin is to familiarize ourselves with demographic and statistical descriptors that are truly shared by all, because they are part of the public record.

## A Statistical Profile

In 1999, 47 million children, more than ever before, enrolled in public elementary and secondary schools in the United States. They represented approximately 90 percent of the nation's K-12 students, a proportion that, despite recent alternatives such as privatization and school choice, has remained relatively constant for 20 years. According to the U. S. Department of Education, "enrollment in public elementary and secondary schools rose 20% between 1985 and 1999" while enrollment in private schools declined slightly, from 12 percent to 11 percent of total enrollment. Public school enrollments are expected to continue rising until at least the year 2006.[4]

Rising enrollments disproportionately affect urban schools for two reasons. First, because the long-term movement of the U.S. population is from rural areas to metropolitan centers, the country is witnessing a rapid growth of new urban areas. One recent analysis showed that between 1990 and 2000, more than fifty places became new Metropolitan Statistical Areas, a federal designation granted to cities with at least 50,000 people or counties with at least 100,000. Such places as Albany, Oregon; New Iberia, Louisiana; and Sierra Vista, Arizona now fit the federal definition of "urban."[5] Clark County (Las Vegas), Nevada is now the fastest-growing urban school system in the country, having grown 75 percent between 1986–87 and 1995–96.[6]

Second, immigration to the United States has been increasing rapidly, and most immigrants begin their life here by joining one of the established ethnic communities found in cities. In 1998 there were almost three times as many immigrants in the United States as there were in 1970, and half of all immigrants were Spanish-speaking. Because many ports of entry are on our coasts and borders, states like New York, Florida, Texas, and California have seen huge jumps in their immigrant populations, and corresponding rises in enrollments in urban schools serving ethnic neighborhoods which are the traditional first stop for immigrant families. In academic year 2000, for instance, the student population of the Los Angeles Unified School District was 71 percent Hispanic, 13 percent black, and 10 percent white.[7]

Skyrocketing enrollment fueled by immigration and increasing urbanization is a long-term trend, not a statistical blip. The highly mobile U.S. population, relocating to the South and West in increasing numbers, continues to create new urban areas and to send its children to public schools. Between 1986–87 and 1995–96, sixteen of the country's twenty largest school districts increased in size by 10 percent or more, and seven grew by more than 20 percent.[8]

Over the next decade urban public schools, and the tangled cluster of educational, financial, political, and social issues of which they are the center, will assume increasing importance in our national life. Yet urban education as a national, not just a local, issue continues to be largely understudied and widely misunderstood. There are, however, starting points for a greater understanding.

One of these is the valuable federal database, "Characteristics of the 100 Largest Public Elementary and Secondary School Districts in the United States,"[9] kept by the National Center for Education Statistics of the U.S. Department of Education and updated with every census.

The National Center provides not just current figures but also comparisons over time. Figures issued in July 1998 contain results from the 1995–96 school year. Among the "Highlights" are these:

- The 100 largest school districts, representing *less than 1 percent* of all school districts in the nation, educated *23 percent of all public school students,* employed *21 percent of all public school teachers,* and accounted for *18 percent of all high school graduates.*
- The 100 largest school districts had larger school sizes and higher mean pupil-teacher ratios than the national averages.
- The *proportion of minority students in the 100 largest districts was almost double* the proportion of minority students in all schools (65%/36%).
- As measured by free lunch eligibility, a larger percentage of students in the 100 largest districts were poor, as compared to the national average (45%/33%).
- Seven of the twenty largest districts have increased in size by over 20 percent since 1986, while only three have grown smaller.
- Three states, Florida, Texas, and California, accounted for over one-third of the 100 largest districts.[10]

These highlights begin to suggest a group of characteristics that, taken in combination, define what we currently recognize as *urban.* Some of these characteristics are: large and growing district size; large average school size; high percentages of "minority" students, and in many cities racially and ethnically mixed student populations composed almost entirely of students of color; large numbers of students whose first or home language is not English; higher than average pupil/teacher ratios; higher than average percentage of students whose families are near or below the federal poverty line; relatively high percentages of Special Education students (students with Individual Education Plans).

The characteristics themselves are not exclusively urban; individually they can be found in other types of school systems. It is the combination of most or all of them in the same place that creates a recognizable "urban" feel. Many rural schools, for example, have high percentages of poor students, high pupil/teacher ratios, and, in parts of the country, high percentages of students of color. Some suburban schools are very large and may be experiencing rising pupil/teacher ratios, but they would not necessarily have large numbers of poor students or high percentages of English Language Learners.

Importantly, even within the "urban" category, schools and systems vary widely. Detroit, for example, the tenth largest system in the country, has a high percentage of students eligible for free lunch (63%), and a large percentage of minority students (94%), but very few English Language Learners, because 90 percent of the school population is African American (in federal terms, "Black/non-Hispanic"). Contrast this with El Paso, Texas, which is in the exact middle of the list of 100 in size, has 59 percent of its students eligible for free lunch, and reports 81 percent of its students as minorities. Of the 81 percent, 76 percent are Hispanic and only 4.5 percent black.[11]

Both Detroit and El Paso are recognizably urban, but differences in composition alert us that, for example, issues around second language instruction and around the cultural relevance of curriculum materials in these two systems will be substantially different. Differences in the way characteristics are combined emphasize the uniquely local nature of urban education, which in turn has implications for reform. To give but a single example, one of the favorite strategies of reform advocates is "scaling up," or taking a program that was successful in one locality or setting and replicating it widely across the country. The gross differences in composition of local school systems evident in the federal database warns us that "scaling up" must be undertaken with great caution. A reading program, for instance, which has been successful with African American elementary school students in one city will not automatically work with a largely Hispanic or Asian population that may be found in another. Differences in cultural and linguistic background translate to differences in learning style, and so in a very real sense all success in urban education is local.

Even within the 100 largest districts there are significant variations in size. Analysis suggests that districts can be grouped into four categories, which I call *mega, midi, mini,* and *composite.*

Systems like New York City, with more than one million students, 55,000 teachers and over 1,000 schools, are really *mega-districts.* If we define a *mega-district* as one with more than 250,000 students, 15,000 teachers, and 300 schools, there are only five in the United States. Besides New York, they are Los Angeles, Chicago, Dade County Florida (Miami), and the Puerto Rico Department of Education, which is a single, centrally administered district serving the entire island. Puerto Rico ranks as the third largest school district in the United States, and, of the 100 largest, the one with the lowest per pupil expenditure. Unlike many treatments of U.S. education, this book will include Puerto Rican students, teachers, and issues in its discussions. Puerto Ricans are U.S. citizens, and in a phenomenon called "return migration" many Puerto Rican students split their school years between island schools and those of mainland cities such as Boston, New York, Hartford, and Allentown, PA. They are thus a major consideration not just for Puerto Rico, but for many school systems on the east coast of the mainland.

After mega-districts come systems with 100,000 to 250,000 students. I call these *midi-districts*, and there were 19 in 1995–96. The largest, at 210,000 students, was Philadelphia. The smallest, at 101,000 students, was Baltimore County, MD. Also in this category were Houston, Honolulu, Detroit, Dallas, San Diego, and several large county school districts such as Fairfax Country, VA, Orange County, FL (Orlando), and Prince George's and Rockville Counties, MD. Not technically but functionally in this category is the city of Atlanta, which is divided into two districts (Atlanta City and Fulton County), together have over 100,000 students.

The bulk of the 100 largest districts fall into the *mini-urban* category, with more than 40,000 students but fewer than 100,000. The largest of the mini-urbans in 1995–96 was Milwaukee with 98,000 students, the smallest St. Paul, MN with 42,000. Included in the 77 mini-urbans are Louisville, Albuquerque, New Orleans, Boston, Cleveland, Fort Worth, Nashville, Tucson, San Francisco, Oakland, San Antonio, El Paso, Anchorage, Omaha, and Charleston, SC.

Finally, there are districts that might best be described as *composite*, because they contain urban, rural, and suburban-type schools within the same district. Composite districts can be maxi, mini, or midi. Several districts I have already mentioned might best be placed into this category. Puerto Rico, for instance, has tiny, rural schools in the mountains as well as large, sprawling, recognizably urban schools in its cities. Similarly, Prince George's County, MD, and Fairfax County, VA are among the 100 largest, but they contain many schools that could be described as rural or suburban, as well as others that are urban. The growing number of composite districts speaks to the local nature of our educational system. In areas of the country where county government is powerful, this type of district is very common. In the near future, composite districts will offer rich fields of study, because they combine characteristics of an educative environment that is stereotypically seen as successful (white, English-speaking, suburban) with one that is stereotypically seen as failing (non-white, non-English speaking, urban). As urban sprawl continues, suburbs on the fringes of cities are seeing rapid change in the composition of their communities, which means rapidly changing student demographics. An understanding of the issues facing urban reform is becoming a necessity for the growing group of educators who work in these mixed or "composite" settings.

### Beliefs

Consideration of definitions, images, and public perceptions, coupled with a close look at the statistical portrait of American urban education, leads me to the final element in my construction of *urban*: a belief statement. The three beliefs on which this book is based are:

1. Urban education is complex.
2. Urban education can be successful.
3. Urban education is connected to the wider story of American education, both historically and in terms of current practice.

These beliefs are central because they focus the gap between words and actions that characterizes our national attitude towards urban education—we say all the right things and often do so many wrong ones. Few would disagree, for example, with the proposition that urban systems are complex. But if we truly believe they are complex, why do we devote so little time and energy to investigating and analyzing that complexity and so much to advocating simplistic, "magic bullet" solutions like privatization (embraced by school boards in Baltimore and Hartford till it proved to be a dismal failure) or wholesale adoption of prepackaged programs whose large-scale success is open to question.

Similarly, how seriously have we explored notions of success that go beyond test scores and take into account parents' and teachers' hopes for children, students' hopes for themselves, and a vision of a society without an educational underclass? How seriously do we ask who would benefit from such a vision, and who would be threatened by it? How seriously have we asked what the realization of America's historic, nineteenth-century ideal of the common school would mean, in the conditions of the twenty-first century? Given the student composition of urban schools today, to take this second belief seriously is to embrace a vision of social transformation.

To believe in such a social transformation requires faith that the calamitist approach is seriously in error, and that today's reform situation, unprecedented as it may seem, is best understood as connected to, not distinct from, longer term trends in American educational and social history.

Finally, most people would agree that urban education is connected to our society as a whole, and would never publicly write off the millions of largely minority students and parents whose futures are being shaped in the public schools of New York, Chicago, Los Angeles, Philadelphia, Miami, Houston, and scores of other cities. But a look at the conditions for schooling in most urban districts—substandard buildings, inadequate and outdated textbooks, large class sizes—raises the question of how important we as a society think urban education really is, when importance is measured not by words but by actions. It is vitally important not to ghettoize urban education, treating it as a dismal third world disconnected from the central currents of American schooling. On the contrary, I will seek to connect urban teaching and learning to the mainstream of American education, both historically and in terms of current practice, for it is only when we are able to see the many ways in which urban education is the same as education in other settings, that we can identify those ways in which it is significantly different.

Patricia Albjerg Graham has compared America's schools to World War II battleships: "large, powerful, cumbersome with enormous crews," responding to social commands issued "by some distant authority, which presumably understands better than anyone on the ship, including the captain, where and why they should go." Society's current command—high achievement for all—is unprecedented, and responding to it successfully will require not just a new course but "support from a fleet" to augment the all-purpose battleships of the past.[12]

Graham's specialized flotilla would include initiatives in the community, in moral development, and in other areas outside schooling. The notion that raising academic achievement in schools will require extended collaboration with entities outside schools—after-school programs, mental health agencies, youth and church groups—is particularly compelling for urban areas where poverty, delinquency, family stresses, and other elements of the social context undoubtedly affect schooling. But implementing such a comprehensive vision of change would involve reformers in something perilously close to social, rather than just educational, transformation. Such an involvement has been anathema to many advocates of systemic reform, who have targeted not the conditions surrounding schooling, but specific changes in curriculum, instruction, and assessment. The implication is that if performance lags it is not the social context that is inadequate, but the school or the students themselves. This leads us directly to the next question: what counts as reform?

## WHAT COUNTS AS REFORM?
## PROGRAMS AND APPROACHES

To extend Graham's metaphor, the number of ships plying the sea of reform is so great, their sizes and cargos so varied, and their destinations so diverse that a comprehensive survey is nearly impossible. *Education Week* has profiled thirty-six major school reform *networks,* each comprising hundreds, and in some cases thousands, of individual schools. The profiles were accompanied by the following disclaimer: "The list is not meant to be all-inclusive. There are far too many reform networks to include them all."[13]

Many schools are part of two or more networks and each network has its own philosophy, goals, and approaches. In addition to whole school change initiatives like Accelerated Schools, the ATLAS Program, The Coalition of Essential Schools, and Success for All, networks profiled provided professional development for individual teachers (Foxfire, AFT Educational Research and Dissemination Program), recruited new teachers (Teach for America), supported administrators (Total Quality Network), developed "cultural literacy" (Core Knowledge Foundation), created curriculum (Galef Institute, Higher Order Thinking Skills), set standards and measured performance (New Standards Project), and sought to "improve student learning through shared governance and action research" (League of Professional Schools).[14] All of these efforts are non-governmental, all have a presence in urban areas, and all are considered part of "school reform."

At the federal level, reform in urban areas is supported by the Comprehensive School Reform Demonstration Act (CSRD-also known as the Obey-Porter bill for its congressional sponsors). The legislative history of CSRD provides a good primer of why it is so difficult to generalize about or categorize reform. Obey-Porter began life as a sort of commonsense proposition: the federal government would short-list a menu of school change programs that had strong research evidence of success, and would provide money for school districts to adopt them. Problems with this approach began to appear almost immediately: some programs, like the reading program Success for All, were already receiving federal money directly and had research evidence of success, but the research was under attack by outside sources because it had been conducted by the program developers themselves and had not undergone peer review.[15] Further, supporters of Obey-Porter differed on the best way to provide support for local school systems: should it come directly from the federal government? Should it go to the states and then be distributed locally (a stance much favored by conservatives since it minimized the federal role)? Should it provide long-term support like Title I and Head Start, or only start-up support? What evidence of local commitment should be required?

In the end, the series of compromises required to get the bill passed shaped a very interesting piece of legislation. The final version set a funding level of $120 million for Fiscal Year 1998 and removed the federal government entirely from the business of defining what was and was not a successful reform program (though the legislation did cite 17 "sample" programs). Instead, that decision was left to the states, who also received the money and administered its delivery to local systems. Federal regulations made it clear, however, what types of programs were to be funded: "proven, research-based models" that "will help expand the quality and quantity of schoolwide reform efforts that enable all children, particularly low-achieving children, to meet challenging academic standards."[16]

This formulation responded to the conservative-leaning desire for higher standards, strict accountability and an expanded role for state government but also to the liberal-leaning desire for equity-driven reforms and a compensatory federal role. CSRD-funded programs would build on and leverage "ongoing efforts to connect higher standards with school improvement at the state and local level" such as Title I, Goals 2000, and School-to-Work Opportunities. Eligibility for funding was tied to the Title I process. Funds were not intended to support special projects or add-ons, but to provide start-up money for programs that would "help schools improve their entire educational operation through, for example, curriculum changes, sustained professional development, and enhanced involvement of parents."[17] A school system's own locally developed programs were explicitly made eligible for funding on an equal basis with outside, national programs, provided the local programs had research evidence attesting to their effectiveness.

Following the passage of CSRD, the U.S. Department of Education requested the Northwest Regional Educational Laboratory (NWERL), assisted by the Education Commission of the States, to develop a *Catalog of School Reform Models* that would help local school districts identify CSRD-eligible programs which matched their local needs. With CSRD providing "financial incentives for schools . . . to implement comprehensive school reform programs that are based on reliable research and effective practices and that include . . . basic academics and parental involvement," CSRD legislation "encourages them to consider adopting externally developed research-based reform models as a central part of their (school improvement) plan." The catalog profiles 26 "entire school reform" and 18 "skill- and content-based reform" models, with the latter divided into Reading/Language Arts Models (7), Mathematics Models (6), Science Models (3), and Other Models (2). Even with the listing of 44 separate models, the NWERL made it clear that the catalog "is not a list of recommended or approved models" and that "a number of models not included here" also had "strong track records."[18]

There is a reason why the federal government declined to name exemplary programs in CSRD, choosing instead to frame criteria which states and schools could use to create or identify them, and why both *Education Week* and NWERL issued what amount to blanket disclaimers. With the reputation of schools at an ebb, and federal, state, and private sources all providing money for change, reform is a seller's market. Claims of success by program developers abound, but evaluating those claims is a difficult matter.

The Holy Grail of current reform efforts is quantitative evidence that changes in areas like curriculum, instruction, or school organization actually improve student achievement. Funders and policymakers yearn for a simple, linear relationship: dollars in, performance out. Few understand the difficulty of what they are asking. Ted Sizer, one of the country's most thoughtful advocates for educational change, recently admitted that when he first began even he was not aware "how hard (reform) would be . . . how fierce the opposition would be, often in the form of neglect," and warned that success will require more than "a few good men and women trying to do the right thing."[19]

Despite decades of research and experimentation, the school change process is in many respects still a black box. The few examples where policy change does seem closely related to student improvement—reduction in class size is probably the best case in point—are hugely expensive and take a relatively long time to show results, not exactly a formula for legislative interest.

Many reform initiatives rely heavily on staff development, seeing the key to success in changing what teachers do in the classroom. Yet establishing a direct link between professional development for teachers and improved test scores for students is one of the most knotty problems in educational assessment, because so many variables affect both teacher change and student performance. When key variables change constantly, as they do in urban schools, linking the two reliably is a near impossibility.

Frequent turnover of staff and administrators, high student mobility rates, large numbers of second language learners, and inadequate educational materials all confound measurement of success. If, say, Malcolm X Elementary School adopts a model reading program and the reading scores go up, is it because of the program's philosophy and teaching methods, or because the program also brought new, additional materials, extra staffing, and attention from the assistant superintendent? The program developer will claim success is due to the program's finely tuned model. Principals and parents will probably not care *why* the scores went up, as long as they went up. Indeed, the principal's job security and pay raise may be tied to higher test scores. Teachers will rejoice over extra funding, more materials, and additional staffing. But replicating Malcolm X's local success will depend on identifying and copying those factors that caused the success, and not others. Since other schools may have enough funding to adopt only parts of the program, or may adopt it in a context significantly different from the one where it was initially successful, it is critical for replication purposes to know what precisely is responsible for the program's success. This is the dilemma facing "exemplary program" replication, one of today's dominant strategies for urban reform.

In fact, when a coalition of education groups commissioned a research-based analysis of twenty-four CSRD-eligible reform programs, fully two-thirds were judged to have either no evidence of "positive effects on student achievement" or evidence rated "weak" or "marginal." The three programs rated as having "strong" evidence had been in existence for 12 years or more and were in use, in October 1998, in 2,140 schools—a handful by national standards. Two of the three "strong" programs, Success for All and High Schools that Work, accounted for 93 percent of the 2,140 schools.[20]

The survey examined implementation studies of these programs in various sites. Of the seven studies reported for High Schools that Work, none were in urban environments. Six of eleven Success for All studies were in urban settings, three were conducted by independent researchers and three by the program's director or a team led by him. The three studies from independent researchers covered nine sites, both "original" and "replicate," and reported partial, problematic, or highly variable implementation tied closely to levels of financing—not surprising given that the first-year cost for full implementation in a 500-student elementary school is estimated at $270,000. The three studies conducted by the program director covered twenty-nine sites. In twenty-eight of the twenty-nine, including both "originals" and "replicates," partial or varied implementation was reported. In one, the program's first site and model, full implementation was reported as well as an increase in mean effect size that increased with years of implementation.[21]

What can we conclude from this survey? First, among twenty-four well-known programs, only three had strong evidence of positive effects on student achievement. Second, of those three only one had achieved widespread replication in urban areas, and implementation was in many cases partial, varied, and problematic. Third, there is a strong suggestion that programs need to survive for at least ten years to develop a sufficient track record for credible evaluation and a sophisticated technical support network for replicant schools to utilize.

These conclusions do not bode well for a vision of reform that seeks quick results at modest cost through "scaling up" a handful of national exemplars. The research evidence provides little grounds for believing that such a quick-and-cheap fix exists, even if we define "fix" in the narrowest possible terms—improved achievement test scores. In most cases, the "exemplars" are far from exemplary and replicating them is fraught with difficulty. Overall, these conclusions suggest that we should view with skepticism the common policy belief that exemplary programs can be successfully replicated on a widespread basis in complex, highly variable, underfinanced urban settings. In Chapter Two I will undertake a deeper analysis of the issues surrounding a systemic reform philosophy whose principal conceptual response to the need for change is the national franchising, at the public expense, of a few highly publicized reform models.

## NOTES

1. *Webster's New World Dictionary of the American Language*, 2nd college ed., s. v. "urban."

2. Tamar Lewin, "Educators Are Bypassed as School System Leaders," *The New York Times*, 8 June 2000, A1, A20.

3. Samuel Freedman, *Small Victories* (New York: Harper, 1991); Tracey Kidder, *Among Schoolchildren* (New York: William Morrow and Co., 1990).

4. *Public and Private School Enrollment, Table 2*, National Center for Education Statistics, *<http://nces.ed.gov/fastfacts/display.asp?id=65 >* (16 August 2001).

5. B. A. Young, *Characteristics of the 100 Largest Public Elementary and Secondary School Districts in the United States: 1995–96*, NCES 98–214 (Washington, DC: National Center for Education Statistics, 1998).

6. Ibid., 5.

7. "Five Year Review LAUSD Ethnic Survey," LAUSDNet, 2001, <*http://www.lausd.k12.ca.us/lausd/offices/bulletins/5_yr_review.html*> (16 August 2001).

8. *Characteristics*, 5.

9. *Characteristics*.

10. Ibid., i.

11. Ibid., Table 5 (enrollment), Table 8 (minority percentage), Table 9 (free/reduced lunch).

12. Patricia A. Graham, "Assimilation, Adjustment, and Access: An Antiquarian View of American Education," in *Learning from the Past: What History Teaches Us about School Reform*, eds. Diane Ravitch and Maris A. Vinovksis (Baltimore: Johns Hopkins, 1995):3–4.

13. *Education Week*, 2 November 1994, 34–41.

14. Ibid.

15. Stanley Pogrow, "What is an Exemplary Program, and Why Should Anyone Care? A Reaction to Slavin and Klein," *Educational Researcher* 27, 7 (1998): 22–8.

16. U.S. Department of Education, "The Comprehensive School Reform Demonstration Program," <*http://ed.gov/offices/OESE/compreform*> (12 December 1998).

17. Ibid.

18. *Catalog of School Reform Models* (Washington, DC: U. S. Government Printing Office, 1998).

19. Theodore Sizer, "Hard Won Lessons from the School Reform Battle: A Conversation with Ted Sizer," *Harvard Education Letter* (July/August 1996): 1.

20. American Institutes for Research, *An Educators' Guide to Schoolwide Reform* (Arlington, VA: Educational Research Service, 1999), my analysis based on data presented on pp. 24, E26–28, E38–40.

21. Ibid.

## Chapter 2

# Taking a Critical Look

Earlier I asked what the realization of America's historic, nineteenth-century ideal of the common school would mean, in the conditions of the twenty-first century. Given the student composition of urban schools today, to take this ideal seriously is to embrace a vision of social transformation, a vision that requires faith that today's reform situation is connected to, not distinct from, longer-term trends in American educational and social history.

What are some of these trends? Lawrence A. Cremin, author of the standard multi-volume history of American education, identifies "three abiding characteristics of American education . . . *popularization,* the tendency to make education . . . increasingly accessible to diverse peoples; . . . *multitudinousness,* the proliferation . . . of institutions to provide . . . that increasing accessibility; and . . . *politicization,* the effort to solve certain social problems indirectly through education rather than directly through politics."[1]

Patricia Albjerg Graham reminds us that, "Traditionally, Americans have considered their schools as mechanisms for improving society. What society has been either unable or unwilling to undertake with its adults, it has expected the schools to accomplish with its children. As the nation's priorities have shifted during this century, so, too, have the goals of the schools."[2]

Basic urban issues like desegregation, bilingual education, and special needs, for instance, can be seen as examples of popularization, for they arise from legislation which extended access to new groups of students. Desegregation is clearly an example of the use of schools as a "mechanism for improving society." Events such as California's recent retreat from bilingual education, charges that Texas' new high stakes achievement tests are racially discriminatory, and Massachusetts' battle to cut special needs programs in favor of more spending on regular education are all examples of both politicization and conflict between equity-based social agendas and new academic demands.

A simplistic, dismissive approach to political, linguistic, and cultural/racial issues that pervade the urban setting has characterized much of reform thinking. If reform is to realize its potential, we need debate based on *all* the knowledge sources and critical tools at our disposal, especially those that have been so far neglected.

If today's systemic reforms are an attempt by schools to adapt to society's new demands, then some of reform's closest observers must be the teachers and principals charged with its implementation. Yet their voices have scarcely been audible. Typically, practitioners lack the time to formulate and the means to disseminate their views. When they do speak out, their opinions and observations are often discounted.

Teachers especially are seen by many as incompetent, self-interested and narrow-minded. Incompetent because, if they had been doing their job in the first place, the schools would never have gotten into this mess. Self-interested because it is *they* who are being asked to change, and thus their observations are nothing more than obstructionist complaining. Narrow-minded because their experience is in a single classroom or school, they lack the "big-picture" necessary to understand reform as a systemic solution.

Reform leaders' decision making processes have often reflected the belief that the further one is from a classroom, the wiser one must be about what needs to go on there. Practitioners are acutely aware of their exclusion: several years ago JoAnne Dowd, a reform-savvy Maine high school teacher and writer, asked me: "How come almost everyone who writes about school reform works someplace other than a school?"

Devaluing practitioner knowledge and opinion is an error. Systemic reforms that call for new types of school organization, new curricular goals, and new teaching techniques represent a significant change in the working lives of teachers and principals. In disregarding their testimony about implementation issues, policymakers, administrators, and the public cut themselves off from first-hand knowledge about the progress of reform. In the long run, disregarding or devaluing teachers is counter-productive because, as Massachusetts elementary teacher Steve Levy reminded me at a conference of the Coalition for Essential Schools, "Ultimately all our questions about reform have to be answered with what happens between a teacher and a student in the classroom."

The dynamics of who gets heard and who gets excluded from the reform debate is ultimately political; it's about power and status. Practitioner resistance to top-down reform can be seen as the latest manifestation of a recurrent, largely neglected theme in our educational history, the ongoing struggle by teachers, the majority of whom are women, to exert some control over their professional lives. As James Fraser has pointed out, "historians of education have paid surprisingly little attention to teachers, as opposed to theorists, administrators, and other leaders of the profession. And when teachers have been the center of attention, the story often has been more in terms of what was done to them by others—politicians, administrators, or union leaders—than in terms of their own role in schools." In the same passage Fraser notes Richard Quantz's observation that historians have a tendency to "treat teachers as nonpersons" and to portray "female teachers especially . . . as objects rather than subjects."[3]

The top-down political bias influences the language we use to describe reform, loading it in subtle ways that prejudice our judgments about reform's outcomes. For example, the term "reform" precludes the thought that current changes may be responsible for harm as well as aid, as far as urban schools are concerned.

## THE GENERATIVE POWER OF LANGUAGE

> So out of the ground the Lord God formed every beast of the field and every bird of the air, and brought them to the man to see what he would call them; and whatever the man called every living creature, that was its name.
>
> —Genesis, 2:18[4]

> It might be a ball and it might be a strike, but it ain't nothin' till I call it.
>
> —Major League baseball umpire

In naming the beasts and birds the biblical first man did more than invent a way of referring to natural creation. For human society, he literally called reality into being. Adam's naming takes place in the middle of the passage in which Eve, the second human, is created. A lone Adam had no need for words; but two humans constitute a society, and society requires the generative power of language. Through the works of Vygotsky and others,[5] the idea that language creates knowledge in social settings has become a seminal one in modern educational thinking.

As the national conversation over school reform unfolds, our "language habits" continually influence our perceptions about what is real and what is possible. The language we use to talk about reform is not objectively given, but is part of a social discourse that is itself subject to the effects of politics and culture. As such, it can be subjected to critical analysis. In the two sections that follow I interrogate two key terms in the national debate about school change: the word "reform" and the term "high standards."

### Reform or Change?

As part of my professional life I work regularly with urban teachers, administrators, parents, and policymakers around the country. Time and again, after the formal meeting is over, I hear privately what people feel they can't say out loud: "Things are changing fast here, but nobody really understands what's going on."

Teachers and administrators say: "The public doesn't understand. Kids aren't the way they used to be. This job isn't what it used to be. Things are really different now." Parents say: "I'm worried about my child. I don't know what the school is doing. I feel out of touch." Policymakers say: "The schools have to do better. Look at the test scores. Millions of dollars are going into these schools, and we've got to have results. Things have to change."

But when they and I talk in public we don't say *change,* we say *reform.* Change is a neutral word that can imply things are getting better, but it also allows the possibility of things getting worse. In contrast, *reform* carries only a positive charge; no right-thinking person could be against it. Used in politics ("a reform slate of candidates"), morality ("we must reform our wicked ways"), or education, it implies that things were in a sorry state before, and that now we are going about the important business of setting them right. To be a *reformer* means to be both virtuous and progressive. By definition reformers can't willfully make things worse, because their intentions are so good; but reforms can and do fail, done in by dark, anti-progressive forces. Thus social reform scenarios—prohibition, campaigns to replace corrupt politicians, anti-smoking activism—are always mini-morality plays with victims and saviors, heroes and villains. I believe that school reform is in danger of becoming such a scenario.

Reform strategy talk now flows easily from the lips of congressmen, mayors, media analysts, national pundits, and segments of America-at-large whose previous interest in education was intermittent at best. Such attention to reform is not an unmixed blessing. Recently one experienced principal said to me, "All through the eighties I kept screaming, why don't the politicians pay attention to education, can't they see how important it is? Now they're paying attention, and I'm scared to death."

If broad interest equals simplistic thinking, we should all be scared—bilingual education, good or bad? Phonics instruction—good or bad? Charter schools, public funding for private schools, high-stakes standardized testing, good or bad? In urban schools the danger of simplistic thinking is greatest of all, for they have the clearest need for reform, yet pose the greatest challenge. They are resource-depleted, organizationally complex, and politically volatile.

Until very recently, reform has been judged mostly on its good intentions and on claims about its work put forward by reformers themselves. The time has come to begin to ask hard questions, to subject reform issues and reform advocates to the kind of scrutiny that has, in recent years, been directed at urban students, parents, and educators; in short, to take a critical view of urban reform.

What might it mean to take such a view? Is anyone who asks hard questions about reform a collaborator with dark, anti-progressive forces? Is agreeing that our schools need to get better the same as agreeing that everything labeled "reform" will make them better? Can good come from questioning the premises of urban reform—the convictions that we are in the grip of an unprecedented educational crisis (what if our current "sorry state" isn't completely sorry after all?), that urban schools are an educational third world where little teaching and learning takes place, and that wholesale change is the only remedy (what if reform, in some instances, does more harm than good?)?

There are multiple meanings for the word "critical," including those of the emerging academic field of "critical studies." By "critical view" I mean a structured way of thinking about urban school reform that starts by drawing on two of the standard dictionary meanings, "characterized by careful analysis and judgement" and "an attempt at objective judging to determine both merits and faults."[6] To these I add tools from critical studies—historical analysis, analysis from the viewpoint of those near the bottom of reform's political and power hierarchies (practitioners, parents), and analyses based in issues of language, race, and culture.

A significant part of my analysis consists of giving credence to "voices from the inside"—the voices of urban teachers, administrators, and parents themselves. They are an important source of knowledge about reform that I believe has been underutilized because they have so frequently been stigmatized as part of the problem, not part of the solution. In contrast to this view, I consistently find that some essential insights about the progress of reform can be supplied only by people in schools who are "doing reform" every day, because their accounts capture the complex, mixed, and contingent nature of authentic change.

I have learned, for example, that reform has created many new pathways to school leadership, both for teachers and principals; but that for those who choose these pathways reform-induced burnout is a significant threat to long-term change. This knowledge has had an important influence on my own work. In the urban leadership doctoral program I direct there are many students who aspire to be teacher-leaders or administrators. Because their participation in the program signals that they are seriously preparing themselves, they are often considered for leadership positions by their school systems quite soon after entering the program, and they frequently ask me to help them consider these new opportunities.

At one time I encouraged students to take advantage of such offers, reasoning that the solid preparation and support they received in our program would make them the kind of leaders-for-change that urban schools so badly need. Now, my practice is to ask them to consider two questions as a pre-lude to any further conversation. The first is this: can this job be success-fully done? By this I mean, within the standards you set for yourself, the job description the school system has created, and the school context in which you will be working, is there a real chance of success on both your terms and theirs? On many occasions, a close look at all three of these fac-tors indicates that no one—not Wonderwoman, not Superman, not God—could succeed in the job that has been created, in the way it is originally structured. In other words, intentionally or unintentionally, the job is a set-up for failure. The only real choice is to go back and try to renegotiate what the job is about, or to turn the job down.

The second question is this: can you do this job and still have a life? In these days of sixty-hour workweeks and 24-hour cellphone contact, the question may seem a bit naive. But it gets at a vital professional, not just personal, issue. Authentic reform is a long-term process, and good leader-ship is critical. Thus a key question for reform becomes, how can urban school systems create and support stable, long-term leadership to manage the change process. Administrators and teacher-leaders are also wives, hus-bands, and partners; they are mothers and fathers of school-age children; sons and daughters of aging parents; members of churches and community groups—in short, they have lives. In my experience, it is possible for a new principal or teacher leader to go all-out to change a school for one year or two years, maybe even three, putting most of their private life aside for the good of the school. But after three years, the need for balance in life starts to re-assert itself, and preserving a key leader from burnout can become a most important issue for a school that wants to sustain the reforms it has started. If the issue is not addressed, the leader leaves and the change ini-tiative is endangered.

Writ large, the issue can be framed this way: if reforming schools are to be environments where students can thrive academically and grow person-ally, they must also be places where principals and teachers are recognized as whole people too, with their own needs for professional and personal renewal. Thus my second question, "can you do this job and still have a life," is really a way of asking, does this situation offer a serious possibility for successful reform, one you can develop in five years or more without burning out; or is it a short-term, quick fix, feel-good reform that's likely to fall apart and leave you feeling used and your staff demoralized and cynical?

### What do we mean by "high standards"?

The meanings we attach to key terms in urban reform, "high standards" for example, are directly influenced by what we understand to be the goals of schooling. Policymakers have repeatedly advanced the claim that mandatory, high stakes tests represent high standards and will improve the quality of schools by "raising the bar" for student performance. In contrast, progressive educational groups such as the Coalition of Essential Schools and Fair Test promote flexible "alternative assessment" strategies that seek to measure a much wider set of educational outcomes than can be reflected in a test score. Largely absent from the debate on standards has been the perspective of the individual classroom teacher in an urban school. To demonstrate how much we miss in not hearing this perspective, I present here a comment on standards by Judith Baker, a teacher at one of Boston's largest high schools and a Boston Public School parent activist. She comments, among other things, on the effects on her teaching of the Massachusetts Comprehensive Assessment System (MCAS), a mandatory test scheduled to be tied to high school graduation for the class of 2003.

### Judith Baker

There are two standards movements, in my mind. One is the fervent hope of parents, many of whom are forced to send their children to schools like the ones where I have taught for 29 years, under-resourced and severely challenged, that their children receive the kind of education which will enable them to enter the mainstream of American life. These parents, myself included, want better schools for our children and are very aware of the deficiencies in our communities' schools.

The other standards movement is partly political electioneering vehicle and partly conservative attack on public education. Alternately espoused by Democrats and Republicans, though seldom with the same bills in mind, this political movement seems to contradict itself over and over, at once arguing that high quality will come with vouchers and free market education in which the private school or home schooler has NO mandates, no controls, no requirements from the government, and arguing that a lengthy set of rules must be followed to make the public schools achieve high standards.

We here in Massachusetts are dropping electives, hands-on projects, and all sorts of proven or successful innovation because we just can't 'cover' the MCAS material and teach the MCAS-required formats for presentation and still stick to quality curriculum. Our professional development time and money is being literally stolen to make room for MCAS strategy time. We are offering less reading in favor of more writing—which may have been valuable years ago when we did little writing, but now we're actually sending the kids home with almost no required reading as their main task is to learn how to write the MCAS answers. We are not really trained to teach test prep anyway, so we are doing things we aren't trained for, while not being allowed to do the things we are trained for. That seems to be a tragedy in the making to me. I'd rather see an expert teach from her/his expert knowledge—in ANY subject—than a novice teach from a prepared curriculum. Kids need to learn things, not hear them, and learning is greatly enhanced by working with an expert in that person's field, even if the field isn't on a state legislator's agenda.

I think the best way to implement higher standards in schools is to give children high quality materials to work with. Show the materials to the parents and teach them to help their children work with them. Give children high quality thinking/writing tasks, and insist they do them. Call home if they don't and engage the parents/guardians in every assignment. Hire enough people in the schools, parents included, so that these phone calls and appointments can really happen on time. Don't let a child's non-performance go unchallenged for weeks, or years. Create a setting where the school is open late, so that children who are having difficulty with a piece of work can stay with expert help until it is finished. Create an environment in every school where the actual work that children do is rewarded, shown, presented, important, and where other children can learn from it. Expose children to the work that adults do—work in unfamiliar fields, different from what their family members do. Make the world of work accessible so that children can aspire to more careers than they see on TV or at home or school. They should know that people make maps, study clams, design toasters, run online services, etc., etc. Surround children with books, at home and at school. Also with maps, lithographs, models of the universe and of DNA, the insides of motors and everything you can find which challenges the imagination and the mind. Let them tinker with these things, and let them watch experts who tinker with them for a living. Take children out to museums, workplaces, sea and lake shores, newspaper press rooms, lawyers' offices and let them shadow people working. We can demonstrate to the public that higher standards are being met by letting the public into the schools on some regular basis, to look at student work, to view whatever data the school has been collecting, to watch classes. A regular report to the public would be a great discipline for a poorly performing school. It would give a school like mine the chance to solicit aid from the public, also, in its quest to offer better services to children. The "higher standards" movement has definitely had an impact on classroom practice.

In my urban high school: we now do more writing in the content areas, and we are beginning to spend more time in common planning. We are more aware of the testing and we take time out of our already overcrowded curriculums to do test prep and test administration. We seem to be developing a more autocratic bureaucracy, as our administrators feel increasingly pressured by their supervisors to produce better test scores. And we may also become more autocratic teachers as the pressure builds on us.[7]

## IS REFORM THE GREATEST THREAT FACING
## URBAN SCHOOLS?

Public perceptions of educational failure are particularly powerful with respect to urban schools, widely considered an educational "third world" within American public education, with all that characterization implies. The images of urban education which form the basis for this perception consist of a narrow set of stereotypic elements: abysmal test scores, difficult and often violent students, crumbling buildings, inefficient and bureaucratic administrators, poorly prepared teachers, and obstructive unions. While each of these elements contains some reality, such images form only a small part of the complex picture of today's urban schools.

We do a real disservice to our ability to address the problems of urban education if we let these stereotypes ghettoize our very thinking processes, making us regard teaching and learning in urban settings as something apart from the major currents affecting American education, and urban students as less than other students. Our ability to create solutions will be enhanced if we move in the opposite direction: to clarify the many ways that urban issues are and have been emblematic of the central trends of American education in this century.

Achieving such clarity is complicated, because there are enormous differences of opinion between policymakers, researchers, and practitioners about the current state of educational reality. Fervent belief in a state of crisis and dire need for reform are political realities, articles of faith sanctioned by the U.S. Department of Education, the National Governor's Council, and almost every state legislature. A Nation at Risk declared that the current generation of students would be the first in America's history to be less well-educated than their parents and warned that: "the educational foundations of our society are presently being eroded by a rising tide of mediocrity that threatens our very future as a Nation and a people. What was unimaginable a generation ago has begun to happen—others are matching and surpassing our educational attainments. If an unfriendly power had attempted to impose on America the mediocre educational performance that exists today, we might well have viewed it as an act of war. As it stands, we have allowed this to happen to ourselves."[8]

These criticisms proceeded from an authoritative, national source; they came at a time, the early 1980s, when Americans were feeling extremely insecure about themselves and their place in the world; and they explicitly linked educational mediocrity to both a foreign threat ("if an unfriendly power") and a domestic one (the first generation to be less educated than their parents). It is worth noting that the report "mentioned a role for the federal government in defining a national interest in education, but it assigned to state and local officials the primary responsibility for initiating and carrying out the recommendations."[9] This they have proceeded to do.

Hundreds of millions of non-federal public and private dollars labeled "reform" have flowed into schools, a commitment of resources that has made it politically risky to question either the need for reform or the shapes it is taking.

At the same time, credible researchers have continued to question the true nature and extent of our "educational crisis" as well as the success of reform initiatives in combating it. Berliner and Biddle,[10] citing data that show American schools performing at least as well as and in some areas better than previously, have argued that the crisis is politically manufactured rather than real. Cremin, citing extensive research on the academic achievement of American children by Stedman and Smith, finds "the predicament of American schooling . . . not nearly so dire as the report of the National Commission suggested" and concludes that there is "no evidence" to support the claim that this generation will the first to be less well educated than its parents.[11] Cuban has pointed out that if schools are to blame for the domestic economic woes and international trade defeats of the 1980s, they must deserve the credit for the booming economy and foreign trade victories of the 1990s.[12] This *reductio ad absurdum* highlights the shallowness of the economic and international competition arguments upon which much of the crisis rhetoric is based.

Researchers have also begun to produce mounting evidence that reform efforts, despite the millions of dollars poured into them, are meeting with limited success. Though it is easy to find individually successful schools or programs, and national reform groups promote their successes while keeping a discreet silence about their failures, there is now enough evaluation research on reform to suggest that few reform initiatives have so far reached their stated long-term goals.[13]

Finally, questions are being raised about the effects of reform on the culture of practice. Are reform initiatives largely just a "churning" or shakeup of existing norms that cannot ultimately lead to a new, more effective culture of teaching and learning?

Research evidence and practitioner criticism have had little impact on the reform juggernaut, possibly because researchers are seen as distant from the field of battle and practitioners as part of the problem that needs fixing, not as part of the group qualified to offer solutions. Overall, the public's dissatisfaction with schools seems both deep and abiding, and doubts about reform are likely to be heard not as constructive criticism but as arguments against better schools, better teaching, better education for our children, and by extension against the possibility of a better society and a better life for all Americans.

Sustained public energy for reform supported by increased public and private funding will not last forever. In the long run, large differences in the points of view of the tax-paying public and its elected representatives on the one hand, and researchers and practitioners on the other, are potentially explosive. When patience ends, we can expect a public backlash that will hold someone accountable. Long-time observers of the disjunction between reform policy and school practice have already anticipated the broad outlines of this backlash:

One has the feeling that the main appeal of the new agenda is that it has not yet failed. When the inevitable unraveling begins, who will absorb the blame? Will it be researchers, who framed the agenda? Will it be state legislators, who passed the comprehensive reforms . . . ? Will it be local school board members . . . ? The answer is probably no. . . . The blame, in all probability, will fall on people who work in schools. Thus does a reform agenda based on the school as the unit of improvement become another device for manifesting hostility and indifference towards schools and the people who work in them.[14]

This prophetic scenario bodes especially ill for urban schools because the conditions attaching to blame are most strongly present there. If in the new reform agenda the school is the unit of change, urban schools represent the greatest challenge because they are the most complex environments for change. Urban buildings are oldest and in poorest repair, books and materials are scarcest and furthest out of date. Urban student populations, with high numbers of immigrant, minority, second-language, and special needs students, do least well on standardized tests, which critics take as proof that their teachers are less competent and less committed than teachers elsewhere.

Urban school systems everywhere are increasingly pressured, and population mobility is creating new urban areas whose schools will soon be facing the same conditions. Unless the current level of understanding about urban education is deepened substantially and shared nationally, the disjunction between political pressure for reform and lack of substantial progress by reform initiatives will eventually create destructive conflicts across the country.

The mixed picture presented by urban reform—lots of activity, some progress, lots of schools where there's still little change—represents a precarious position, because the public's patience is limited. As reforms grow more publicly visible, the consequences of failure grow direr. The stakes are extremely high. Calls have already begun for abandonment or wholesale transformation of the whole enterprise of urban public education, in the form of vouchers, privatization, or some other form of competitive, market-economic system of allocating educational resources. As the saying has it, "No good deed goes unpunished." Reform is undoubtedly a good deed, with people of goodwill working daily to make it happen. If success does not come with the speed demanded by intense public interest and large public expenditure, who will pay the bill—who will be punished?

Will it be urban students, who are largely poor, African American, Hispanic, and Asian? One researcher has estimated that in Texas over a recent five-year period at least 100,000 black and Hispanic students did not graduate as a result of the state's high-stakes assessment system.[15] Is this evidence of successful reform—a courageous legislature drawing an Alamo-like line in the sand to show it's serious about high standards; or proof of institutional racism—a thinly disguised attempt on the part of the white, English-speaking dominant culture to deny immigrants and "minorities" access to a basic qualification for both employment and entrance to college, a high school diploma?

Will it be teachers? In one school system I know, an "exemplary" reading curriculum achieved measurable success in a summer program with motivated students and a 10-to-1 student-teacher ratio. In the fall an administrator wanted to mandate it in a classroom with 33 students and a student body that locked the teacher out of class more than once. If those students don't achieve the same measurable gains as the summer group, should the teacher be fired?

Will it be principals? As urban systems realize that a key to good schools is strong leadership, superintendents are demanding much more from principals and holding them more directly accountable for student learning. At the same time, conditions for learning—up-to-date textbooks in sufficient numbers, paper and pencils, a school library, a decent physical plant, adequately trained teachers—are still woefully inadequate in all too many cases.[16] High turnover rates for principals are increasingly common— approximately 25 percent of principals are new each year in New York City, and in the early years of reform in Chicago the rate was even higher—and in many cities principal openings attract many fewer candidates than they did only a few years ago. In contrast, superintendents are looking for well-trained, hard-working principals who can move reform forward in their buildings. One new principal I know who fits this description was taken out of his building last year in an ambulance because of the workload, the stress, and the hours. In schools that combine multiple simultaneous reforms, high-stakes standardized testing, and a chronically inadequate resource base, the urban principalship is fast becoming a job that punishes those who try hardest to do it well.

One antidote to the "blame game" is to understand how impervious to change the deep structure of American schools has been over the last 100 years. Another is to grasp the close connection between social and economic conditions and school success, particularly in urban areas, and to understand equity issues as attempts to alter decades-long legal and illegal denials of educational opportunity to minority children. Chapter Three examines these issues in detail.

## NOTES

1. Lawrence A. Cremin, *Popular Education and Its Discontents* (New York: Harper and Row, 1990), vii–viii.

2. Patricia Graham, "Battleships and Schools," *Daedalus* 124, no. 4 (1995): 43.

3. James Fraser, "Agents of Democracy: Urban Elementary-school Teachers and the Conditions of Teaching," in *American Teachers: Histories of a Profession at Work,* ed. Donald Warren (New York: Macmillan, 1989).

4. Herbert May and Bruce Metzger, eds., *The New Oxford Annotated Bible with the Apocrypha, Revised Standard Version* (New York: Oxford, 1977), 4.

5. L. S. Vygotsky, *Mind in Society* (Cambridge: Harvard, 1978).

6. *Webster's New World Dictionary of the American Language,* 2nd college ed., *s. v.* "critical."

7. Judith Baker, *<JudithBakr@aol.com >* "High Standards," 22 October 1999, *<care@yahoogroups.com>* (24 October 1999).

8. National Commission on Excellence in Education, *A Nation at Risk: the Imperatives for Educational Reform,* (Washington, DC: U.S. Department of Education, 1983).

9. *Popular Education,* 39.

10. David Berliner and Bruce Biddle, *The Manufactured Crisis: Myths, Fraud, and the Attack on America's Public Schools* (Reading, MA: Addison-Wesley, 1995).

11. *Popular Education,* 31.

12. Larry Cuban, "The Great School Scam," *Education Week,* 15 June 1994.

13. Gary Anderson, "Toward Authentic Participation: Deconstructing the Discourses of Participatory Reforms in Education," *American Educational Research Journal* 35, no. 4 (1998): 571–603; L. Christensen, "Reconstituting Jefferson," *Rethinking Schools* 13, no. 1 (1998): 1, 8; Richard Elmore, "Getting to Scale with Good Educational Practice,"*Harvard Educational Review* 66, no. 1 (1996): 1–26; Richard Elmore and Milbrey McLaughlin, *Steady Work: Policy, Practice, and the Reform of American Education* (Santa Monica, CA: Rand, 1988); Michael Fullan, "Turning Systemic Thinking on Its Head,"*Phi Delta Kappan* 77, no. 6 (1996): 420–23; Michael Fullan and Matthew Miles, "Getting Reform Right: What Works and What Doesn't," *Phi Delta Kappan* 73, no. 10 (1992): 744–52; James Hoffman, "When Bad Things Happen to Good Ideas in Literacy Education: Professional Dilemmas, Personal Decisions, and Political Traps," *The Reading Teacher* 52, no. 2 (1998): 102–11; Edward Miller, "Idealists and Cynics: The Micropolitics of Systemic School Reform," *The Harvard Education Letter* XII, no. 4 (1996): 1–3; Donna Muncey and Patrick McQuillan, "Preliminary Findings from a Five-year Study of the Coalition of Essential Schools,"*Phi Delta Kappan* 74, no. 6 (1993): 486–89; David Tyack and William Tobin, "The 'Grammar' of Schooling: Why Has It Been So Hard to Change?" *American Educational Research Journal* 31, no. 3 (1994): 453–79.

14. Elmore and McLaughlin.

15. Walt Haney, "The Myth of the Texas Miracle in Education," *Education Policy Analysis Archives* (electronic journal) 8, no. 41 (2000).

16. Jonathon Kozol, *Savage Inequalities: Children in America's Schools* (New York: Crown, 1991).

*Chapter 3*

# Deepening Our Thinking About Reform

While proponents of the new reform agenda are eager to dissociate themselves from the mistakes of federal reform since 1960, they are likely to repeat many of these mistakes in the absence of a clear understanding of that experience. The emphasis may have shifted from federal to state and local policy, but the issues are much the same.
—Richard F. Elmore and Milbrey W. McLaughlin[1]

To judge from the ahistorical character of most current policy talk about reform, innovators may consider amnesia a virtue.
—David Tyack and Larry Cuban[2]

## WHY LISTEN TO HISTORY?
## PRESENTISM VS. THE HISTORICAL RECORD

Americans care about education. Among topics the public considers important, polls consistently show it at or near the top. Schooling is regularly in the news, and a position on education is an essential part of most campaign platforms. But both media and politics are lured by simple answers to complex questions, quick fixes for long-standing problems. As a result, the public's interest in education reform has been passionate without being deep. Media and public policy have given little consideration, for example, to reform as a recurring feature of American schooling. Even less have they explored the American public school's abiding roots in the past and long record of resistance to change.

This systematic forgetting is a serious flaw in current reform efforts, for it deprives us of knowledge that can help shape the planning and implementation of necessary change. Among major reform programs only Ted

Sizer's Coalition of Essential Schools is structured with a recognition of the significant past. Sizer's historical knowledge of American high schools was essential to the development of his designs for change.[3] Perhaps not coincidentally, these designs have been widely and voluntarily adopted by schools across the country.

I will begin this chapter by giving our public amnesia its scholarly name—"presentism"—and suggesting why historical knowledge is particularly important to those who propose to reform *urban* education. I will move to a review of selected interpretive frameworks from four prominent educational historians. I will then use these frameworks to identify points of intersection between the mainstream narrative of American schooling and the educational histories of the three non-mainstream groups who make up the vast majority of today's urban students: African-, Hispanic-, and Asian Americans. Throughout I will call attention to the role that politics, language, and culture (including race) have played and continue to play in urban schooling—a role that is seldom acknowledged by policymakers, who are likely to be members of mainstream culture with little first-hand knowledge of urban contexts for teaching and learning.

### Combating Presentism

I often ask colleagues who know I work in Boston this question: when was the first desegregation suit brought against the Boston Public Schools? Aware of the city's stormy history of mandatory busing, most people guess the late 1960s or the early 1970s. They are wrong by over 100 years.

My colleagues' knowledge of school desegregation begins with the 1954 federal court decision in *Brown v. Board of Education*. Often they know of the contentious and sometimes violent struggle to desegregate the Boston schools through court-ordered busing in the early 1970s. Some are old enough to remember nightly news footage of buses full of black children being stoned by white anti-busing demonstrators; others have read *Common Ground*,[4] the context-rich, Pulitzer-Prize winning account of black and white families with children in Boston's schools during this time.

My colleagues are surprised, then, to learn that the first organized attempt to gain equal schooling for Boston's black children took place shortly after the American Revolution and the first school desegregation suit was brought before the Civil War. In 1787, Prince Hall unsuccessfully sought access to public schools for African American children. In 1834 a local white merchant endowed a separate school for blacks. Throughout the 1840s Boston's African American community campaigned for equality in schooling.

These events led directly to the filing of Boston's first school desegregation litigation, the Roberts case. In 1848 Benjamin Roberts attempted to enroll his daughter Sarah in each of the five white public schools that stood between their home and the Smith School. When Sarah was denied entrance to all of them, Roberts sued the city. On April 8, 1850 the Massachusetts Supreme Court ruled against Roberts. The decision was *not* based, as we might expect, on inequality of access—in fact, both sides stipulated that facilities were unequal. Instead, the court ruled that the law clearly gave Boston's Primary School Committee the authority to make the racial distinctions that it made, therefore the court had no obligation to take equality of facilities into account. Nell and his group then filed bills in the state legislature to end public school segregation; a first bill failed in 1851, but an amended version passed in 1855. In the fall of 1855, black children in Boston began attending the public schools closest to their homes.[5]

The 1972 Boston desegregation case, following the famous ruling in *Brown* that "separate but equal is inherently unequal," addressed the question the Massachusetts Supreme Court had sidestepped more than 120 years before. The plaintiffs proved that the school committee had created and maintained a separate, black public school system within the Boston Public Schools, and that this shadow system was grossly inferior in essential areas like physical plant, learning resources, and teacher qualifications, denying black children equal access to education.

Though the 1850 and 1972 Boston desegregation cases differ in the basis on which a decision was rendered, they share a common pattern: a black community concerned for the education of its children being denied equity at the local level, and seeking redress at higher levels, through state and federal courts and the state legislature. Later in this chapter I will provide evidence that this pattern, in which minority parents are forced to become adversaries rather than allies of school authorities in order to secure a quality education for their children, is common throughout the nineteenth and twentieth centuries not just in the black community but also among Asian and Hispanic Americans. In many ways, it forms the typical or normative frame of reference for minority communities towards their local schools.

Why is this knowledge significant in the context of urban school reform? For one thing it opens for white teachers and administrators, who make up the huge majority of professionals in urban schools, the possibility of seeing race issues in a new way. If, for instance, you are a principal or teacher in Boston and you think desegregation as an issue started in the 1970s, then the progress we have made to date, though inadequate, may not seem too bad. But what if you know that the desegregation case filed in 1972 asked for a remedy to the same problem Benjamin Roberts had tried to address over 120 years earlier? Your notion of "progress" and your level of faith in "the system" will be quite different. You will have begun to understand some of the anger, frustration, and despair felt by many black parents, teachers, and political leaders in Boston, members of a community which at the dawn of the twenty-first century had been fighting for over 150 years to achieve the same simple goal: a quality public education for its children. As the city histories in Section Two will show, Boston is hardly unique in this regard.

The lack of historical knowledge about desegregation in Boston is a small example of a larger phenomenon which affects much of the thinking behind urban reform: "present-mindedness" or "presentism." Historians use these terms to refer to "an obsession with the recent and the present"[6] that seems endemic to our now-oriented culture. When headlines scream that American schools are worse than they have ever been, official reports claim we're facing an educational crisis that's "unprecedented," or unions claim teachers have never been treated worse, their exaggerated claims are presentist. By treating today's perspective as the only valid one, presentism causes us to think, speak, and act as if current events are entirely unconnected to their roots in the past.

In fact, attempts to achieve widespread change have been a recurring feature of American educational history, they have been regularly studied by educational historians, and those studies can yield important lessons for today. If we ignore these lessons we can gain only a limited understanding of current problems, and therefore we are in a much poorer position to solve them. Combating presentism, then, requires that we take the historical record seriously, listening to history not as an infallible oracle but as one way to deepen our thinking about positive change in urban schools and effective ways to accomplish it. With this in mind I will consider now a small number of relevant concepts, frameworks, and analyses from four widely respected guides to the history of American education—Lawrence Cremin, David Tyack and Larry Cuban, and Patricia Albjerg Graham. I will follow this with a short, historical look at the struggles of immigrant and minority communities to gain the advantages of education.

### Educational Ecology, Education vs. Schooling, the "Cacophony of Teaching"

The late Lawrence Cremin is among the most eminent of American educational historians. Throughout his work he develops three concepts which can help us understand why reforming urban education is so complicated. These concepts also suggest shapes effective reform might take. The first is his "ecological approach" to education, the second his development of John Dewey's distinction between *education* and *schooling*, and the third his notion of a "cacophony of teaching."

Cremin defines an "ecological approach" to education as "one that views educational institutions and configurations in relation to one another and to the larger society that sustains them and is in turn affected by them." Significantly, he illustrates this definition with the following comparison:

what we have traditionally thought of as the extraordinary influence of the nineteenth-century common school . . . derived not so much from the common school per se as from a configuration of education of which the common school was only one element. Ordinarily including the white Protestant family, the white Protestant church, and the white Protestant Sunday school along with the common school, it was a configuration in which the values and pedagogies of the several component institutions happened to be mutually supportive. Other contemporary configurations were fraught with internal conflict . . . if one considers the Indian reservation as a configuration of education, one is immediately impressed by the tensions between familial instruction and missionary instruction, between Indian values and white values, between the virtues of resistance and the virtues of accommodation. . . .[7]

Considered as configurations of education "fraught with internal conflict," many urban public schools may have more in common with reservation schools than with their supposed ancestor, the common school. Such conflicts—between family and school attitudes towards pedagogy, between "white values" and the values held by communities of color, between resistance and accommodation—are well documented in recent literature on urban schooling.[8] Though such language-, culture-, and race-based conflicts are enacted in school settings, their sources lie not just in the school, but in social conflicts outside it.

When curriculums are driven by mandated standards and high stakes testing, ecological effects both positive and negative are magnified, because "standards involve much more than determinations of what knowledge is of most worth; they also involve social and cultural differences, and they frequently serve as symbols and surrogates for those differences." If, for example, parents place their children "in predominantly White private schools, which they perceive as having high standards, instead of racially integrated public schools, which they perceive as having low standards . . . the perceptions may or may not conform to reality . . . but the very choices on the part of parents may create a measure of mutual support between home and school . . . (that) makes a self-fulfilling prophecy of the choice." On the other hand, citing the work of anthropologist John H. Ogbu as well as his own studies, Cremin considers the case of "groups that perceive themselves as outside the system." Certain sub-communities of African Americans, working-class whites, and ethnoreligious minorities may resist schooling because they see schools as "instruments for socializing their children to subservient roles . . . given the reality of compulsory attendance, their only option other than truancy is to fail."[9]

It should be no surprise, then, that the ecological approach led Cremin to conclude that what happens in the classroom—*schooling*—is only part, and often the least dramatic part, of a student's learning. *Education*, on the other hand, includes familial circumstances and influences prior to, during, and after schooling, as well as learning that takes place in babysitting and day care, boys and girls clubs, scouting, church groups, museums, clubs, gangs, peer groups, the armed services, job-related training programs, and myriad other formal and informal settings.

Popular media form an illustrative case in point. Radio, television, computers, video games, the internet, movies, and music play an educative role that, for good or ill, has grown increasingly powerful. Cremin called this multiplicity of educational influences a "cacophony of teaching," citing Marshall McCluhan's observation that "The electronic environment makes an information level outside the schoolroom that is far higher than the information level inside. . . . The child knows that in going to school he is in some sense interrupting his education."[10] Schooling competes for attention with other educative values and forces in the student's environment, a reality that classroom teachers know all too well.

### The Lessons of One Hundred Years of Reform

In *Tinkering Toward Utopia: A Century of Public School Reform,*[11] David Tyack and Larry Cuban review the progress of educational reform in the twentieth century and attempt to answer some basic questions about change, including:

Why have Americans believed in progress in education for over a century but have come to doubt it in recent years?

How have schools changed reforms, as opposed to reforms changing schools?

Why has the grammar of schooling—the organizational forms that govern instruction—persisted, while challenges to it have mostly been evanescent?

Why have outsiders' attempts to reinvent schooling—break-the-mold strategies—generally been short-lived shooting stars?[12]

They conclude that our schools are neither as bad as they are currently painted, nor as likely to see rapid, systemic change as many current reformers believe, because "The ahistorical nature of most current reform arguments results in both a magnification of present defects in relation to the past and an understatement of the difficulty of changing the system."[13]

Tyack and Cuban believe that making change "at the heart of education—classroom instruction" is both the most important goal for reform and the hardest to achieve. Such a change "will result in the future more from internal changes created by the knowledge and expertise of teachers than from the decisions of external policymakers," particularly if reforms are designed to be "hybridized" by schools, by which they mean "adapted by educators working together to take advantage of their knowledge of their own diverse students and communities and supporting each other in new ways of teaching." They also stress the importance of involving parents in such reforms, particularly when change involves new structures or teaching methods that depart significantly from traditional notions of what constitutes "real school."[14]

One clear lesson they draw from 100 years of school reform speaks eloquently to today's reformers: "Unless practitioners are also enlisted in defining problems and devising solutions adapted to their own varied circumstances and local knowledge, lasting improvement will probably not occur in classrooms."[15]

### Schooling's Response to Social Demands: A Century of Change

In a set of recent articles Patricia Albjerg Graham outlines the responses public schools have made, over the past 100 years, to changing demands of the larger society.[16] She identifies four social goals schools have been asked to meet—Assimilation, Adjustment, Access, and Achievement—and argues that schools have responded successfully to the first three. The fourth and current goal, high academic achievement for all, is unprecedented, and will require an unprecedented commitment from both schools and society.

In the *assimilation* period (1900–1925), "the schools performed the astonishingly successful transformation of taking many children whose family culture and often . . . language was foreign and converting them into adults who were Americans . . . the school was the primary means through which the children of immigrants encountered American institutions."[17] High academic performance was neither sought nor achieved for the majority of students, because "the schools' principal goal was moral, to create citizens who possessed the habits of heart and will to function well in this new land and who were sufficiently if minimally literate."[18]

But these successes were achieved with European populations who were, to use Ogbu's term, "voluntary migrants." In contrast, says Graham, "Little effort was made to assimilate the 10 percent of the population who were of African ancestry." For them, as well as for Native Americans, Hispanics, and some Asians, "melting pot rules applied differently . . . often particular efforts were made . . . to rid them of their own cultural traditions and get them to accept uncritically the dominant culture."[19]

For all cultural groups, graduation from high school was neither required nor expected. Young men could enter the work force with few academic skills; young women were assumed to be headed for futures as wives, mothers, and homemakers. In New York, considered the best urban school system of the time, "of 1,000 children entering city schools in 1908 . . . only 263 would reach eighth grade and a bare 56 the fourth year of high school."[20]

As the pace of immigration slowed and the schools made assimilation a reality, social emphasis shifted to *adjustment* (1925–1954). Schools took on two new missions: educating the "whole child" and social sorting. The Progressive Education movement, even as it argued for developing the whole child, "implicitly . . . defined (the child) by his or her social contexts."[21]

The later Life Adjustment movement held that one in five students should receive a college preparatory education, another one in five vocational training, and the remaining 60 percent a general track curriculum. The academic side of schooling—curriculum, pedagogy, academic testing—took a back seat to social and civic goals. With more students staying past the eighth grade, schooling was strongly influenced by the U.S. Bureau of Education's Seven Cardinal Principles of secondary education: health, command of fundamental processes, worthy home membership, vocation, civic education, worthy use of leisure time, and ethical character. In sharp contrast to today's reforms, of the seven principles only one, command of fundamental processes, "even hinted at academic activities, and it conveyed a sense of primitive academic mastery. The remaining six all were nonacademic in their content. High school educators took this emphasis to heart and developed programs that matched the goals . . ." which led them "to minimize the significance of academic learning . . ."[22]

In the *access period* (1954–1983) a new social direction was signaled. The 1954 Supreme Court decision in *Brown v. Board of Education* pushed schools to provide access to those previously denied it. Specifically, "separate but equal" educational arrangements were declared to be "inherently unequal."[23] For schools conditioned to maintaining the status quo, this was a new and unfamiliar task: "Few educational leaders in mid-century envisioned their role to be that of increasing social justice . . . but most elementary and secondary schools found themselves assigned this obligation by the courts."[24] Emphasis on access continued with attention to economically disadvantaged children in the Elementary and Secondary Education Act of 1965 and to special needs children with the Education for All Handicapped Act (PL 94–142) in 1975, as well with state and federal legislation aimed at easing the academic transition of students whose first language was not English.

The current *achievement* period (1983–present) was kicked off by the publication of *A Nation at Risk*.[25] Its attempt to make high academic achievement a goal that all students should reach is unprecedented in the history of American education. The new goal arises from new economic and social realities. Prominent among these are the country's rapid transformation from a manufacturing economy to one based on information and services, and a huge and continuing surge of non-European immigration. Together these create the need for an increasingly educated work force and put increasing pressure on public schools to supply it. Fewer and fewer good jobs are available to those who attended public school but did not achieve academically. Though universal achievement and high test results have been announced as goals, "Nowhere do we find from our national leadership constructive proposals on the means by which these goals can be achieved."[26] Graham concludes that "A national strategy that relies on ringing alarm bells, proposing goals, and providing tests as its key elements but fails to address the conditions of either children or schools is unworthy of America."[27]

### Ecology, Cacophony, and Reform

State legislatures can mandate rigorous curricula, high stakes testing, and greater accountability and can provide funding to support these mandates. But history suggests that such reforms are likely to have greatest effect on those communities least in need of them: relatively well-funded, adequately performing suburban systems with a high level of congruence between the goals of schooling and the surrounding educational ecology. By contrast, America's urban teachers labor on the raw edge of a sad contradiction: the richest country in the world has levels of child poverty "substantially higher—often two-to-three times higher—than that of most other major Western industrialized nations."[28] The positive effects of reform on urban schools will be limited unless school-focused change is accompanied by parallel improvements in the educative environment—adequate food and shelter, affordable day care and health care, a living wage for working parents, opportunities for involvement with museums, clubs, churches and youth organizations, and other, similar steps.

Further, there is little in today's reforms to address the historic gap between those outside schools who dictate reform and those inside who must implement it. Current reforms focus on the school as the unit of improvement and on high achievement on the "new basics" of curriculum as the primary measurable outcome. This approach leaves little room for ecological questions. In stark contrast, urban teachers must deal firsthand with both reform and ecology. They face, on the one hand, mandated standards and high stakes testing, and on the other, social realities like widespread poverty, "electronic babysitting," students working 20 or more hours a week for minimum wage, fallout from family stresses, and the closing of neighborhood libraries and youth centers. Teaching large classes with few resources, they must make their lessons heard amidst the "cacophony of teaching," competing against powerful electronic, cultural, and economic messages which bombard students in the 18 hours a day they spend outside school. It is hardly surprising, then, that the "culture of practice" is at times reluctant to embrace reform. Many urban teachers understand, even if they don't dare to articulate, that in the long run they and their students stand a good chance of becoming not the beneficiaries of reform, but its victims.

## THE PERCEPTION OF CRISIS AND THE DIFFICULTY OF CHANGE

History sharpens our appreciation of painful ironies, and educational history is no exception. Some examples:

- Judged by the standards applied in the past, today's schools are no worse and in many ways better than they have ever been. The nation is not, in fact, at risk from a badly failing educational system. By and large, parents still think that the school their child attends is doing a good job; but parents of school-age children form a much smaller percentage of the overall population than previously. As fewer and fewer Americans come into direct contact with schools, the demands on schools grow greater and the level of dissatisfaction grows higher. This dissatisfaction is part of a more general loss of confidence in public institutions. Yet reform policies developed by these institutions, particularly executive and legislative bodies, are our chief means of curing ailing schools. As in the access period, the judicial branch of government often serves as arbiter-of-last-resort in politically controversial areas like school finance reform and provision of education to immigrant and second-language students. It is not surprising then, that non-governmental groups, both for-profit and not-for-profit, have a growing voice in school reform, or that direct or indirect privatization schemes are being increasingly urged as "the answer." When the reform "question" is framed simplistically and government is seen only as part of the problem, this answer can look attractive. When both the reform question and public institutions are seen in their full historical complexity and schools are viewed as responding to social demands, we begin to glimpse the immense national effort it will take to actually achieve aims like those so facilely set out in documents like *A Nation at Risk* and *Goals 2000*.

- Schools are not being judged by the standards of the past, but by the goals of the future. This may not be fair, but it explains a great deal. To say that American schools have not declined and have even improved in some areas, while historically and educationally true, misses the political point, and school reform is a deeply political issue. When voters say "our schools are failing," what they often mean is something like, "I'm afraid for the future of our children" coupled with "schools are the only viable institution our kids have left." If achievement is the new social directive for schools, then as in the access period schools are being asked to take on a vanguard role for society as a whole. But the public does not see school improvement in this light; rather it sees schools as having declined from a golden age of previous success, an age that never actually existed.

- Expectations of mandatory attendance, universal access, and high academic achievement by *all* students are unprecedented, and meeting them will require both new teaching approaches and high levels of additional resources, as well as major contributions from surrounding societal structures in which schools are imbedded. Past efforts suggest that reforms aimed at administrative structures and systemic change are among those least likely to succeed. Yet reform to date has concentrated almost exclusively on such changes: school-based management, more authority for principals, new basics of curriculum, high-stakes testing. Largely ignored has been historical evidence that improvement in urban schools is immensely aided by policies that address not just school structures, but the surrounding ecology. Successful urban school reform will require partnerships (between school and community, public sector and private) that promote strong families, active churches and community groups, affordable housing, more equitable distribution of economic benefits, accessible health care, and the dismantling of social barriers based on race and ethnicity.

But securing adequate resources and changing societal attitudes are long, contentious processes. This suggests a political use for presentism: it masks the consensus-building necessary to reach these goals. It's easy for diverse constituencies to agree, for instance, that all children should learn to read by the third grade. It is immensely more difficult and more divisive to acknowledge the changes it would take to achieve this goal, and to campaign for the resources necessary to meet it. Is making sure all children can read by grade three more important than more missiles? More important than extending the war on drugs to Latin America? These are the kinds of trade-offs it would likely take to expand the federal role to the extent necessary to meet *Goals 2000*. Presentism as a political strategy helps insure such a debate will never take place.

The success of instructional reform lies in what happens between teachers and students when the classroom door is closed. Because of this, the attitudes reform programs take towards teachers are of major importance; it is troubling that in so many instances that attitude is so negative. Teachers are often perceived as underprepared, too old, too set in their ways, too demoralized, and too restricted by union contracts to do the job that reform requires them to do. Prescriptive "exemplary programs" try to change behavior in ways that implicitly or explicitly deny teachers' knowledge, expertise, and autonomy. While there are certainly poor teachers as well as good ones, blaming teachers is another of the simplistic reform strategies that history has proven to be unsuccessful. Even if all of today's teachers were to be replaced tomorrow—a solution I have heard advocated more than once by frustrated urban principals—it is unlikely that a new generation of teachers would prove to be substantially different, unless the conditions in which they teach and the leadership of their schools improved as well.

More realistically, there is on the horizon no undiscovered cadre of teachers who will ask fewer uncomfortable questions, get more advanced training, and work more hours for less money and fewer benefits. In fact, the rate at which new teachers are leaving urban schools suggests the opposite. Significantly, fewer minority candidates are entering teaching. According to the National Education Association, data from the National Center for Education Statistics show that "by the early twenty-first century, the percentage of minority teachers is expected to shrink to an all-time low of 5 percent, while 41 percent of American students will be minorities."[29] A recent review of teacher education programs revealed a discouraging lack of preparation for this diversity.[30] If current trends continue, change will come about, if it comes, largely through the cooperation of the current teaching force, or one much like it.

History suggests strongly that devaluing the contributions of teachers may be the single biggest mistake reformers can make, because no reform succeeds without teachers' explicit or implicit assent. Schools differ in size, in culture, in functioning, in their attitudes towards change. Under the best conditions, policy-based reforms require adaptation to local settings and individual school needs. When they choose to do so, teachers and principals are adept at minimal compliance, outright sabotage, or just "laying low" till the current reform blows over, then going back to business as usual. In large, urban systems repeated attempts at reform produce layers of complexity which themselves become barriers to change. Tyack and Cuban, citing New York City's regular attempts to decentralize and re-centralize its schools, note that "Each governance reform builds on layers of previous changes going back more than a century. Under such circumstances, the complexity of running a vast system makes 'school governance' sound like an oxymoron."[31]

At the moment, systemic reform seems to proceed on the assumption that the farther one is from the classroom, the greater one's credibility in designing solutions. In contrast, a long history of previous attempts at reform warns us that, if reform is to have any chance of success, teachers cannot be made the scapegoats of change, they must be enlisted as its allies. This means that they must be respected as professionals and as people, their input must be sought and taken seriously in the planning stages of change as well as in the implementation stages, and their views of what works in schools must be attended to, not disregarded.

### The Importance of "Minority" Perspectives

Economic and cultural groups who have historically been minorities form the majority student population of today's urban schools. In bellweather states like California, Texas, and Florida they constitute or will soon constitute the majority of *all* public school students. Recent statistics on the preschool population of Suffolk County, MA, the county where I work and which includes Boston and three nearby towns, give some indication of the rate at which demographic changes are occurring. U.S. Census data for 1999 showed 13,790 white children under the age of four, as compared to 20,630 African American children, 10,815 Hispanic children, and 4,704 Asian children. Similar figures for 1990 showed 19,165 white, 16,447 black, 8,275 Hispanic, and 2,689 Asian children.[32]

With rates of change like those shown in Table 3.1, it is difficult to over-emphasize the importance demographic factors will have for schools in the immediate future. If we are to enrich our thinking about reform by delving into the relevant past, it is important to ask what the experience of this emerging majority has been in relation to the mainstream of American education.

Table 3.1
Percent Change by Race/Ethnicity, Children Under Age Four, Suffolk Co., MA, 1990, 1999

|          | White   | Black   | Hispanic | Asian   |
|----------|---------|---------|----------|---------|
| % change | –28%    | +25%    | +31%     | +75%    |
| 1999     | 13,790  | 20,630  | 10,815   | 4,704   |
| 1990     | 19,165  | 16,477  | 8,275    | 2,689   |

Cremin, Tyack and Cuban, and Graham all touch upon this experience in their larger historical accounts, and Graham's four-stage schema can provide a platform for further exploration. From a mainstream perspective, the concerns of minority communities erupt with seeming suddenness in 1954, triggering what Graham calls the *access* period (1954–83). But recent research in educational and social history can help us recover a deeper story: the exclusion from education of America's Hispanic, African American, and Asian communities going back to the assimilation period and beyond. Familiarity with this story can provide us with a better understanding of deep-seated political, linguistic, and cultural forces at work in schools today, forces that represent significant but often hidden barriers to reform.

For example, today's urban areas are experiencing a second great wave of immigration, the first being the years from immediately prior to the assimilation period to the 1920s.[33] It is common (and true) to point out the most obvious difference between new immigrants and old: the vast majority of new immigrants are not white Europeans but immigrants of color from Asia, Mexico, Central and South America, the Caribbean, and Africa. But there is a danger in this truism. It may lead us to assume that because the rate at which "new immigrants" are appearing is unprecedented, their presence in the American social landscape is also unprecedented. Nothing could be further from the truth. Asian Americans have been in the United States longer than many European immigrant groups, and thousands of Chicanos in Texas and the Southwest are descended from ancestors who never immigrated at all, they just kept living in villages and on farms where their families had been for over 100 years. Treaties between the United States and Mexico made their lands and villages part of the United States.

Between 1880 and 1920 millions of European immigrants entered the United States. The sheer numbers had an impact, but understanding who the immigrants were in the eyes of mainstream America is the key to understanding the role public schools were asked to play in educating them. They were largely Catholic and Jewish; Irish and southern or eastern European; unskilled; poorly educated; and fleeing war, famine, and poverty. "Ellis

Island" stories which mythologize the European immigrant experience have passed into national folklore. Such stories generally focus on two themes: triumph over economic obstacles and elbowing out a place in the American social order. What those obstacles were, particularly in terms of educational attitudes, is less explicitly remembered. The religious, cultural and (in the terms of the time) racial backgrounds of the new immigrants were seen as highly questionable. Even progressive leaders such as Ellwood Cubberly, Dean of the School of Education at Stanford University, held sentiments like these expressed in 1919:

These southern and eastern Europeans were of a very different type from the North and West Europeans who preceded them. Largely illiterate, docile, lacking in initiative, and almost wholly without the Anglo-Saxon conceptions of righteousness, liberty, law, order, public decency, and government, their coming has served to dilute tremendously our national stock and to weaken and corrupt our political life . . . popular education everywhere has been made more difficult by their presence. . . . The new peoples . . . have come so fast that we have been unable to absorb and assimilate them, and our national life, for the past quarter of a century, has been afflicted with a serious case of racial indigestion.[34]

"Racial indigestion" caused by European immigrants arriving faster than they could be absorbed may have been unpleasant, but at least it presumed that in time, through schooling, they *could* be absorbed and the dilution of "our national stock" reversed. This presumption rested, in turn, on an implied kinship between all Europeans, whether "noble" Anglo-Saxons or "degenerate" Irish, Italians, Poles, or Russians. No such kinship was presumed to exist with non-European groups: Native Americans, Asians, Mexicans, Puerto Ricans, African Americans. There was therefore no argument for assimilation-through-education, and their widespread exclusion from mainstream activity (including education) or relegation to second-class status was a common practice.

When Asians began to arrive in significant numbers, as Sucheng Chan has pointed out, "four of the major groups—the Chinese, Japanese, Asian Indians, and Filipinos—were each excluded by law two or three decades after their initial arrival."[35] The Chinese Exclusion Act of 1882 (renewed in 1892 and extended in 1902), insured that Europe—albeit southern and eastern Europe—would remain the primary source for new Americans. The Act's effects were immediate and striking. It was as if an iron gate had suddenly been slammed down, closing America to the Chinese: in 1882, 39,579 Chinese immigrants were recorded; three years later the total was 22.[36]

Exclusionary laws slackened but did not stem the tide of Asian immigration. Japanese in particular continued to come, 256,196 arriving between 1900 and 1925.[37] Not only was gaining legal entry into the United States significantly more difficult for Asian immigrants, once they arrived they faced an additional barrier: a federal law barring non-whites from becoming naturalized citizens.[38]

From the late 1800s legal barriers to immigration and assimilation were regularly challenged by West Coast Asian Americans, particularly the Chinese American community. According to legal scholars Charles and Laurene Wu McClain,

> Contrary to the popular image of the Chinese in the United States as passive victims of racial discrimination . . . while the Chinese were indeed victims, they were not passive. Angered by the discriminatory laws enacted to humiliate and exclude them, the Chinese decided to take their grievances to the American courts . . . their cases did profoundly affect the course of American jurisprudence, contributing in a significant way to the molding of due-process and equal-protection jurisprudence under the fourteenth amendment.[39]

From this perspective it should come as no surprise that *Lau v. Nichols*, the 1974 legal challenge that ultimately resulted in congressional bilingual education legislation, was brought in a federal court against the San Francisco public schools by a Chinese mother, with the full support of San Francisco's Chinese American community. *Lau v. Nichols,* a key access period event, turns out to be another instance, like that of Boston's 1970s desegregation case, where what seems on the surface to be a contemporary response to a contemporary problem is in fact the latest battle in an ongoing, historically-rooted struggle by a community of color to gain equal treatment under the law. As we will see in the upcoming city profiles of Chicago, Bay Area, and Boston, historically rooted local conditions of politics, language, and culture have strong effects on top-down, nationally inspired systemic reforms.

Immigration from Mexico, Central and South America, and the Caribbean began to gain momentum during the assimilation period. In our current anti-immigrant climate it is difficult to imagine, but for a good portion of the twentieth century our border with Mexico was for all practical purposes non-existent. Because of the huge volume of European immigrants during the assimilation period, U.S. authorities were geared up to process new arrivals who came by boat. Before 1908 no counts were made of "walk-ins" who arrived by land through either Canada or Mexico. Even after 1908 not all entering aliens were recorded. According to a U.S. government source, "Before 1930, no count was made of residents of a year or longer of . . . Mexico who planned to remain in the United States less than 6 months."[40]

Between 1930 and 1945, immigration status was often based on the "announced intentions" of the newcomer. Land immigration, of course, then as now included Central Americans who entered through Mexico. In some government records a separate immigration category called "Other

America" was used to report Central and South American and West Indian (Cuban, Dominican, and Haitian) immigrants, whether they arrived by land or by boat.

Though it is extremely difficult to determine the full extent of Mexican and Central American immigration, it is clear that official figures even when available greatly underrepresent this population. Even so, the recorded numbers are substantial. One source estimates that in 1924, 87,648 Mexicans were legally admitted and that this number is equal to 45 percent of southern and eastern European immigration for the same year.[41]

Table 3.2 shows a comparison of one set of official statistics on immigration from Mexico, other America, and Ireland at five-year intervals between 1910 and 1930. Clearly, in the early decades of the twentieth century the European immigrant experience was not the only one of significance.

In fact, throughout most of the twentieth century the United States made it easy for Mexicans and other Americans to come to "El Norte" because U.S. agriculture and industry needed controllable, expendable, low-wage workers. The workers in turn were simultaneously pushed and pulled by forces similar to those which affected Irish and southern and eastern European immigrants—civil war, famine, and lack of opportunity at home, the lure of higher wages and a better life in the United States. During World War II the United States recruited Mexican workers to meet the wartime labor shortage, using buses to transport laborers from inland villages in Mexico to American industrial centers. As a result, vigorous Mexican American communities are part of today's urban landscape not just in southwestern and western cities like Houston and Los Angeles, but in northern cities like Detroit and Chicago.

No one should underestimate the difficulties faced by the European immigrants, or their strength and resiliency in overcoming them. But it is equally important to understand that the legal, social, and attitudinal obstacles faced by non-European immigrants differed not just in degree, but in kind. Mexican children, for example, were segregated from the main-

Table 3.2
**Immigrants by Area of Origin, Five-Year Intervals, 1910–1930[42]**

|      | Mexico | Other America | Ireland |
|------|--------|---------------|---------|
| 1910 | 18,691 | 14,280        | 29,855  |
| 1915 | 12,340 | 16,651        | 14,185  |
| 1920 | 52,361 | 20,280        | 9,591   |
| 1925 | 32,964 | 5,779         | 26,650  |
| 1930 | 12,703 | 10,147        | 23,445  |

stream socially and linguistically, and frequently received an intermittent and substandard education. Ronald Takaki's *A Different Mirror,* one of the few multicultural accounts of American history, recounts compelling examples of assimilation and adjustment period attitudes towards schooling for Mexicans in the southwest. These include an educator's comment that "There would be a revolution in the community if the Mexicans wanted to come to the White schools"; the beliefs of a ranch manager's wife, "Let him (the Mexican) have as good an education but still let him know he is not as good as a White man. God did not intend him to be . . ."; a sugar beet grower's concern that "If every (Mexican) child has a high school education, who will labor?"; and a farmer's candid admission that "If I wanted a man I would want one of the more ignorant ones. . . . Educated Mexicans are the hardest to handle."[43]

Recognizing the place assigned to them in every social situation was a necessary survival skill for Mexican Americans, as it was for blacks, whether in the Jim Crow south, the industrial north, or the agricultural west. Takaki offers this portrait of the racial rules in Texas in the 1920s and 1930s:

In the presence of Anglos, they were expected to assume "a deferential body posture and respectful voice tone" . . . they were permitted to shop in the Anglo business section of town only on Saturdays. They could patronize Anglo cafes, but only the counter and carryout service. "A group of us Mexicans who were well-dressed once went to a restaurant in Amarillo," complained Wenceslao Iglesias in the 1920s, "and they told us that if we wanted to eat we should go to the special department where it said 'For Colored People.' I told my friend that I would rather die from starvation than to humiliate myself before the Americans by eating with the Negroes."[44]

The racial hierarchy reflected in Iglesias' remark was informally codified in the black community in a colloquial rhyming expression regarding hiring. If you were white, you were "all right," if you were Brown, you could "stick around," but if you were black, you'd better "get back."

America's entry into World War I began an era of social change that led ultimately to the undermining of many overt segregationist practices. As Asian and European immigration slowed prior to and during World War I, America's still-voracious labor needs fueled another long-term population shift: the "Great Migration" of rural blacks to the industrial cities of the Midwest and Northeast. The changes to northern cities, as well as to the social and geographic patterns of America's African American communities, were dramatic. According to Takaki, between 1910 and 1920 Detroit's black population rose from 5,000 to 40,800, Cleveland's from 8,400 to 34,400, Chicago's from 44,000 to 109,400, and New York's from 91,700 to 152,400.[45]

Blacks traveled north for the same reasons that Irish, Italians, Greeks, and Poles crossed the Atlantic and Mexicans crossed the Rio Grande: to

Table 3.3
Percent Rise in Black Population Due the Great Migration between 1910–1920

|           | Detroit | Cleveland | Chicago  | New York |
|-----------|---------|-----------|----------|----------|
| % change  | +816%   | +409%     | +249%    | +166%    |
| 1920      | 40,800  | 34,400    | 109,400  | 152,400  |
| 1910      | 5,000   | 8,400     | 44,000   | 91,700   |

get a better job, to escape oppression, to build a better, freer life. Once in the north, blacks encountered larger, more organized schools, compulsory attendance laws, and expanded opportunity. They also encountered discrimination in housing and, when the boom economy turned bad, the "last hired, first fired" syndrome in the labor market. As internal migrants, blacks were in an ambiguous position. According to historian Spencer Crew, "Northern schools, despite their shortcomings, offered better training. . . . Nearly twice as many black students completed northern high schools as finished southern ones, and many adults after moving north returned to school to complete their education." At the same time, segregation in housing and schooling was both legal and near-universal, and as a rule "the higher the percentage of black students in a school, the lower the percentage of funds it received."[46] Thus, though life in the north was often better, it was not equal.

During World War II a second outpouring of southern blacks headed north and, increasingly, west. Between 1940 and 1960, 3 million blacks left the south headed for traditional destinations like Chicago and Detroit, but also to Los Angeles, Oakland, Seattle, and Portland.[47] When the first black children of the post-war baby boom began to reach school age, the stage was set for the landmark legal confrontation on school desegregation that permanently changed American education and American society, the *Brown* case.

### Political Struggles for Access

A knowledge of the legal and attitudinal barriers to assimilation outlined above should inform our efforts at school change, because integration with the larger society—or the lack of such integration—has a profound effect on schooling. As Irish, Italians, Poles, Eastern European Jews, and other European groups achieved a certain degree of assimilation, they began to gain political power at the local level (mayor, city council, school committee). Since schools were locally controlled, this assured at least a minimal level of responsiveness of public schools to their concerns. In fact, so powerful did some white ethnic politicians become that the schools became famous as patronage homes for their supporters, and one of the important reforms of the adjustment period was the "professionalization" of school administration to protect educational hiring from the ravages of corrupt (ethnic) politicians. In addition, the parochial school system in cities like Chicago and New York provided an important, ethnically based alternative to public education, since the schools were based in Catholic parishes that were characterized by identification with a predominant ethnic group.

A connection between political assimilation and school achievement is suggested by the work of researcher Joel Perlmann.[48] He studied the relationship between immigrant communities, school structures, and student achievement in Providence, Rhode Island between 1880 and 1935, and found that in the earlier part of this period the academic performance of Irish students was below that of "native" white students (the children of previous immigrants from northern and western Europe). But as the Irish moved into politically powerful positions and began to achieve economically and socially, their school performance rose significantly. This is an intriguing finding, because it suggests that for non-mainstream groups political, economic, and social progress can be *causes*, as well as effects, of improved school performance. This in turn argues that social policies which promote bias-free political and economic access and affordable housing, day care, and health care can be effective educational reforms.

Historically, as migration and immigration brought large numbers of non-Europeans and their children into the educational arena in the cities of the north, west, and southwest, this was not the pattern that emerged. In fact, in almost every case, legal and illegal discrimination created barriers to full political and social participation. Even today Asian, Hispanic, and African American communities are underrepresented in standard measures of civic participation like voter registration and in "meat-and-potatoes" political positions like city council seats, state representative positions, and mayoral and gubernatorial posts. As long as these communities lacked political and economic power, the response of school systems was quite different than it had been for European immigrant groups.

The result was that minority communities turned to the courts for enforcement of their legal rights, beginning a long tradition of adversarial relationships with local school systems which neither provided nor wished to provide equitable services. The prototype case in this regard, *Brown v the Topeka, Kansas Board of Education* (1954), was not the opening of this strategy, but the culmination of efforts in the black community that been building for twenty or more years. *Brown* signaled the beginning of the access period because, in its wake, other groups began to adopt a similar strategy, which pitted citizens against the school system to gain rights which they saw as basic.

Desegregation cases were brought by local NAACPs across the country, including the Boston case. In many places the Hispanic community joined these efforts as a co-plaintiff. Eventually, parent advocates for Special Needs students used this same strategy, as did advocates for children whose first language was not English and advocates for the rights of girls and women. The success of resulting court challenges led directly to state and federal legislation: the Elementary and Secondary Education Act of 1965, the federal special needs law (PL 94–142), and Title IX, the basic gender equity law that governs education today.

Efforts by parents of color to gain an equal education for their children, then, have had an effect on schools that extends far beyond race. The effect on urban schools has been particularly great, because they are the most directly affected by desegregation, but also have the most students in need of compensatory services, the most second-language students, and the highest proportion of special needs students. Any time we go into an urban school and see racial/ethnic diversity, or a bilingual classroom, or special classes for students with physical or learning disabilities, or a girls' basketball team with coaching and equipment equal to the boys' team, we are seeing the results of parents using judicial and political means to force schools to do what they did not initially want to do. To date, reform efforts have systematically ignored this basic political fact about the relationship between urban schools and the communities of color they primarily serve. For example, almost every reform plan includes language about the importance of parent outreach, but calls for outreach almost never include an honest assessment of the adversarial relationship that has traditionally existed between urban parents and their schools.

Like reforms in other areas, judicial and legislative attempts to make schools more equitable have been only partly successful. In the current achievement era, even these gains are under attack. But the hard-won partial victories of one generation neither disappear nor blend easily into reforms championed by the next. In Graham's words, "Citizens viewing the schools . . . often fail to recognize the profound external forces that have buffeted the schools in earlier decades. Thus, they often find it difficult to understand why remnants of previous social agendas for the schools persist in the face of new, contradictory demands."[49]

Using Graham's categories, I would argue that ongoing political battles between advocates for Bilingual Education and proponents of English Only legislation, for instance, can be seen as a dispute between the contradictory visions of "American-ness" which underlay the assimilation period and the access period. In the first, becoming an American meant jettisoning one's heritage to melt into the white, Anglo mainstream; in the second, "American-ness" included the possibility of retaining core elements of ethnic and racial identity while still enjoying full participation in society. Similarly, battles against tracking pit the institutionalized values of the adjustment period, when the social function of schools was to sort, against new values associated with access and achievement for all. Basic elements of urban school life such as special needs classes, free or reduced lunch, and before- and after-school programs are rooted in a vision of the whole child that arose in the adjustment period and became extended by law, in the access period, to previously disenfranchised populations. Now in the achievement period schools are seeing these reforms curtailed so more resources can be devoted to test preparation and remediation.

## SUMMING UP

I began this chapter by suggesting that "historical amnesia" is one of the principal shortcomings of today's efforts at systemic reform and that combating presentism is an essential strategy for promoting lasting change. What would such combat look like? It would mean, at the very least, acknowledgement by reform architects that the urban student body and learning environment differ substantially from the mainstream template currently used by reform planners. It would mean enlisting teachers as agents, not victims, of reform, by respecting them professionally and taking seriously their experience and knowledge, particularly about issues surrounding the implementation of reform. It would mean taking into account, as reforms are implemented, that for much of the nineteenth and twentieth centuries American public schools have intentionally obstructed efforts by communities of color to secure a quality education for their children. Legal and illegal barriers have been placed in the way at every step, and the history of minority communities in relation to education is filled with decades-long efforts to remove these barriers. The legacy of these barriers and these efforts will not disappear just because today's policymakers choose to ignore it. Reformers may have the best of intentions, but as representatives of the mainstream culture they carry a heavy historical burden. Whether they acknowledge it or not, that burden affects their efforts at reform.

In fact, it affects teaching and learning in urban classrooms at every level, every day, in ways both visible and invisible. Urban parents are acutely aware that their schools need to be better if their children are to move towards full economic and social participation. But the guiding narrative for their view of schools is not the "decline from a golden age" of the op ed page, or the need to meet an outside threat of A Nation at Risk, but the steady and ongoing struggle to wrest from an unwilling public school system a decent education for their children. It is in this context that reformers should view the willingness of segments of the minority community to embrace nearly any means to achieve this goal: vouchers, privatization, charter schools, and publicly funded all-black or all-male schools have in various communities won the support of black leaders in particular.

Can a systemic reform movement which ignores questions of race, language, and culture hope to succeed in its goal of high achievement for all? As new immigrant groups arrive, they enter a public school arena already polarized around the past. If efforts at systemic urban reform continue to ignore the past and concentrate only on curriculum, testing, and administration, we will have missed a major opportunity for change.

In particular, we must find ways to make high academic achievement work with, not against, equity for students of color, poor students, and students whose first language is not English. We must believe, and act as if we believe, that equity and achievement are *not* incompatible goals. For urban populations above all, achievement is linked to equity, academic success to equality. Any "reform movement" which does not recognize this, in deeds as well as words, is no reform at all but a return to the mistakes of the past.

## NOTES

1. Richard Elmore and Milbrey McLaughlin, *Steady Work: Policy, Practice, and the Reform of American Education* (Santa Monica: Rand, 1988): 15.

2. David Tyack and Larry Cuban, *Tinkering Toward Utopia: A Century of Public School Reform* (Cambridge, MA: Harvard, 1995), 6.

3. Theodore Sizer, *Secondary Schools at the Turn of the Century* (New Haven: Yale, 1964).

4. J. Anthony Lukas, *Common Ground: A Turbulent Decade in the Lives of Three American Families* (New York: Knopf, 1985).

5. *The African Meeting House in Boston: A Source Book* (Boston: Museum of Afro-American History, 1988).

6. Daniel Boorstin and Ruth Boorstin, eds., *Hidden History* (New York: Harper and Row, 1987): xxvi. See also Peter Novick, *That Noble Dream: The "Objectivity Question" and the American Historical Profession* (Cambridge: Cambridge University, 1988).

7. Lawrence Cremin, *Public Education* (New York: Basic Books, 1976): 36.

8. See, for example: Lilia Bartolome, *The Misteaching of Academic Discourses: The Politics of Language in the Classroom* (Boulder, CO: Westview, 1998); Lisa Delpit, *Other People's Children: Cultural Conflict in the Classroom* (New York: The New Press, 1995); Michelle Fine, ed. *Chartering Urban School Reform: Reflections on Public High Schools in the Midst of Change* (New York: Teachers College, 1994); Signithia Fordham, *Blacked Out: Dilemmas of Race, Identity, and Success at Capital High* (Chicago: University of Chicago, 1996); Donaldo Macedo, "Literacy for stupidification: the pedagogy of big lies," in Pepi Leistyna, Arlie Woodrum, and Stephen Sherblom, eds., *Breaking Free: the Transformative Power of Critical Pedagogy* (Cambridge, MA: Harvard, 1996); Martha Montero-Sieburth, and Franicisco Villaruel, eds. *Making Invisible Latino Adolescents Visible: A Critical Approach to Latino Diversity* (New York: Garland, 1999); John Ogbu, and M. Gibson, eds., *Minority Status and Schooling: A Comparative Study of Immigrant and Involuntary Minorities* (New York: Garland, 1991).

9. Lawrence Cremin, *Popular Education and Its Discontents* (New York: Harper and Row, 1990): 9–10.

10. *Popular Education*, 51.

11. *Tinkering*, (1995).

12. Ibid., 5.

13. Ibid., 134.

14. Ibid., 135–36.

15. Ibid., 137.

16. Patricia Graham, "What America Has Expected of Its Schools Over the Past Century," *American Journal of Education* 101 (1993 February): 83–98; Patricia Graham, "Assimilation, Adjustment, and Access: An Antiquarian View of American Education," in *Learning from the Past: What History Teaches Us about School Reform*, Diane Ravitch and Maris Vinovskis, eds. (Baltimore: Johns Hopkins, 1995): 3–24; Patricia Graham, "Battleships and Schools," *Daedalus* 124, 4, (1995, Fall): 43–47.

17. *Learning from the Past*, 10.

18. Ibid., 11.

19. Ibid., 12.

20. Ibid., 11.

21. Ibid., 14.

22. Ibid., 14.

23. *Brown et al. v. Board of Education of Topeka, Kansas et al., 347 U.S. 483* (1954).

24. "What America," 92.

25. National Commission on Excellence in Education, *A Nation at Risk: the Imperatives for Educational Reform* (Washington, DC: U.S. Department of Education, 1983).

26. "What America," 96.

27. "What America," 96–97.

28. "Child Poverty Fact Sheet," National Center for Children in Poverty, 2000, *<http://cpmcnet.columbia.edu/dept/nccp/ycpf.html>* (3 October 2001).

29. "Fact Sheet on Teacher Shortage," National Education Association, 1996, *<http://www.nea.org/teaching/shortage.html>* (18 October 2001).

30. Gloria Ladson-Billings, "Preparing Teachers for Diverse Student Populations: A Critical Race Theory Perspective," *Review of Research in Education* 24 (Washington, DC: American Educational Research Association, 1999).

31. *Tinkering*, 63.

32. Cindy Rodriguez, "Minority Children in Majority in Boston," *Boston Globe*, 30 August 2000, A1, A16.

33. Joan Lowy, "Reconsider Immigration Policies, Study Advises," *Quincy Patriot Ledger*, 6–7 January 2001, 8.

34. Wayne Urban and Jennings Wagoner, *American Education: A History* (Boston: McGraw-Hill, 2000), 214.

35. Sucheng Chan, *Entry Denied: Exclusion and the Chinese Community in America, 1882–1943.* (Philadelphia: Temple University, 1991), vii.

36. U.S. Bureau of the Census, *Historical Statistics of the United States, Colonial Times to 1957* (Washington, DC, U.S. Government Printing Office, 1960), 57–58.

37. *Historical Statistics*, 58.

38. Ron Takaki, *A Different Mirror: A History of Multicultural America* (Boston: Little, Brown, 1993): 207.

39. Charles McLain and Laurene Wu McLain, "The Chinese Contribution to the Development of American Law," in *Entry Denied* (1991): 21–22.

40. *Historical Statistics*, 48.

41. *Different Mirror*, 329.

42. *Historical Statistics*, 56, 58.

43. *Different Mirror*, 327.

44. Ibid.

45. *Different Mirror,* 340–41.

46. Spencer Crew, *Field to Factory: Afro-American Migration 1915–1940* (Washington, DC: National Museum of American History, 1987): 58–59.

47. Ibid., 73.

48. Jonathon Perlmann, *Ethnic Differences: Schooling and Social Structure among the Irish, Italians, Jews, and Blacks in an American City, 1880–1935* (New York: Cambridge University, 1988).

49. *Learning from the Past*, 3.

*Chapter 4*

# Imaginary Gardens and Exemplary Contexts: Language Arts Reform in the Urban Elementary School

## INTRODUCTION

As America enters the twenty-first century, elementary schools across the country are striving for reform. Improvement of reading and writing skills is central to reform everywhere, but in urban schools it takes on special urgency. Large numbers of English Language Learners, high percentages of students with language-related Individual Education Plans, and the widely publicized "achievement gap" in reading scores between white students and students of color create intense pressure on principals and teachers to achieve measurable gains quickly.

Increasingly, schools and school systems engaged in reform turn to universities and outside networks for assistance. Given the intense pressure for rapid, dramatic improvement and the embattled state of many urban classrooms, there is a ready market for prepackaged "exemplary programs" and other forms of assistance that implicitly or explicitly deny teachers' autonomy and efficacy. In contrast, a track record of attempted reforms of curriculum and instruction stretching back to the 1970s suggests a single lesson: changes implemented from the top down or the outside in are almost bound to fail unless they gain not just the nominal assent but the active support of teachers and principals who must be their key implementers. This historical lesson suggests a strategy for collaboration that is the opposite of the prepackaged, exemplary, one-size-fits-all gospel that many reformers currently preach. Milbrey McLaughlin has pointed out that,

if teachers lie at the heart of successful efforts to enhance classroom practices, then the professional networks that engage teachers comprise promising vehicles for change . . . change strategies rooted in the natural networks of teachers—in their professional associations—may be more effective than strategies that adhere solely to a delivery structure outlined by the policy system.[1]

My interest in these issues is long-standing. As director of a doctoral program in Urban School Leadership, my students are teacher-leaders, principals, and systemwide administrators in more than twenty urban communities in Eastern Massachusetts. As Director of the Boston Writing Project (BWP) and a member of the leadership team of the National Writing Project's Urban Sites Network,[2] I work with teachers and administrators locally and from across the country who are practicing and promoting urban literacy reform.

In both of these roles, I have recently begun to glimpse a recurrent pattern in urban reform. Large amounts of time, effort, and money are poured into a troubled school in a short period of time, with the expectation that both "defective" teachers and long-standing problems of school achievement will be permanently "fixed." The money is tied to specific reform programs the school must adopt. In some cases these are publisher-sponsored workshops or for-profit educational innovations, in others they are programs funded by initiatives like the private Annenberg Challenge or the federal Comprehensive School Reform Demonstration Act (CSRD).

Reform starts with an initial flurry of activity and funding lasting eighteen months to two years, then this initial momentum slows noticeably. Multiple causes contribute to this slowing: a supportive principal or key teacher leader leaves to take another assignment and is replaced by someone less charismatic; burnout begins to set in among the most active staff members; grant funding which supported release time and new materials is withdrawn by the central office to be reallocated to the latest high-priority "school in trouble." Under these conditions reform proves difficult to sustain and in the end the school sees little long-term change in either teaching practice or student performance.

If this pattern is as common as my experience suggests, it raises serious questions. If urban schools are to be permanently improved, we need to begin by honestly analyzing both the forces driving reform and the school-based contexts which make it so difficult to achieve.

I offer here three connected approaches to the problem of permanently improving literacy education in urban elementary schools: first, a portrait of an imaginary, composite urban school—East Elementary—that illustrates some of the hidden reasons why lasting change is so difficult to achieve; second, consideration of some relevant research findings concerning reform and language arts instruction; third, suggestions for a new way to think about change. Portrait, research, and suggestions share an important additional dimension: they highlight implementation issues that occur in schools when outsiders—reform experts, university faculty, content-area "coaches"—attempt to work closely with insiders—teachers and principals—to create lasting change. If such collaborations are ever to succeed, I believe we must shift the focus of effort from *exemplary programs* created by outside agents and supported by short-term funding, to the creation of *exemplary contexts,* the set of conditions that will allow a particular school with a unique history and faculty to integrate outside interventions into a process of sustainable success on its own terms.

## AN IMAGINARY SCHOOL WITH REAL ISSUES: EAST ELEMENTARY

The poet Marianne Moore once referred to her creations as "Imaginary gardens filled with real toads."[3] Her poems were products of the imagination, but the issues about life they raised were real. The poetic form allowed her to talk about these difficult realities in unique and effective ways.

Taking a cue from Moore, I've tried to create "an imaginary school filled with real issues." Drawing on published research, interviews, and my own experience, I've described a composite urban school—East Elementary—staffed with a principal and teachers who are both individuals and representative of larger realities. I'll ask you to join me on my initial visits to East, seeing the school through my outsider's eyes; then to sit in on conversations with school insiders while I think through ways to help East move forward and recommend first steps in the change process.

### East's Profile, Principal Alice, and Teacher-Leader Barbara

East is a historically low-performing school and its relationship with parents has never been strong. It has 800 students and, using the federal government's categories, reports 50 percent as African American, 25 percent as Hispanic, 10 percent as Asian, 10 percent as white, and 5 percent as "other minority." About 25 percent of East's students, disproportionately African American and Hispanic boys, are in special education classes at least part of the day. There is a substantial Spanish bilingual cluster. East is a Title I school; 35 percent of its students read below grade level and 60 percent are eligible for the federal free lunch program. The average age of East teachers is in the late 40s; most have been teaching for 15 years or more. The teaching staff is predominantly white and female.

East's teachers are working hard to move forward together under the leadership of Alice, a committed and active African American principal who came to the school one year ago. Alice is under tremendous pressure from above to move East forward in two areas: implementation of new curriculum standards and improved student performance on statewide tests keyed to those standards. She also feels tremendous internal pressure to succeed based on three factors: she has been a high achiever her entire life and is determined to meet the professional challenge of "turning East around";

she is among the first generation of women and "minority" administrators in the school system, and is aware that many eyes are on her; and she feels a special responsibility to the "minority" parents and children who make up the majority of the school's population.

Alice has spent her first year developing with her staff a mandated school-wide change plan that is now on file with the central office and for which she and the school will be held accountable. To improve language arts instruction, this plan relies heavily on adoption of an "exemplary literacy program" that is paid for by federal CSRD funds. The program's philosophy holds that the school must develop "ownership" of the program for it to be successful.

As part of the process of taking ownership Alice has asked a "coach" from the university, myself, to help East identify change issues raised by adoption of the program in the context of the state's new language arts curriculum standards and high stakes tests. In what follows I present a picture of the setting for change at East just prior to the initiation of the program, as seen through my outsider's eyes.

On my first visit to East, Alice suggests that I talk with Barbara, a third-grade teacher who is successful with students and widely respected by other teachers in the building. Though she holds no leadership title other than membership on the school council, Barbara is one of three or four influential teacher-leaders in the building whose support is absolutely essential if the change process is to have a hope of succeeding.

In a long conversation with Barbara a certain picture of teaching at East starts to emerge. Self-contained, regular education teachers, the majority in the school, have widely differing philosophies and teaching styles. There are animosities between some individuals, but in general there is a "live-and-let-live" attitude about teaching as long as colleagues feel that you are working hard and care about the children entrusted to you.

The most "progressive" teachers share a holistic approach characterized by anti-basal, anti-skill and drill, anti-prescriptive instruction that tries to address all four language skills—reading, writing, speaking, and listening—in a developmental manner that looks at the whole child. They value classroom activities that meet multiple curricular goals, and do not seek a strict one-to-one correlation between a single activity and a single outcome in reading or writing. They are deeply troubled by those who interpret the new curriculum as connecting a single classroom activity to a single curricular goal, an approach they see as pedagogically regressive.

A number of other teachers in the building have tried such a "progressive" approach and abandoned it for a much more traditional one, which is also favored by a vocal set of East parents. I recall Alice's words at our first meeting: "Take the whole language approach to reading. Many teachers here say they tried it but are now saying it doesn't work for urban low income kids because they believe our children need a more direct and structured approach to reading, therefore they are going back to a heavy phonics approach. But the best teachers found that they have to use a balance of a whole language and structured phonetic approach."

A small number of teachers are clearly unsuccessful. Their classes have frequent discipline problems, their students make little progress, and savvy parents visit Alice early in the year to insure that their children do not get assigned to these teachers.

## The Wave Theory

The following week I spend a good deal of time sitting in regular education classrooms by invitation, watching East's teachers at work and talking with them about why they do what they do. At the end of the week I meet with Alice and Barbara to offer first impressions.

We are sitting in the tiny principal's office on a Friday afternoon. The school has just gone from the noise and activity of dismissal to the quiet that follows, and Alice and Barbara have just come in from bus duty. Luckily, today no buses were late, no children got sick, and no neighbors have called to complain about noisy East students running through yards on the way home.

I struggle with what to say. I'm finding it very difficult to generalize about teaching at East, especially based on only a single week of observation. I decide to start with a comparison. The regular education teachers here, I say, are like beachcombing artists, constructing individual, eclectic pedagogies by combining insights from years of classroom experience with treasures left on shore by successive waves of pedagogical innovation.

Alice and Barbara look at me like I'm crazy; it's an uncomfortable moment. Clearly I need to explain myself. Aware that I'm beginning to sound like someone who works in a university, I go on. I explain my "wave theory" of language arts teaching. Most East teachers are old enough to have seen at least three distinct waves of "new pedagogy" in reading and writing break over schools and recede. The first wave, writing process/writing workshop pedagogy, began in the late 1970s and crested in the mid-1980s; the second wave, whole language, began gathering force as writing process receded; and the third wave, multicultural children's literature, began to really take off in the mid-1990s. None of the three "waves" completely receded, and all are being advocated and practiced simultaneously today. But staff development programs in school systems tended to adopt them in succession as each became the "hot" pedagogical innovation of its time, and so teachers were likely to experience them sequentially.

As an outside observer, it seems to me that most East teachers have constructed their own synthesis of techniques from these three waves, combined with their undergraduate or graduate training in the teaching of reading. Now they must comply with curriculum mandates, struggling to craft a pedagogy that is true to their beliefs and also meets the new demands of standards and testing.

Interested but skeptical, Alice asks me a question which is also a challenge: "How will understanding 'the waves' help East move forward?" I take this to mean: "I need to turn this school around in a hurry and I'm in a vulnerable position. If what you're explaining can help improve things here for teachers and kids in measurable ways, I'm still interested, if it won't, I can't afford to spend time on it."

### Deeper into The Waves

Accepting the challenge, I jump in, explaining that writing process pedagogy challenged, for the first time, the primacy of reading as the focus of staff development, curriculum time and textbooks. But over time teachers learned experientially what researchers have confirmed: in many cases there is little difference between the classroom practice of teachers who label themselves "writing process" teachers and teachers who do not. Many teachers who got the training to make this pedagogy work in their classrooms experienced a remarkable transformation for themselves and their students. For others, change consisted of replacing the 1970s jargon "brainstorming" with the 1980s jargon "prewriting" and replacing a publisher's wall poster listing The Elements of the Five Paragraph Theme with a similar poster listing The Five Steps of the Writing Process.

The second wave, whole language, enfolded writing in an inclusive approach to language arts, reclaiming some of the ground the reading community had lost to advocates of writing process. But as Alice and Barbara know, political pressure has made East's school system step away from officially embracing whole language, though many teachers in the building use elements of whole language pedagogy.

The third wave was children's literature. The recent emphasis on quality children's literature, particularly multicultural children's literature, is warmly embraced by the majority of East teachers. Many are spending their own money to equip classroom literature libraries while their school system continues to spend millions of dollars on a new series of basal readers.

The new basal has further confused pedagogical issues. The school system ordered basals by grade level, but so many of East's students are reading below grade level that the basal is useless for achieving the principle benefit for which it was adopted—providing a unifying element to the curriculum in a school system with a high level of student mobility. And just as the basal series of the 1980s adopted the nomenclature and trappings, but not the spirit, of writing process pedagogy, the basals of the 1990 have adopted superficial elements of whole language and whole literature while missing their essence, and have added a renewed emphasis on phonics.

Barbara responds that most East teachers have chosen a middle way, using some basal stories but supplementing them with whole works of children's literature. Many wonder if what they are doing is "right," she adds, and feel uncertain about the decisions they have made. "But," says Alice, "you still haven't answered my question: what's the connection between the waves, improved language arts instruction, and whole-school change?"

I see that she's right, and that to provide an answer I have to talk to more than just the regular education teachers. I need to find out how the Special Needs, Bilingual, and Reading teachers fit into the picture. Alice and Barbara suggest I spend the next week getting the perspectives of Jackie, a Special Needs teacher, Francisco, a bilingual education teacher, and Phyllis, a Title I specialist. At the end of the week, this is what I have found out.

### Jackie

Jackie is struggling with the redefined professional role that special needs inclusion demands of her. For years she has used a prescriptive approach to language development based on the need to construct discrete objectives in her students' Individual Educational Plans (IEP's), with each instructional activity tied to a measurable outcome. Now she is being called on to re-create herself in the more flexible role called for in the inclusion classroom, in which she is a second teacher paired for part of the day with various regular education teachers with whom she shares her "mainstreamed" SPED students. She still feels uncomfortable entering some of her colleagues' classrooms, and they are uncomfortable having her there. The training in Special Education she received fifteen to twenty years ago and her years of experience writing, implementing, and monitoring IEP's are based on philosophies of learning substantially different from those held by Barbara and other teachers with whom she must now team.

Jackie has, on her own, sought out workshops and classes in new, holistic pedagogies, but she is still facing a complex professional transition. Now she must work each week with five or more mainstream teachers whose styles are widely divergent from each other. Further, East students have done poorly on the recent state reading tests. Because the scores of Special Needs students are not figured into the school's testing average, she now feels pressure to help raise the school's average by classifying poorly performing students as special needs cases, even though she can identify no serious learning or emotional disability. Because this pressure runs directly counter to the philosophy of inclusion which the school has publicly adopted, Jackie feels doubly uneasy.

A schoolwide approach to language arts would ease Jackie's transition by providing common ground for the collaborative planning she does with mainstream teachers. But if the proposed schoolwide language arts initiative is to be successful, she and her mainstream colleagues need a chance to discuss not just what they do, but *why* they do it. Because of the sensitive nature of this discussion, it must take place in a trustful setting, one which assumes that good teaching can look many different ways, that because one person does things differently from another does not mean that one is right and the other is wrong.

### Francisco

Francisco teaches in the school's Spanish bilingual cluster. For him the single biggest issue around language is equity. He struggles daily not to be marginalized as a professional, and not to have his students and his program marginalized within the life of the school because their first language is not English. Pedagogically, his graduate level training has given him a sophisticated set of tools to analyze students' proficiency in both their native language (L1) and their acquired language (L2). Other teachers in the building seem to care about only one thing, "Are you teaching them English?" Yet Francisco knows that one key to building English proficiency in his students is to strengthen their Spanish, because research on language learning has shown that strengthening native language skills results in improved English skills.[4] He also knows that older children must maintain their cognitive development in areas such as math, science, and social studies if they are not to fall behind, and therefore must receive some content-area instruction in L1. Outside his own cluster no one in the school is familiar with this way of looking at language, and so it is difficult for him to talk about language development with colleagues. He knows from the way other teachers react that he is using a vocabulary and developmental framework with which they are not familiar.

Further, Francisco has studied persuasive evidence that it takes six or more years of support for students to make a successful transition to a level of English that will allow them to succeed academically in the mainstream classroom, but because of laws governing bilingual education he is under tremendous pressure to push students into the mainstream in three years or less.[5] In these circumstances, he knows that some are bound to fail. If he attempts to do what his professional training dictates—hold on to his students for more than three years—the rest of the school sees him as "coddling" or "sheltering" them; if he pushes them into the mainstream, he knows he is setting them up for a failure which will confirm, to other staff members, negative stereotypes of Hispanic students as academically inadequate. Not only does Francisco bring a different developmental framework to the language arts discussion, he also brings powerful political issues around language status. These issues directly affect him and his students, but if he expresses them openly, he may be branded a "troublemaker" and find that he, his bilingual colleagues, and his program become even more marginalized. Francisco is angry, but he dare not express his anger.

### Phyllis

When Phyllis started as a Title I reading teacher years ago, regulations confined her to one-on-one or small group reading instruction in a closely defined, diagnostic/prescriptive framework. Over the years Title I regulations have become more holistic, recognizing that reading and writing are developmentally intertwined, and she has taken graduate courses and workshops in the teaching of writing as well as in whole language and children's literature. Though she still sees students individually or in small groups, her teaching philosophy is close to Barbara's. This is her first year at East, and she is still feeling her way along. She receives students from Barbara, Jackie, and Francisco, and she would like to synchronize her instruction with what goes on in their classrooms, but she really doesn't have a clear idea of what *does* go on, and she's never had a chance to talk to them about it. Already, though, she realizes that each one of them teaches with different assumptions. Right now, Phyllis relies heavily on her own accumulated, eclectic style that incorporates pieces of previous Title I philosophy and her graduate training, and concentrates her energy on her students while she feels out the other adults in the building.

## TOADS IN THE GARDEN: CAUTIONARY RESEARCH AND ANALYSIS

At the end of the week, back in my office, I put my notes in order in preparation for Monday's meeting with Alice and Barbara. Then I put my university hat back on and begin to consider East in a national, research-based context. At this early stage, I see two large "danger zones" threatening instructional improvement. The first is a set of conditions described by systems thinker Michael Fullan as *fragmentation and overload*.

According to Fullan

There is an overwhelming amount of evidence that educational change is . . . non-linear. This means that the most systemically sophisticated plan imaginable will unfold in a non-linear, broken-front, back-and-forth manner. It will be fragmented. . . . Overload and fragmentation . . . take their toll on the most committed, who find that will alone is not sufficient to achieve or sustain reform.[6]

In the face of fragmentation and overload, success relies heavily on time and support for teachers to make sense of proposed changes at the school level. Diverse beliefs about how children learn to read and write represent an important element of fragmentation at East and schools like it, and as long as these beliefs remain unexamined they are a major barrier to success, no matter what "exemplary program" is being put in place. For East to move forward Barbara, Jackie, Francisco, and Phyllis must begin to work together, rather than separately, for they serve the same group of children. But this will require time for the sharing of knowledge, activities for building mutual respect, and reflections that discover common ground in their divergent teaching philosophies and assumptions.

The second danger zone is this. At East both the motive force for change and the important ideas about how change is to be accomplished come from outside the school, indeed outside the teaching profession, implying that East and its teachers are part of the problem, not part of the solution. Yet for change to succeed, these very same problematic teachers must be the carriers and implementers of the new ideas. In this paradox East reflects education reform nationally over the last thirty years. A major study of federal reform efforts in the 1960s, 1970s, and 1980s identified as a "core irony" the fact that federal policies were based on "a fundamental mistrust of the judgement and knowledge of educators, but successful implementation of those reforms relies on those very educators."[7]

Efforts to improve language arts over the last 20 years—the waves-in-the wave theory—represent a particular instance of change efforts thwarted by fragmentation, overload, and mistrust of the judgment and knowledge of teachers. Writing process pedagogy can be seen as the paradigmatic example of this phenomenon. As the process gospel spread rapidly in the late 1970s and early 1980s, language arts curricula mandated process steps, peer response, and the author's chair. But without high-quality, sustained professional development for the teachers on the receiving end of these mandates, little systemic change resulted.[8]

Succeeding innovations—literature-based reading, "big books," whole language, the reader's workshop, DISTAR, and others—met a similar fate. New ideas backed by strong research evidence were effectively adopted by small numbers of teachers, but their widespread implementation existed in name rather than in fact. A recent review of these efforts reached this conclusion: "It's clearly much easier to change the top half of the system than the bottom half. 'Reform' efforts are underway in every state in the country. It is less clear that these reform efforts have had any effect at the classroom level. . . . At best, we can argue that the "systemic" reform may set the stage for innovations in practice, but does not assure them."[9]

The lesson here seems clear. Successful, research-tested techniques for improving language arts instruction have been developed. It is easy to find outstanding individual classrooms and teacher exemplars of success for any given technique, and these exemplars are publicized widely by advocates of a particular reform. But no reform has achieved success that could be termed widespread, and in too many cases the original spirit and intent of the techniques has been undermined by other factors. Seen from this perspective, the "eclectic" pedagogy found at East is more normative than unusual.

For example, Barbara Batton and Linda Vereline of the New York City Writing Project conducted an intensive analysis of literacy instruction in a 1,200-student New York City elementary school designated for "corrective action" due to low test scores.

Batton and Vereline found a school that was 100 years old and badly overcrowded, working at 125 percent of student capacity and with a long waiting list for kindergarten placement. Students new to the United States were a regular part of the student population, and each grade from K-5 had three bilingual classes.

A large number of "exemplary" literacy practices were in use, including twenty-minute blocks of silent reading time directly after lunch; ninety-minute literacy periods every day for monolingual and bilingual students; homogenous reading groups in grades 2, 3, and 4; specific reading assessments for group placement; remedial reading initiatives; classroom libraries; and a "reading buddies" program across grades. Writing practices included book making and publishing; a schoolwide writing-across-the-curriculum program; and daily journal writing. Professional development for all teachers was being provided by the publisher of the school's new basal series, and mandatory ESL workshops for monolingual teachers were being given by an outside consultant.

Batton and Vereline's survey of literacy practices made clear that the majority of the student's day, no matter what grade level, was being spent in activities related to reading and writing. And yet test scores continued to decline. This caused them to take a deeper look at the educational context in the building, a look that uncovered hidden sources of difficulty. These included a "culture of mistrust" created by years of scrutiny linked to constantly changing district mandates, which in their report to the district they described in these terms:

This steady diet of prescribed packaged kits and history of continually replaced mandated programs across the curriculum for which staff is then given "training" has sent a message of mistrust for teachers as independently capable and competent educators and has contributed to undermining teachers from taking responsibility for their own practice.[10]

Batton and Vereline also found that though there were many literacy activities, the definition of literacy embraced by the school was a narrow one that relied heavily on the constructs in the basal series. In addition, they noted that the school was having limited success reaching out to parents, that there was a widespread perception of inequity in distribution of materials on the part of bilingual staff, and that teachers were very concerned about the absence of schoolwide art, music, and movement programs. Taken together with the "culture of mistrust," these factors neutralized or outweighed the effects of the many "exemplary practices" which were in use daily in the school.

Confident that I now have a sense of the "local context" at East as well as a grasp of relevant national patterns in systemic and language arts reform, I begin to construct the recommendations I will give to Alice and Barbara on Monday.

## CREATING EXEMPLARY CONTEXTS

My thinking starts with the context East shares with hundreds of other urban schools struggling to change. These schools are widely perceived by the voters and elected officials who fund them to be not just failing but incapable of reforming themselves. Because of this, their instructional agenda is heavily influenced by ideas and structures from the outside: mandated curricula, high stakes tests, and systemic reforms embodied in "exemplary programs." To date there is little evidence that these curricular and systemic reforms have achieved widespread success.[11]

Analyses of existing reforms suggest two conclusions. The first is that limited, short-term interventions are bound to fail because "the problems addressed by current state-driven reforms or change-agent programs are not acute; they are chronic."[12] The second is that success ultimately depends not on the externally generated exemplary program or curricular innovation, but on the internal context—the school itself. Well-designed reform programs try to account for this by devoting attention to the "fit" between program and school or the balance between fidelity to "exemplary" techniques and adaptation to local needs.[13] But this still leaves the emphasis on the change program, not on the school.

At the moment, policymakers, reformers and school systems typically proceed as if adoption of exemplary programs and development of strong local contexts are non-conflictual goals, complementary parts of an overall school improvement strategy. From what I have seen, this is a naïve assumption. The experience of urban teachers and principals across the country is often that of development *versus* adoption, not the development *through* adoption that is assumed to be the norm. From their point of view, systemic reform is often an "imaginary garden" filled with "real toads" like the following:

• Top-down and outside-in reforms in curriculum and staff development from the 1960s to the 1990s achieved individual successes, but produced little evidence of widespread, lasting change, whether measured on their own terms (fidelity of adoption) or the school's (improved performance by students and teachers). There are few reasons to believe the current wave of exemplary programs and systemic reforms will achieve a different fate, for few of these programs address the major stumbling block to such reform—they devalue teacher knowledge and expertise by starting from the assumption that the knowledge and commitment necessary for change reside chiefly *outside* the school, in the university, policy center, or private consulting group sponsoring the exemplary program.

- Momentum for reform often comes from disinterested advocates seeking only to improve education. But in an educational system like ours, based in state and local political structures, other motives play a role as well. Reform can be driven by officeholders responding to the short-term election cycle rather than the long-term cycle we know is necessary for renewal; or by a beleaguered superintendent's need to *do something right now,* to respond to disastrous test scores; or by persuasive, high-profile academics seeking prestige or profits through national adoption of their reform plans; or by a frustrated, job-threatened principal's need to show the superintendent he is a "team player" by adopting a reform favored by central office. Or all of these motives may operate at once to create a political, strategic, and educational maelstrom that takes its toll on classroom instruction as well as on teacher and principal morale.

- Devaluing teachers' potential for contributing to reform is not a problem particular to urban education or to the current wave of reform. In seeking to answer the question of why the organizational forms that govern instruction have persisted while challenges to them have been "mostly evanescent," Tyack and Cuban reviewed 100 years of historical evidence and drew this conclusion:

To bring about improvement at the heart of education—classroom instruction . . .—has proven to be the most difficult kind of reform, and it will result in the future more from internal changes created by the knowledge and expertise of teachers than from the decisions of external policymakers.[14]

## MY RECOMMENDATIONS

After considering these "real toads," the starting point for my recommendations to Alice and Barbara will be this: East's primary emphasis should be placed not on the outside element, the *exemplary program,* but on the internal task, making East an *exemplary context* for learning. This is a problematic recommendation from some perspectives, because it implies that the professionals who work in the school are to a large degree intelligent, competent, and caring enough to begin addressing their own problems, a proposition that, given the current state of urban schools, seems to many to be untrue on its face.

What is an exemplary context? First and foremost, it is unique. An *exemplar* is an example to be learned from, not a rigorous template to be unthinkingly copied. Thus exemplary contexts are neither wholly transportable nor entirely copyable. Elements in them, approaches to particular problems, strategies for particular situations, can certainly be transported and adopted. But the exemplary local context represents its own unique mixture of history, location, staff, and leadership.

Second, exemplary contexts require stable, long-term leadership that goes beyond the principal. One recurring figure in school reform is the charismatic principal, the catalyst for change. These inspiring figures enable change in others, provide administrative support and vision, and give a sense of purpose and direction to a school's change process. But charismatic principals are often also ambitious principals, and they move on to other opportunities. Many schools have found that when a charismatic principal departs, the momentum for change goes too. An exemplary context requires a strong principal, but also strong teacher leadership to provide continuity in times of transition.

Third, exemplary contexts are places where the leadership maximizes budget resources by managing people well. It is a truism of the leadership literature that effective leaders create healthy school cultures. Often overlooked are the budgetary effects of good management. Personnel costs (salaries and benefits) make up from 70 to 90 percent of most school budgets, so a school in which personnel are reasonably satisfied and productive is a school where the budget is being managed well. Conversely, a school full of dissatisfied, factionalized personnel is a school where the leadership is wasting a great deal of money. In resource-poor urban environments the skill of managing well a school's principal financial asset, its personnel, is an essential one for creating an exemplary local context.

How does East go about becoming an exemplary context? The first step is to focus on the long-term success of the school and the long-term needs of its teachers, students and parents, and then ask how mandated reforms can help the school get to where it needs to go. This is the opposite of what currently happens in many schools, where the school is felt to be adrift and directionless and outside mandates and change programs are seen as filling a vacuum of leadership and confidence.

Four areas, sustained over time, can provide both common direction and respect for differences, enabling Barbara, Jackie, Francisco, Phyllis, and the rest of East's staff to move forward together to implement an effective schoolwide language arts plan. These approaches can be undertaken singly or as complementary parts of an overall plan. They are compatible with both state curriculum initiatives and exemplary reform programs.

The *first* is regular discussion of a range of real work from East students. One formal way to start this process is to create a gradewide writing sample, typically at a grade in which students are also taking a state- or city-wide test tied to the new curriculum, and to conduct a modified holistic scoring session with the faculty using this sample. In this process, teachers rate and respond to anonymous, gradewide samples of best, worst, and average student writing on a given topic, and then discus them and identify characteristics of low, middle, and high performing writers in that grade. In such a discussion, Barbara, Jackie, Francisco, and Phyllis would all be commenting on the same pieces of writing, and both the commonalities and differences in their approaches to language would quickly become apparent. This, in turn, would provide grounds for further discussion as the year went on, discussion that could also be grounded in student artifacts from other grades and in areas besides writing. This is especially possible if teachers in the building already keep portfolios of such student artifacts, or agree to begin keeping them for this purpose. An important outcome of such discussions may be creation of a schoolwide reading and writing philosophy that is simple, jointly created, and agreed on by *all* the faculty. The philosophy can then be posted in the principal's office, at the entrance to the school, and in every teacher's room, as well as translated into appropriate languages and sent home to parents with an explanatory letter.

The *second* is in-depth analysis, again on a regular basis and in a group, of the learning patterns of individual students using a simple but formal process that insures that this is more than just gossiping or complaining about students. One such process is the "descriptive review" developed by the Prospect School in Vermont, and now used by schools in other parts of the country; another is a reflective case study or case story, a technique now used regularly in educational leadership.[15] Whatever process is used, it must insure confidentiality, be respectful of students, show students' strengths as well as weaknesses, and invite multiple perspectives on and interpretations of students' behavior and learning styles. This is particularly true in the multiracial, multilingual contexts of many urban schools.

The *third* is regular reflective writing by teachers, and sharing of that writing with colleagues. Writing and sharing starts group discussions on common ground, lets teachers reflect on their own processes as language learners, and leads naturally to further discussions about teaching language arts. It can also be combined with other methods mentioned: reviews of student work or looks at individual students can provide the ground for reflective writing which can then be shared and responded to, moving program planning along in a grounded way. Such writing can also take for its subject the process of using state curriculum frameworks, the impact of mandated high-stakes testing on students, teachers, and parents, or reflections on the implementation process of an exemplary program.[16]

The *fourth* is school-based teacher research, and discussion of data produced by such research, to check on progress of schoolwide initiatives or promote inquiry approaches to teaching. Variations of this technique—teacher research, action research, and practitioner inquiry are three frequently used labels—have been growing rapidly in schools, and they can undergird long-term change in schools like East, because they unlock both power and positive energy that can fuel connections across disciplines or teaching philosophies.[17]

These four strategies—looking closely at student work, in-depth group analysis of student learning issues using a formal process, regular reflective writing, and school-based research—are effective and doable, and in the real world are often found in various combinations adapted to what a school views as its greatest needs.

Here, to demonstrate some ways these techniques work in the real world, I will mention three examples I know well because I have participated in or observed them.

- In Boston, the school system's Center For Leadership Development funded forty-six school-based inquiry groups in 1999–2000 and many of them, in response to a systemwide priority, are looking closely at student work. This is the fourth year of the inquiry group program. Steve Gordon, a Lead Teacher with the program since its inception, wrote in a recent Inquiry Group newsletter of both his belief in the program and the need to take it to a higher level:

I am convinced of the necessity of this work, its value to teachers, and the seriousness of teacher commitment. My big question is: what is the identity of the Inquiry Group Program as an institution in Boston's professional development plans? What is its place in building knowledge and methods that influence instruction and school culture? . . . Most of our professional development involves "training" and workshops, which are considered essential methods for sharing "best practices" although they often do not seem to result in enduring change. I feel a need to establish a permanent "bottom-up" methodology for professional development—to argue for inquiry groups as *equally* essential, a necessity rather than a luxury.[18]

- A Massachusetts professional development network, the Massachusetts Field Center for Teaching and Learning, has since 1996 sponsored a statewide Teachers Academy which supports school-based action research teams. Over a twelve month period these five-member teams identify, research, and address a school-wide change goal. Regular reflective writing by participating teachers is a formal and important element of the program. Evaluations show the program is successful both in creating change in individual teachers' beliefs and practices, and in creating schoolwide change.

- In my own work with schools I have seen how a simple shift in the use of a standard reflective writing technique can open new areas of awareness for a whole school. Several years ago I was part of a team conducting a year-long professional development series at a large Boston elementary school. The school had low test scores, high enrollment, and a student body that was highly diverse, including a majority of African American students and bilingual programs in both Spanish and Haitian Creole. At the second after-school workshop, which included the whole faculty and the principal, we asked participants to do a piece of short, memory-based personal writing—a standard technique used many in-service situations. This time, we added a single sentence to the directions: "Please feel free to write in whatever language you feel most comfortable in." Immediately, the dynamics in the room changed. When it came time to share aloud, we encouraged those who had not written in English to read what they had written just as they had written it, and then to provide an impromptu English translation.

- The discussion that followed was rich and animated, and opened up in an unprecedented way major issues of language status, "correctness," pedagogy, and philosophy that had been boiling just under the surface. Some of the bilingual teachers said they had never before felt free to express themselves as professionals in their first language, and that it was a liberating experience. Others, both bilingual and regular education teachers, wondered if we were sending the wrong message, devaluing the importance of English which was, after all, the key to school success for both bilingual and monolingual children. Some teachers pointed out that the situation of those African American children who spoke nonstandard English at home was in some ways similar to the situation of the Spanish and Haitian-speaking children.

Among several of the Haitian teachers there was conflict over whether their "real" first language was Haitian Creole, an emerging language, or the traditional French in which much Haitian schooling is conducted. At the end of the time period few wanted to leave. It had become clear to all that the beliefs revealed in this conversation were affecting teaching and learning in the school in a powerful, hitherto hidden way.

The read-aloud in three languages was a breakthrough moment for that workshop series; it acted like a lightning bolt suddenly illuminating the true tension and complexity inherent in literacy learning in the school. After that moment neither teachers nor workshop leaders pretended that better reading and writing could be achieved simply by applying an appropriate selection of "best practices." Something far deeper and more personal was at stake. By June, the school had made substantial progress in defining for itself its own shared philosophy of writing, based on those things the whole staff could agree on, and individual teachers and clusters of teachers had shared and learned new techniques, analyzed student work and their own teaching, and made significant change in their classroom approaches to literacy.

The philosophy statement, when viewed from the outside, contained little that was surprising—writing was a process, writing should be done regularly and in a variety of forms at all grade levels, there are many different "correct" techniques for teaching writing, parents should be regularly informed both of writing lessons and of why the lessons were designed as they were, improved literacy in the first language strengthened English language learning, all the school's students had the right to regular instruction in English fluency and usage—its importance was that it embodied a set of negotiations around differing and strongly held beliefs that had started the teachers and principal on the road to schoolwide change—to becoming not a replication site of a national exemplar, but their own "exemplary context."

With these three examples in mind, I now feel ready to meet with Alice and Barbara, but I'm apprehensive. The recommendations I'm making are not easy to implement and may not be favored by the district superintendent because they take too long and don't achieve directly measurable student results. This puts Alice in a difficult position; and without Alice's support my recommendations will go nowhere. East is already suffering from fragmentation and overload: both principal and teachers are stretched for time by the extra meetings required for the mandated curriculum reforms and the exemplary program. On the other hand, my visits with Jackie,

Phyllis, Francisco, and the regular education teachers have given Alice, Barbara, and me a way to talk about the dirty little secret of mandated whole school change—before you can make a school *change* you first have to make it *whole*. Wholeness comes from dealing, on the school's own terms, with internal fragmentation and internal goal-setting. Francisco, Phyllis, Jackie, and Barbara must have ways to talk to each other not just about what they do, but about why they do it, as professionals working in the same building with the same set of children and parents. And all four must be able to talk as professionals to Alice, and she to them. The externally generated reforms can be either an obstacle or an opportunity, depending on whether East can achieve a core wholeness and identity as a school that is larger and more central than the external change forces. If it can, then outside reforms may bring additional resources, opportunities for professional development, and links to external networks that can enrich East. But if mandated external solutions take the place of internal coherence, initiative, and identity, then the battle for reform is already lost. The core focus must not be on the *exemplary program,* but on how to make East an *exemplary context* for teaching and learning, in the long term and largely with the personnel already in place. I look forward to Monday's meeting with excitement, hope, and a little fear.

## CONCLUSION

At the outset of this chapter I argued that increased funding for reform brings increased opportunity but also presents a dilemma: how can reform succeed if urban teachers and principals are central to its successful implementation, yet reformers routinely regard them as part of the problem, not part of the solution?

I argued that we must shift the focus of collaboration from *exemplary programs,* which explicitly or implicitly deny practitioners' autonomy and efficacy, to the creation of *exemplary contexts,* the set of conditions that will allow a particular school with a unique history and faculty to integrate outside interventions into a process of sustainable success on its own terms.

To focus on exemplary contexts we must clarify our thinking about change. Rather than uncritically accepting the change process often promoted by national reform advocates, "scaling up" exemplars for reproduction across the country, we must advocate for "scaling down," which Joseph P. McDonald defines as "working on the real problems of redesign at the actual sites, where new beliefs must be adopted, new structures and cultures worked out, and new ways imagined. . . ."[19]

Locally based networks are both scaled-down and relevant, and can help schools build exemplary contexts because the outside collaborators know the local terrain and have a theory of action that, in McDonald's words, "takes teachers' actual contexts seriously, that nonetheless introduces teachers to outside areas, that offers them an appealing new identity rooted in new competencies, and that manages not only to forgive but to encourage and support learning on the job."[20]

Such networks offer hope for the future because they recognize two realities that have remained constant through repeated attempts to change American schooling since the 1970s: teacher knowledge and commitment lie at the heart of successful change and, at the school level, individuals change systems as much as systems change individuals.

## NOTES

1. Milbrey McLaughlin, "The Rand Change Agent Study Revisited: Macro Perspectives and Micro Realities," *Educational Researcher* 19, no. 9 (1990): 15.

2. The National Writing Project is the nation's oldest, largest, and arguably most successful professional development network for teachers. It now comprises more than 160 sites in all 50 states, the District of Columbia, and Puerto Rico and reaches more than 100,000 teachers each year. Each site is a local university-school collaboration; sites share a common philosophy and training model, but differ according to local circumstances.

3. Marianne Moore, "Poetry," *Collected Poems* (New York: Macmillan, 1951), 40–41.

4. Jim Cummins, *Negotiating Identities: Education for Empowerment in a Diverse Society* (Ontario, CA: California Association for Bilingual Education, 1996). Z. F. Beykont, "Academic Progress of a Nondominant Group: A Longitudinal Study of Puerto Ricans in New York City's Late-Exit Bilingual Programs" (Ed. D. diss., Harvard Graduate School of Education, 1994). J. D. Ramirez, "Executive Summary," *Bilingual Research Journal* 16 (1992): 1–62.

5. Ramirez (1992). Virginia Collier, "Age and Rate of Acquisition of Second Language for Academic Purposes," *TESOL Quarterly* 21 (1987): 617–641. Jim Cummins, "Age on Arrival and Immigrant Second Language Learning in Canada: A Reassessment," *Applied Linguistics* 2 (1981): 132–49.

6. Michael Fullan, "Turning Systemic Thinking on Its Head," *Phi Delta Kappan* 77 (1996): 421.

7. Richard Elmore and Milbrey McLaughlin, *Steady Work: Policy, Practice, and the Reform of American Education* (Santa Monica, CA: Rand, 1988).

8. Arthur Applebee, *Contexts for Learning to Write: Studies of Secondary School Instruction* (Norwood, NJ: Ablex Publishing, 1984) and Donald Graves, *The Enemy is Orthodoxy: A Researcher Learns to Write: Selected Articles and Monographs* (Exeter, N H: Heinemann, 1984).

9. James Hoffman, "When Bad Things Happen to Good Ideas in Literacy Education: Professional Dilemmas, Personal Decisions, and Political Traps," *The Reading Teacher* 52, no. 2 (1998): 108.

10. Barbara Batton and Linda Vereline, *Literacy Practices at C. E. S. 28 and C. J. H. S. 117* (New York: Institute for Literacy Studies, 1997), 10.

11. Applebee (1984); Gary Anderson, "Toward Authentic Participation: Deconstructing the Discourses of Participatory Reforms in Education," *American Educational Research Journal* 35, no. 4 (1998): 571–603; Linda Christensen,

"Reconstituting Jefferson," *Rethinking Schools* 13, no. 1 (1998): 1, 8; Richard Elmore, "Getting to Scale with Good Educational Practice," *Harvard Educational Review* 66, no. 1 (1996): 1–26; Michael Fullan and Matthew Miles, "Getting Reform Right: What Works and What Doesn't," *Phi Delta Kappan* 73 (1992): 745–52; Elmore and McLaughlin (1988); Graves (1984); Hoffman (1998); Edward Miller, "Idealists and Cynics: The Micropolitics of Systemic School Reform," *The Harvard Education Letter* XII, no. 4 (1996): 1–3; Donna Muncey and Patrick McQuillan, "Preliminary Findings from a Five-year Study of the Coalition of Essential Schools," *Phi Delta Kappan* 74 (1993): 486–89; David Tyack and Walter Tobin, "The 'Grammar' of Schooling: Why Has It Been So Hard to Change?" *American Educational Research Journal* 31, no. 3 (1994): 453–79.

12. McLaughlin, 1990.

13. Tom Chenoweth, "Emerging National Models of Schooling for At-Risk Students," *International Journal of Educational Reform* 1, no. 3 (1992): 255–69.

14. David Tyack and Larry Cuban, *Tinkering toward Utopia: A Century of Public School Reform* (Cambridge, MA: Harvard University, 1995), 134–35.

15. For descriptive review in an urban elementary school: Rhoda Kanevsky, "Descriptive Review of a Child: A Way of Knowing About Teaching and Learning," in *Inside/Outside: Teacher Research and Knowledge*, Marilyn Cochran-Smith and Susan Lytle, eds. (New York: Teachers College, 1993), 150–62. For reflective case studies and case stories: Richard Ackerman, Patricia Maslin-Ostrowski, and Charles Christensen, "Case Stories: Telling Tales about School," *Educational Leadership* 53, no. 6 (1996): 21–3 and UCLA Graduate School of Education and Information Studies, *Center X Quarterly* 8, no. 2 (1996).

16. Grace Hall McEntee, "Diving with Whales: Five Reasons for Practitioners to Write for Publication," *The Quarterly of the National Writing Project* 20, no. 4 (1998): 21–6 and Simon Hole and Grace Hall McEntee, "Reflection is at the Heart of Practice," *Educational Leadership* 56, no. 8 (1999): 34–37.

17. Emily F. Calhoun, *How to Use Action Research in the Self-Renewing School* (Alexandria, VA: Association for Supervision and Curriculum Development, 1994) and Joe Check, "Teacher Research as Powerful Professional Development," *The Harvard Education Letter* XIII, no. 3 (1997): 6–8.

18. Steve Gordon, "A Lead Teacher Reflects," *Inquiring Together Teacher Inquiry Group Newsletter* (November 1999): 1.

19. Joseph P. McDonald, *Redesigning School: Lessons for the 21st Century* (San Francisco: Jossey-Bass, 1996), 245.

20. Ibid., 248.

## Part II

# Policy Versus Reality: Implementation Dilemmas in Urban Reform

### GENERATION VS. IMPLEMENTATION:
### TWO ANALYTIC FRAMES

Analysts make a basic distinction between *policy generation* and *policy implementation*.[1] I began this study by discussing *generative* dimensions of urban reform: What is urban? What is reform? What can history tell us about the contexts and outcomes of past reforms? In the *Imaginary Gardens* chapter I began to shift the focus to *implementation*. In the chapters that follow I will present a more detailed look at the implementation process in three urban areas: Chicago; Bay Area, California (Oakland and San Francisco); and Boston. I will use these cities as lenses to focus, respectively, on issues of politics, language, and culture as they affect the implementation of reform, and particularly on the uniqueness of the three local contexts. I will make extensive use of the testimony of those most familiar with the implementation of reform, and least represented in the national conversation on it—professionals who work in schools.

A starting point for understanding the relationship between generation and implementation is the fact that the United States unlike, for example, Japan or Britain, has local rather than national control of schooling. Federal influence on education is weak because many Americans want it that way. Until the 2000 election the platform of the Republican Party, the long-standing majority in Washington, had for years called for elimination of the U.S. Department of Education. In financial terms, the U.S. government's share of public school costs has traditionally hovered below 10 percent.

Money is not the only way of exercising influence, however. In the area of educational equity, the statutory and symbolic role of the federal government has been major. Between 1954 and the 1990s, federal courts and Washington legislators repeatedly made common cause with parents and advocates against local educational authorities, mandating change in areas such as school desegregation, bilingual education, special needs, and gender equity. Compensatory federal breakfast, lunch, and reading programs represent additional interventions. Because the basis of these interventions is equity, they affect urban schools much more greatly than suburban schools. With the single exception of Title IX (gender equity), all of these interventions deal with predominantly urban populations.

Between Washington and local districts stand the states, whose role in education has grown rapidly since the Reagan administration. Currently states supply about 45 percent of the funding for K-12 schooling, but in urban areas the state share is sometimes less, a fact some regard as evidence of anti-urban bias. In Chicago in the 2001 fiscal year, for example, the total school budget was estimated to be $3.5 billion, with the local share comprising approximately $1.6 billion (46%), the state share $1.3 billion (37%), and the federal share $590 million (16%).[2]

Typical state interventions include mandated curriculum frameworks, high-stakes assessments, organizational changes such as school-based management, stricter testing for new teachers, and provision of supplementary funding for professional development. States also administer federal Obey-Porter (CSRD) funds to support local adoption of whole-school reform models. But neither Washington nor the states operate schools. So while one can generalize about federal and state policy goals, it is difficult to make similar broad statements about implementation.

This is because urban schools must implement simultaneously three sets of policy demands: federal, state, and local. Those demands can be contradictory. If local districts had been willing to provide equal opportunity to black, Hispanic, and Asian students, their parents would never have had to seek federal court rulings and to lobby for compensatory education programs. The same can be said for parents of special needs students and bilingual parents.

In response to federal mandates on equity and state orders about what to teach and how to test, districts translate policy into practice, legislation into programs. Wide variation in local resources, attitudes, and methods is inevitable. Educators must implement best-practice changes while complying with federal mandates on equity and state mandates on high standards and high-stakes testing, all within a context that is underresourced and crisis-driven. Lawmakers may mandate change, but educators ultimately determine its success or failure. In this conundrum lies reform's great weakness, and also its greatest potential strength, particularly for urban settings.

## POLICY VS. PRACTICE: DIVERSE IMAGES OF REFORM

The relationship between policy and practice can be viewed as a dialogue between "should" and "is." State policies and district reform plans advocate practices that *should* be followed, set performance goals that *should* be met, and project student learning gains that *should* occur as a result. Step-by-step implementation timetables are supported by carefully calibrated budgets and monitored by periodic benchmarks for achievement. But schools, especially urban schools, live in the messy world of *is*. This world is non-linear, subject to frequent and violent change, and buffeted by political and social stresses whose causes lie far outside the dictates of *should*.

The more complex a social structure is, the greater the number of plausible explanations that exist for its behavior.[3] We need to be open to the full range of explanations for the current condition of the complex social structure called urban education. It is vital to urban parents and students, as well as to the health of our cities and our nation, that urban schools do a better job of educating children. Our chances for success in this difficult enterprise are not enhanced by a one-sided conversation that amplifies the voice of *should* and silences the voices of *is*. Urban schools are not simple, mechanistic environments that respond directly to top-down, command-and-control approaches to reform; they are complex human environments that respond in an indirect fashion characterized by false starts, incomplete compliance, and partial success. The better we understand processes of implementation, the *is* of teachers and principals responding to the *should* of administrators and legislators, the greater chance we have for success.

Let me provide some examples. Several years ago I attended a conference at which practitioners and school-based consultants were asked to share characteristic images of urban school reform.[4] Practitioner and scholar Joseph P. McDonald offered this four-word summary of the current situation: "good intentions/bad design." His point was that we need to devote as much attention and support to the "how" of reform, the implementation side, as we do to the "what," the goals side. Another panelist characterized reform as a "quagmire of good intentions" that was swallowing up dollars, time, and energy without seriously addressing its own procedural flaws. A third panel member, my friend and colleague Peter Golden, introduced two images that illustrated characteristic perversions of reform that, as a practitioner, he found professionally demeaning.

Peter, a veteran of more than twenty-five years in middle and high school English classrooms in Boston, named his images "reform as photo op" and "reform as Potemkin village." The first, he explained, describes a scenario familiar to many urban teachers and principals. Central office personnel accompanied by political figures, business partners, or philanthropic donors show up at a school with reporters and television crews in tow. They are there to award a large grant or launch a reform initiative. In teachers' eyes, the school is reduced to a visual prop, a backdrop which serves a convenient political purpose for a few hours. And if, as often happens, the initiative launched with such fanfare should wither away over the next two or three years due to lack of adequate resources and attention from the same cast of central office characters, no camera crew will be there to see it. According to Peter, the real message is this: the *perception* of change is all. The halting, complex, frustrating *reality* of change, the daily stuff of teachers' professional lives, is of little value, because it can't be packaged as a photo op or sound bite that will fool outsiders into thinking that real progress is being made. The celebratory photo op thus becomes a source of bitterness and demoralization for teachers, one more proof that what goes on in their classrooms is increasingly dictated by people far removed from the daily give-and-take of teaching and learning.

Peter's second image, "reform as Potemkin village," is drawn from Russian history. About the time our thirteen colonies were throwing off Britain's colonial yoke, the vast Russian Empire was governed by the world's most powerful woman, Catherine the Great. Among her lovers was Grigori Potemkin, a dashing and ambitious army officer who gained her support for a far-reaching plan to colonize the Ukrainian steppe. Potemkin "spared neither men, money, nor himself . . . but he never calculated the cost, and most of the plan had to be abandoned when but half accomplished." When Catherine undertook a royal tour in 1787 to view his reported successes, it was "a triumph for Potemkin, for he disguised all the weak points of his administration."[5] A widely repeated but probably apocryphal tale held that he erected entire villages of false-front houses and shops, like Hollywood sets, and populated them with cheering peasant "extras" to provide his patron with the appearance of success as her ornate carriage rolled by. Soon, "Potemkin village" came to refer to "something that appears to be elaborate and impressive but in actual fact lacks substance."[6]

These two visual metaphors accuse reform advocates of valuing smooth image over rough substance and of using reform to advance their own ambitions. Both images imply that, in their implementation, reforms are frequently insulting to the professionals who labor every day in schools, and that individuals in leadership positions often advance themselves at the expense of teachers, students, and parents.

Peter's images resonated with his largely practitioner audience that day, because he had named something that most of them had experienced in their own professional lives: the elevation of form over substance in the implementation of change, and the subsequent scapegoating of practitioners as the main obstacle to improved schools. The perspective of teachers and principals who have bought into reform, and then felt betrayed by it, is a crucial one for understanding the current dynamics of change in urban settings.

But practitioners' views on reform are far from monolithic. Another veteran teacher who was at the conference—I'll call her Myra—pointed out that many teachers have conflicting feelings about their changing role. An immigrant and a native Spanish speaker, Myra has experience as a self-contained elementary teacher, an ESL teacher, and a bilingual literacy specialist. Most recently, she has been a literacy coach working with three quite different elementary schools.

In a note to me after the conference, Myra agreed that there were schools where Peter's metaphors applied, but felt that as an overall response they were too cynical:

As a practitioner myself, and facilitator of school reform, I see this reaction every day. We resist; we criticize; but the fact is that our teaching profession is well known for being one that promotes "habit formation." We sign in every morning at a specific time; we teach in the same school for as many years as we can, and when we are forced to leave, due to cutbacks, or whatever, we do so screaming and kicking. How can we leave our friends; our predictable ways? Who wants to start all over again?

I go every morning to my schools with a sense of urgency. When I look around I see lots of veteran teachers who have been teaching the same way for twenty years. Fortunately, this doesn't happen across the board. Last Saturday I spent the day with the whole faculty of one of my schools, brainstorming and reflecting on how they are going to improve teaching and therefore learning. I was impressed by their depth of knowledge and their lack of complaining for having to spend several weekends doing this—and they aren't getting paid for it. The reality in my other schools is the caring teacher, (I never met a teacher who doesn't care), but caring, until we have to look at our practice and at our results, and do something about it. So, if we take the cynical view, then what?

I would like to point out that what school reform is proposing, in many cases, is not bad: teachers as reflective practitioners; teachers making more decisions; teachers looking at students' work to design instruction; teachers knowing intimately their students' reading behaviors, or lack of, to guide the reading lessons; teachers being aware of cognitive, developmental and culturally appropriate teaching methods. If this is reform, I totally embrace it, because it makes sense. I think that we teachers are the ones who can generate knowledge about teaching and learning, but how can this happen when teachers resist, resist, resist, and have this negative view exhibited in the Potemkin village image. How can this happen when teachers ignore the culturally different? Sometimes I think that we have a dual personality: on one side is a good teacher with good intentions; on the other side, a cynical resister entrenched in the politics of a dying school system. I've seen many caring teachers who lack a sensitivity to the fact that teaching that is culturally appropriate allows for a greater range of students to succeed; that writing in a second language imposes different cognitive demands that must be studied and promoted.

Foucault once said "the most insightful way to understand society is to consider it from the perspective of the professions that have emerged to contain its failures." School reform has emerged to contain OUR failure to teach this diverse population—and as a teacher I am responsible. The buck stops here, as they say. And school reform, at least in the schools I know, is no longer a photo op, or a fake village. Principals are being observed and evaluated. Schools are panicking because of In Depth Reviews. Teachers are being held accountable for having two-thirds of their pupils reading three grades below level and not doing anything different about it. And I think it is about time.

Personally, I strongly believe that resistance and cynicism function as ways to preserve the status quo, by protecting the structure of schooling—that only reflects the society at large. This, in my understanding, is that white, private and suburban schools support and maintain the powerful, and urban schools are a warehouse for the Latinos, African Americans, and white poor. So, is it too much to ask principals and teachers to do something about it? Is school reform such a bad idea? And if it is a quagmire of good intentions, what can be done to replace it? Was something being done before school reform? Were teachers up in arms years ago because 60% of high school students graduated every year barely knowing how to read? As a non-mainstream teacher, my images are: if people didn't want to climb Mount Everest because it is terribly high, then what? If scientists felt defeated by the prospect of finding a cure for AIDS, and gave up before even starting, then what? If someone doesn't attempt school reform to stop the intellectual genocide that goes on every day in our school system, then what?

It is crucial to recognize that neither Peter nor Myra are "right" or "wrong"—both views reflect something real about current reform efforts. In any large city it is possible to name schools or situations that support Peter's conclusions, and other schools and situations that support Myra's. Variables that critically affect successful implementation—resources, leadership, composition of the faculty and the student body—vary widely from school to school and even grade to grade.

Because of this, policy stances that appear consistent at the top levels often degrade badly by the time they reach the school level. District administrators, for example, point out that "photo ops" are important to reform, because rebuilding the public image of urban education is a critical step in obtaining badly needed additional resources. No mayor or legislator can risk investing in a system perceived to be bloated, inefficient, and badly failing in its instructional mission. Similarly, superintendents find willing listeners when they publicize exemplars. Recognizing success demonstrates that change is possible, aggressive leadership rewarded, good teaching recognized. Political stakes are high, and the practitioners' perspective is often seen as of little importance compared to the urgent need to show that success, though not yet achieved, is a realizable goal. But if success is claimed on questionable grounds to make those at the top look good, then what the superintendent parades as an exemplar, practitioners may know as a "Potemkin school."

I have discussed five images that emerged from a single conference in Boston—good intentions/bad design, photo op, Potemkin village, climbing Mt. Everest, intellectual genocide—in some detail for a reason. Interviewing urban educators around the country for the last several years, I have encountered teachers from many cities telling essentially these same stories.

These teachers believe that change is needed and are working hard for reform, but are increasingly frustrated because they are experiencing not one reform but two: the one school systems announce in press conferences and post on their Web sites, and the one teachers, principals, and students actually live in the schools. My fear is that the largely hidden "two reforms" phenomenon may become a national Potemkin village if we consistently silence practitioners who are the primary witnesses to the implementation of reform.

The first reform reality, the one that gets all the attention, consists largely of four elements: state-mandated curriculum frameworks and high-stakes tests, the school system's own ambitious goals, outside programs to help achieve those goals, and highly publicized sets of numbers—number of dollars spent, number of schools and teachers involved, number of students passing or failing the reading test. The second, hidden, classroom-level reality is characterized by a do-it-or-else, standards-based pressure that takes little account of issues teachers actually face: frequent turnover in principals, high student mobility rates, intermittent attendance, large class sizes, high numbers of English language learners and special needs students.

Practitioners in many cities describe a widening gap between these two realities—the reform vision outlined in the superintendent's press conference and the frantic but halting pace of school-level change. Trying to live a professional life that straddles this gap can be frustrating and demoralizing, and teachers are not the only ones who realize this. Systems thinker Michael Fullan points out that educational change is nonlinear and that the continuous stream of planned and unplanned changes that affect schools are major barriers to systemic reforms. When the powers-that-be mandate linear progress in a nonlinear environment, "(o)verload and fragmentation combine to reduce educators' motivation for working on reform. Together they make the situation that the schools face seem hopeless, and they take their toll on the most committed, who find that will alone is not sufficient to achieve or sustain reform."[7] In the second half of this book I will attempt to show both the public and the largely hidden aspects of reform, and to trace the ways in which they are connected to each other as two faces of the same dynamic reality of change.

## GOALS AND ORGANIZATION OF PART II

The dynamics of change can be devilishly hard to see, if by "seeing" we mean being able to describe them in a way that is true simultaneously to history, to statistical data, and to the felt experience of the full range of players involved. These players include teachers, administrators, and students, as well as parents who entrust their children to their city's schools and are so often disappointed. They also include the prosperous army of consultants, business partners, and funders who have become an established part of urban change efforts as well as elected officials who hold the purse strings of reform, and policymakers who draft its blueprints.

To really see urban reform we need analytic equivalents of both a wide-angle lens and a zoom, both panoramas and close-ups. In my initial chapters I provided wide-angle views; in Part Two I will take close-up looks at reform in three urban areas, Chicago, the Bay Area, CA, and Boston. Each area will be used as a focal point for discussing one of the critical concerns of this book: politics (Chicago), language issues (Bay Area), and race and culture (Boston).

The city chapters follow a common format. They begin with an introduction to the critical theme, followed by a brief history of language and cultural issues in the educational politics of that city. They continue with a discussion of local reform issues that makes central use of the testimony of expert practitioners, and close with a short list of conclusions. Practitioner testimony is drawn from interviews, discussions, and focus groups with teachers, administrators, coaches, and consultants from more than 20 urban school systems that I have conducted over the past five years.

In general, I have defined an "expert practitioner" as a school-based educator who is able to bring multiple perspectives to the discussion of reform. In choosing "expert practitioners" I used the following criteria: 1) have had five or more years of teaching experience in urban schools; 2) hold a master's degree or higher; 3) have been involved in reform at the school level for at least two years; 4) have been responsible for something larger than a single classroom at some point in their careers, for example, serving in a district level position, conducting citywide staff development, working as a coach or literacy coordinator; and 5) have significant involvement with one or more outside networks such as the National Writing Project, Foxfire, the Coalition for Essential Schools, or a local, university-based collaboration. Practitioners quoted also represent a wide range of cultural, racial/ethnic, and linguistic backgrounds, with a special emphasis on African American, Hispanic, and Asian American educators.

I chose teachers and administrators who met these criteria because I wanted to hear from those whose support and commitment is essential if reform is to succeed: school-based leaders who are experienced, engaged, well-trained, and professionally active. In the course of my interviews I came especially to value the fourth and fifth criteria, experience outside the classroom and involvement with an outside network. Practitioners who maintain teaching as their principal identity after working outside the classroom have a focus on children that grounds them in an important way and makes their observations particularly valuable. Many of them have chosen not to accept invitations to take on a higher-paying position because they believe being with students is where the action truly is. Similarly, practitioners involved in outside networks demonstrate powerfully that "teachers are willing and eager to be involved in activities that challenge them and promote their professional growth," their involvement serves to "illuminate a fundamental lesson for policymakers: *the context in which educational change is pursued is everything.*"[8]

The role of urban principals under reform is a subject urgently in need of more study, as is the role of "middle management" personnel in large systems—the array of coordinators, assistant superintendents, and project leaders who seem to multiply almost organically as part of the change process. In this book I have chosen to concentrate on the role of teachers, principals, and "insider/outsiders"—coaches, consultants, program coordinators, change facilitators—who are rapidly becoming a permanent fixture of school life under reform. These are the front-line players of reform, yet they are the least heard from. Understanding their roles will become critical over the next ten years as aging faculties in cities across the country give way to a new generation of teachers. It is unclear where this new generation is going to come from or how long they will stay—planners in Chicago were surprised to learn that in 2000, 60 percent of the city's new teachers were career-changing adults rather than recent college graduates.[9] The more we know about the teacher's and principal's experiences of reform, the better we will be able to prepare and support the new generation that is taking over urban classrooms and schools.

Finally, I must note the obvious. While for purposes of analysis I have separated the issues of politics, language, and culture and assigned each to a city, in reality they are inextricably intertwined. The discussion of reform politics in Chicago, for example, inevitably touches on issues of language and culture, just as the discussion of language issues in the Bay Area inevitably involves culture and politics.

By linking a single issue to a single city, my intent is to illustrate in concrete terms the power, complexity, and uniqueness of local contexts. Policymakers and reform strategists consistently underestimate the extent to which the implementation of reform is influenced by local histories, alliances, and configurations with roots far deeper than the effects of exemplary change models and best practice pedagogical strategies. At the same time, the testimony of practitioners from widely separate locales supports some general conclusions about the implementation of reform in urban areas, and these too will emerge from the city chapters. The true picture of urban reform lies somewhere between, in a combination of the unique and local with the generalizable and national.

## NOTES

1. James L. Gallagher, "Models for Policy Analysis: Child and Family Policy," in *Models for Policy Analysis,* eds. R. Haskin and J. Gallagher (Norwood, NJ: Ablex, 1985): 49.

2. Chicago Public Schools Web Site, "CPS at a Glance," 2001, <*http://www.cps.k12.il.us/*> (4 January 2001).

3. Frank Fischer, *Evaluating Public Policy* (Chicago: Nelson-Hall, 1995): 229.

4. "School Reform: Looking Back, Looking Forward," 21 September 1999, University of Massachusetts Boston.

5. *Encyclopedia Brittanica*, 2001 ed., s. v. "Potemkin."

6. *American Heritage Dictionary of the English Language,* 4th ed., s. v. "Potemkin village."

7. Michael Fullan, "Turning Systemic Thinking on Its Head," *Phi Delta Kappan* 77 (1996): 420-3.

8. Ann Lieberman and Milbrey McLaughlin, "Networks for Educational Change: Powerful and Problematic," *Phi Delta Kappan* 71 (1992): 677.

9. Sharon Ransom, conversation with author, Milwaukee, WI, 24 November 2000.

## Chapter 5

# Chicago: A Primer in Reform Politics

### INTRODUCTION

If, as Tip O'Neill famously said, "All politics is local," then public schools must be counted among the oldest political institutions Americans possess. The Massachusetts Bay Colony, founded in 1630, had already hired a town schoolmaster by 1635 and opened a grammar school by 1636. In 1647 the Massachusetts General Court passed the "Old Deluder Satan Act," which set the pattern for local funding and control of schools for generations of New England towns: "(it) asserted that Satan, master of deception, was keeping people from true knowledge of the Scriptures. Acknowledging dissent and a fear that the learning of the church and civic elders might not survive into future generations, the law required that towns with fifty or more families must make provision for instruction in reading and writing. . . . Noncompliance could result in a fine levied against the town."[1]

The Act was passed in a climate of dissension, responded to a perceived outside threat (the wiles of Satan), was motivated by fear of decline from a "golden age" of learning (the deep scriptural knowledge of Puritan elders), and carried sanctions for non-compliance. Like many of today's school laws, its intent was reform-minded and it was deeply political.

Public schools are political in many ways. They invariably consume the lion's share of municipal budgets, insuring that voters take at least a financial interest in their success or failure. They are a significant source of publicly funded employment; and many a legislative career has been launched with election to a local school committee, the entry-level job of American politics.

But starting with the Watergate scandal and continuing through Irangate and "Monicagate," the American public's opinion of politics and politicians has sunk ever lower. Loss of faith in the political process has led to widespread distrust of public institutions, and since schools are the one public institution that touches most Americans, calls for education reform can be seen as part of the spirit of the times. In discussing the politics of education, therefore, we must take care not to begin from the solely pejorative definition of popular usage, but to recover the full range of meanings, positive and negative, that *politics* can hold.

Among those meanings are the following:

* the methods or tactics involved in managing a state or government,
* intrigue or maneuvering within a political unit or group in order to gain control or power,
* the often internally conflicting interrelationships among people in a society.[2]

No better venue could be found for studying the role that politics play than Chicago, political city *par excellence* and home to the nation's most ambitious effort at urban school reform.

Chicago holds a storied place in American political mythology. For decades under Mayor Richard J. Daley it was a bastion of ethnic machine politics, and schools were very much a part of the political mix. Chicago lore holds that John F. Kennedy gained the presidency in 1960 because, at the critical moment, Daley's machine manipulated enough votes to swing the crucial state of Illinois to the Democrats.

This story was much cited by national media during the even closer 2000 presidential race. Uncited was what many believe to be the second half of the story, the impact of Daley's actions on Chicago's schools. Delivering the needed vote may have created a political debt that put the new Democratic administration in a poor position to enforce federal school desegregation decrees in what was perhaps the most ethnically and racially divided major city in America. Thus, while President Kennedy personally intervened in the desegregation of the University of Mississippi in 1963, highlighting southern resistance to educational equity, in 1965 the Johnson administration backed off from a federal desegregation order in Chicago that would have affected many times the number of black and white students.

At the dawn of the new century, Chicago's public schools are nearly devoid of white students. In the 1999–2000 school year, approximately 90 percent of the system's 431,750 students were "minorities"; more than half were African American, more than one-third Latino. Eighty-five percent came from low-income families and sixteen percent were classified "limited-English-proficient."[3] In the rough-and-tumble of Chicago's political process, who looks out for the interests of these students? Overrepresented in the schools, blacks and Latinos are still underrepresented in basic power structures: city council seats, the mayor's office, state and federal legislative posts, corporate boardrooms, and top levels of the reform hierarchy.

One recent study concluded that, "Since 1995, all but one of the top management team have been white males, after a decade of African American superintendents . . . the hierarchy of managerial positions is being re-stratified, with whites at the top, and African Americans and Hispanics in the middle and bottom."[4]

The shifting racial and ethnic dimensions of educational politics are germane because, in Chicago, "school reform" does not refer to a single initiative, idea, or entity but to a long series of intertwined political and educational events. Since 1986 Chicago's schools have been subject to a more or less continuous series of reforms, the scope and complexity of which surpass anything else in the nation. Observers frequently divide the changes into two broad waves. The first dates from 1988 when the Illinois legislature dismantled the huge and wasteful Chicago Board of Education and replaced it with a decentralized, school-based management (SBM) model. Responsibility for staffing, budget, and curricular decisions was vested in powerful Local School Councils (LSC's) made up of parents, teachers, community members, and the principal. In the second wave, dating from a second state legislative action in 1995, LSC's remained but control of the schools was re-centralized in the office of Mayor Richard M. Daley. Daley appointed his chief budget officer, Paul Vallas, to head the schools. In this neo-corporate administrative model, staffing, curriculum, instructional methods, and testing are ultimately dictated from, and accountable too, the mayor's office.[5] Vallas instituted sweeping policy changes, balanced the school budget for six consecutive years, and oversaw $2.6 billion in construction projects. Unfortunately, when test scores became stagnant and then declined, Daley publicly criticized him and in June 2001 Vallas announced his resignation.[6] This suggests that corporate-bred superintendents, even when handpicked by the mayor, may enjoy little more longevity than their education-bred counterparts.

To capture the flavor of more than a decade of continuously mutating reforms, in this chapter I will present the views of three long-term participant-observers of the process, one whose role has been external, one whose role has been primarily internal, and one who bridges both roles. All hold leadership roles in the Chicago Area Writing Project, a university-school collaboration that is a major provider of school-based professional development in literacy. Personal experience, a passionate commitment to urban education, and a sense of wider perspectives inform their views. My own commentary will connect their experiences in Chicago to larger, national patterns in reform.

The first of these viewpoints is from Professor B. J. Wagner of Roosevelt University, a scholar-activist and director of the Chicago Area Writing Project who has worked closely with Chicago's schools for more than thirty years. Wagner describes the long history of cultural and racial tensions that have characterized schooling there, tensions that remind us of a powerful social subtext to current reforms. In particular, she looks at the educational histories of immigrants and linguistic and racial minorities, groups who now form the vast majority of students in the Chicago public schools.

## THE POLITICS OF RACE, ETHNICITY, AND REFORM IN CHICAGO'S SCHOOLS—BETTY JANE WAGNER

### Immigration and Ethnicity

Chicago has grown up as a city of ethnic enclaves, with each wave of newcomers clustering in carefully demarcated neighborhoods and schools. Neighborhood-based enclaves grew from the 1850s through the turn of the century, when Chicago was second only to New York in the number of first- or second-generation immigrant children in its schools.[7] Today, as the country's fourth largest gateway for immigration, Chicago remains a city divided by race and ethnicity.[8]

In the mid-1800s immigrants faced schools suffering from severe over-crowding, with student-teacher ratios of up to 100:1.[9] Most immigrant children could not even go to school because there were too few seats, and non-immigrants filled the available places first.[10] Half of Chicago's school-aged children were foreign born, but they represented only 16 percent of the school enrollment.

In subsequent years Catholic immigrants from Germany and Ireland, who in the mid-1800s each made up 20 percent of the city's population, started the Catholic school system, partly in response to what they perceived as an "Anglo-Saxon bias"[11] in public schools. The Archbishop of Chicago allowed ethnic groups to form schools in their own parishes, so the members of different ethnic enclaves enrolled in separate Catholic schools in much the same way they attended separate public schools.[12]

Over the next few decades, immigrants were finally able to attend schools in large numbers and influence the curriculum, especially around issues of language. In the late 1800s, Germans across the Midwest made sure their children went to schools taught in the German language, bilingual schools, or at least schools where the children studied German.[13] At this time about twenty-five percent of all Chicago's school children were learning German in public schools[14] and still more attended Catholic schools taught in German.

In the late 1800s, public fears of bilingualism and pressures for assimilation led to the downfall of the German language programs. But by the turn of the century, the immigrant population had formed their own po-litical organizations to influence representation and decision making in the schools, and Germans in particular united to "resist this encroachment on their language rights."[15] In Chicago, according to a newspaper report in 1902, the mayor appointed the school board "largely to accommodate certain geographical, racial and political considerations."[16]

Today, Chicago's largest immigrant group comes from Mexico, followed by the Philippines, India, Poland, and Korea. Once again bilingual programs flourish in the city and provide teaching jobs for members of the immigrant communities. According to state law, newcomers stay in transitional bilingual programs for three years and then are mainstreamed if they can pass a test of English proficiency. Although details of the programs often become topics of contention, the underlying concept of providing at least a three-year transitional program has been well accepted.

### African American Struggles

Chicago's African Americans now make up more than half of the enrollment in public schools. They have struggled harder than any other group to gain access to adequate schooling and have profited little from their efforts or the efforts of others on their behalf.

The early African American population in Chicago was required by an 1863 "Black School Law" to attend separate schools from whites. In 1874, however, the Illinois legislature outlawed segregation. Nevertheless, neighborhoods were segregated, schools served neighborhoods, and schools, *de facto,* remained segregated.

Over the years, poor facilities and crowded conditions plagued the African American schools, with conditions worsening as the population increased. Southern blacks began migrating to Chicago during World War I and then again in even larger numbers during and just after World War II. In the 1940s, Chicago's black population increased by 77 percent; between 1950 and 1960 the black population increased by another 65 percent, to 813,000; "At one point 2,200 black people were moving to Chicago every week."[17]

After the black population explosion from the 1940s through the 1960s and the passage of *Brown v. Board of Education,* the NAACP (National Association for the Advancement of Colored People), CORE (Congress of Racial Equality), and the Urban League began working for school integration in Chicago. In 1956, these groups called the neighborhood schools policy a cover-up for continuing segregation and complained about the crowded conditions of the black schools. The density of the population in new housing projects, coupled with the rapid growth in the black population, led to severe overcrowding in the segregated all-black schools. School superintendent, Ben Willis, enacted policies to bring down overcrowding that served to perpetuate segregation.

Instead of integrating the adjacent and usually half-empty white schools, Willis put the black schools on double shifts, eight to noon and noon to four, and installed "Willis Wagons"—trailers converted into temporary classrooms—in their playgrounds, thereby creating an urban equivalent of the inferior rural black school systems of the South.[18]

In 1961, a group of parents filed suit (the *Webb* case), charging that ger-rymandering had created the overcrowded all-black schools. As part of an out-of-court settlement, the school district instituted a voluntary pupil trans-fer plan and created a study panel "to make recommendations on desegre-gation."[19] The settlement led to little, if any, change in either school segregation or the conditions of the black schools.

In 1963, the Coordinating Council of Community Organizations, founded by a high school teacher the year before, staged a school boycott to protest Willis' segregationist policies. This "single largest civil rights protest in the history of Chicago" resulted in 200,000 students staying out of school for a day.[20] In the same year, the federal government threatened to cut funding to the Chicago schools because they remained segregated, but when Mayor Richard J. Daley agreed to follow the desegregation rec-ommendations of the study panel from the *Webb* case, the suit was sus-pended. Daley, however, did not keep his word.

In 1965, the U.S. Commission of Education withheld 30 million dollars from the Chicago schools from the first Title I ESEA (Elementary and Sec-ondary Education Act) grant "pending an investigation of complaints from community organizations of discrimination in the system."[21] The funds were restored within five days, "following intervention by the President (at the urging of Mayor Richard J. Daley and leading Congressmen from the city)."[22] With their powers all but stripped, federal regulators could only ask Chicago to voluntarily desegregate its schools. Not surprisingly, Chi-cago schools maintained their segregated ways.

In the early 1970s, new pressures emerged at the state level, where ma-jor battles were waged over plans to bus students to desegregate the schools. In 1973, the Illinois legislature prohibited busing, effectively ending state pressures for desegregation and ultimately leading to renewed federal pres-sure in the form of further funding threats. Given the new federal interest, in 1977, Chicago school leaders agreed, as a stopgap measure, to balance the faculties at each school by race, educational background, and teaching experience. The following year district officials proposed a desegregation plan for students, which included a system of voluntary transfers, open enrollment in the high schools, and expanded magnet schools and academic interest centers. This plan failed, so by 1979, the U.S. Office of Education declared Chicago schools out of compliance with their 1977 faculty de-segregation plan and charged the schools with continued pupil segregation. Finally, in April of 1980, the U.S. Department of Justice pressed charges against Chicago schools.

Meanwhile, the Chicago schools were experiencing severe financial dif-ficulties. The superintendent resigned, and just before the Justice Depart-ment suit was filed, the mayor gained control of the school system and appointed a new school board with a majority of minority members. This school board, knowing a suit was imminent, negotiated a consent decree as soon as the 1980 suit was filed and accepted. The consent decree called for increased integration of students and educational compensation for schools that could not be integrated because of the demographics of Chicago, a city with few whites and large numbers of blacks. Only an additional 4 percent of students of color attended schools that were at least 15 percent white. The vast majority of students —77 percent—were in segregated schools, and of these, 43 percent were in "racially isolated" schools with no white students at all.

In the years following the consent decree, Chicago has hired more teachers of color than any city other than Detroit: 46.1 percent are African American, 8.7 percent Latino, 1.5 percent Asian, and 16 percent Native American/Alaskan Native as of 2000. Thus, Chicago students are more likely to find role models who are persons of color among the staff than they are in most other major cities in the United States. However, faculty desegregation also has had its negative side. The policies have eroded staff morale, and principals in all-black schools complain about the restrictions on teacher hiring. Many feel that the only available white teachers are poorly qualified and so resent the quotas in the consent decree that keep them from hiring stronger black applicants.

Many of Chicago's white ethnic groups have historically resisted school desegregation. In response to integration efforts, many whites left the public schools, moving their children into parochial and other private schools or to the suburbs.[23] Sanders notes that the Catholic school system began serving non-Catholic whites who "wished to avoid the colored invasion of the public schools"[24] starting in the 1930s. Catholic schools maintained separate schools for whites and blacks until the 1960s.

Today, in spite of some integration in selected schools, both the Catholic system and the public schools remain essentially segregated. Some argue that the desegregation plans have actually favored whites, who make up only 11 percent of the school population but get 35 percent of the highly prized slots in magnet schools where the bulk of the compensatory funds have gone. According to Hess, "Black and Hispanic leaders [are] . . . frustrated by past intransigence and current demographic limitations" and essentially have given up on their original goals of an integrated school system.[25]

### Current Political Climate

Chicago's public schools continue to operate in a difficult financial and political climate set in large part by the Illinois General Assembly. Like most state governments, Illinois faced a severe financial crisis in the 1990s. This affects Chicago disproportionately. The Chicago public schools face three serious constraints. First, Illinois has been for decades and continues to be one of the lowest states (48th out of 50) in the proportion of its gross wealth spent on education. Second, state and local resources are distributed to schools inequitably, making Chicago comparatively disadvantaged. This is somewhat offset by programs targeted for the children of the poor, but cutbacks in federal funding have diminished even these. Third, Illinois, like many states, is split into strongly held urban and non-urban attitudes. The legislature, despite the return of the Democrats to a majority in the House in 1996, has been dominated by non-Chicago representatives, termed "Downstaters," who share an anti-urban bias with many of the suburban representatives in northern Illinois. The widespread perception in Chicago is that the state legislature is biased against persons of color.

The most glaring example of the city versus non-city bias was the law that would not allow the Chicago Public Schools to open unless they could show a balanced budget. Other school districts in the state continued to open each fall with serious deficits, but not Chicago. In the fall of 1993, it took a series of judicial decisions to open the Chicago schools at all, and then only after delays in the start of school. Another example of anti-city bias was the state funding formula for additional money for low-income students. Although over 80 percent of Chicago public school students come from low-income homes, the state legislators, in order to limit the proportion of funding coming to Chicago, stipulated that districts could be funded for no more than 62.5 percent of students as low-income. In 1988, the funding formula was changed; the amount of funding per student is now determined by the total number of low-income students according to the most recent federal census divided by the average daily attendance of the best three-month period in the prior school year. The same formula is used for the rest of the state.

The development in Illinois with the greatest potential for improving the lot of the Chicago public schools is school reform. In 1988 the Illinois General Assembly enacted the Chicago School Reform Act. It has been called, perhaps with some exaggeration, the most radical experiment in the history of public education. It has three major components: (a) a set of ten goals to provide urban students the same academic opportunities as suburban students and a stipulation that all schools reach national norms in academic subjects and graduation rates; (b) a reallocation of the system's resources from the bloated central administrative offices of the 1980s to the local school level; and (c) a system of site-based management.

Given the history of Chicago's ethnic enclaves and its desegregation struggles, it is not surprising that school reform in Chicago is less about multiculturalism or racial balance in schools, than about local control and according to Wrigley, "the power of ethnic groups to control jobs."[26] Changes in governance are at the heart of the reform experiment. Each local school elects a ten-person Local School Council (LSC) made up of parents, community residents, and teachers, who along with the principal and a student representative (if the school is a high school), comprise the LSC. The LSC has three functions: (a) to adopt a school improvement plan each year, based on a needs assessment; (b) to adopt a local school budget, designed to implement the improvement plan; and (c) to decide to retain or change the principal of the school.

One of the more noticeable effects of school reform is principal turnover. By December of 1995, 83 percent of the principals in Chicago's 557 public schools had no more than three years of experience.[27] A higher proportion of Chicago principals is now African American and Latino and a lower proportion is white.[28]

Especially at the high school level, reform has had more of an impact on the ways schools are governed than on the ways children are taught.[29] Although there is great variation from one school to another, most teachers simply find they have more work to do outside of class as they take on school improvement, budgeting, and governance duties. There has been steady gain in student achievement in reading and mathematics. There is some debate about whether the gains can be attributed to the reforms or to the fact that students took the tests seriously because the school district imposed the consequence that students who scored below a certain threshold would have to go to summer school.

After the steady rise, reading scores leveled out slightly in 2001. Mayor Richard J. Daley and Chief Executive Officer Paul Vallas expressed great dismay even though the reading scores on the Iowa Tests of Basic Skills approached the national norm. Neither policymakers nor those in the press pointed out that test scores correlate closely with family income, and that for a school system with 85.7 percent of its students from low-income homes, to approach the national average is quite an accomplishment. The large population of immigrant children added to the high proportion of low-income students challenges Chicago's teachers. The fact that students are doing as well as they are is a credit to their dedication and skill.

## BARBARA KATO: A CHICAGO TEACHER SPEAKS ABOUT REFORM[30]

B. J. Wagner's mini-history, in the previous section, illuminates the contentious past of Chicago's schools, where successive waves of newcomers and outsiders have attempted to carve out a viable education for their children. Her account reminds us that definitions of reform that focus solely on management, testing, curriculum, and pedagogy tell only part of the story. To understand the full dynamics of change, we must never lose sight of the social tensions which underlie the technical aspects of reform. In a similar way, a story of reform told only from the outside is incomplete. To supply an insider's view, we next turn to a veteran Chicago teacher.

Barbara Kato's relationship with the Chicago Public Schools (CPS) spans more than thirty years and many different roles. She attended CPS as an elementary and secondary student, and as a CPS teacher since 1976 has

handled pre-school, kindergarten, primary, and upper elementary classrooms in six different schools. Since 1991 she has been released from teaching in certain years to direct the staff development work of the Chicago
Area Writing Project (CAWP), a university-based, nationally networked
collaborative program that offers Chicago's teachers in-service training in
the teaching of writing and reading. For the 2000–2001 academic year
Barbara returned to a fifth grade classroom and in 2000 she completed a
doctoral dissertation titled "For better and for worse: Veteran teachers trying to teach well under eleven years of Chicago school reform." Her comments are informed not just by her own experience as a teacher and staff
developer but by a thorough grounding in the research literature on reform
in Chicago and by her own interviews and case studies of "exemplary teachers who choose to teach in difficult settings."[31] In the sections that follow
I will alternate excerpts from my interviews with Kato, with my own reflections on her story.

### Two Waves of Reform

I began my conversation with Barbara by asking, "What's political about reform
in Chicago?"

In Chicago, everything is political! Let's talk about the first wave. Mayor Richard J. Daley had for years been "robbing Peter to pay Paul" to keep the schools
open. When he died in 1976, there was nobody to intercede in Board-Chicago
Teacher Union negotiations, and we proceeded to have five strikes between 1980
and 1987. Educational reform groups had been talking about and planning alternative site-based structures well before the September 1987 teachers' strike. So when
it happened, they already had a model for restructuring and just needed the
groundswell of support. They were ready to channel the anger and organization
of the grassroots parent and community groups into a more organized political
force. It's naïve to think that the design of school reform, the money to get it started,
and political clout in Springfield to get the law passed were the result of parent
and community groups. They provided some fuel, but the train and tracks had been
laid already.

By 1987, Harold Washington had been re-elected for a second term as mayor,
but died of a heart attack in November 1987 just as the groundwork was being
laid to reorganize the schools. The city council spent all their time arguing with
each other about who would be the next mayor rather than worrying about the
schools. Chicago business leaders, civic and community groups, and others lobbied
state legislators to pass the 1988 school reform law. Downstate legislators were
unwilling to give any increased financial support to the Chicago schools unless it
was tied to school reform. So Chicago was expected to restructure without having
any additional funds.

The Chicago Teachers Union was a latecomer to the coalition and might not
have had any input into the restructuring had they taken the rigid and negative
stance that the Principals Association had. The principals lost all seniority rights
and ended up with four-year contracts voted on by a local school council made up
of six parents, two community members, and two teachers. They ended up with

much responsibility but not much control.

The Chicago business community was heavily involved in School Reform. It pushed for the Chicago School Finance Authority to be established in 1980 which was headed by business people and had final approval of all school finances and all budgetary decisions of the Chicago Board of Education. They didn't trust the superintendent nor did they have faith in the city government. No school budget could be passed without their approval.

Once new mayor Richard M. Daley was well-established, the business community helped push the state legislature to pass the 1995 amendment to the School Reform law giving all the power to the Chicago mayor. They could dissolve the Chicago Finance Authority. They took away the right of Chicago teachers to strike. But lo and behold, the $150 million dollar shortfall projected for 1995–96 disappeared almost overnight. Suddenly, the system had money to pay its bills. Amazing. This was all political.

Under the second wave, the mayor appointed his chief of staff as School Reform Board president and his budget director as Chief Executive Officer, and sent dozens of people from city hall over to the Chicago Board of Education. The interesting thing is that there doesn't seem to be anyone left who is looking critically at this second wave of school reform. It's my belief that no one wants to take on the mayor, but I'm not sure. There are very few stories in the news critical of the initiatives of the present Chicago Board of Education.

This may be connected to the fact that the former education writer from the Sun-Times now works at the Board, and the former education writer from the Tribune is the mayor's press secretary. The former reform activists are working for the Board now. My sense is that there are actually lots more outside people who were involved in the first wave of School Reform who are now employed by the Board. Parents who were active in the first grassroots movement have moved on to other things. I remember calling parents of my kindergarten students in 1987 to show up for a rally. Well, those kindergarten students just graduated from high school last June. So why would their parents still be actively involved in Chicago public school activities?

## First Reflection

Imbedded in Kato's account are important political themes—I count nine of them—that in varying degrees are characteristic not just of Chicago but of urban reform nationally. Taken as a group, these themes go far to explain the current state of affairs in urban educational politics in the United States. They are:

1. calamitous loss of faith in the adequacy of the schools, and the competence of the professionals who work in them, by the voting public;

2. loss of status and bargaining leverage by teacher's unions, resulting in an increased workload for teachers and significant alterations to their duties;

3. an even greater loss, for principals, of control over their professional lives, and a new set of expectations of what it means to be a principal;

4. significant participation by state legislatures, both financially and educationally, in the planning and implementation of local change;

5. direct and prolonged involvement of the corporate community, at the highest levels, in the planning and implementation of change;

6. concurrent attempts to decentralize management at the school level and re-centralize it at the system level, with power often flowing directly from the mayor's office;

7. appointment of a corporate-style manager as CEO of the schools;

8. a time span for reform activity so lengthy that reform effectively becomes the new status quo;

9. a prolonged "honeymoon" period in which media criticism of reform is largely suspended and progress claimed by top reform advocates is accepted uncritically. For the media, calling a city's power structure to account—its mayor and cor-porate and legislative leaders—is a much riskier task than blaming highly vul-nerable teachers and disenfranchised minority communities.

If we reflect on these nine themes in light of Wagner's mini-history, three basic political realities of urban reform become apparent. First, the major energy for change has come from outside the schools rather than inside; second, the structure, governance, staffing, and financing of schools are political in ways that teaching and learning are not; and third, political solutions shaped by social tensions have frequently produced educational policy fraught with internal contradictions.

The third reality, discussed earlier as the more general dilemma of policy generation vs. policy implementation, is visible in Chicago in a striking way. There is ongoing tension between the minority communities who send their children to the public schools and powerful mainstream groups promot-ing top-down change (local- and state-elected officials, educational research-ers, corporate leaders, reporters and editors). There is also a tension created when democratization is mandated at the building level while top-down control is the operating principle at the system level.

The first tension is most easily seen in the struggle of Chicago's large and politically active African American community to become authors of change, rather than just recipients. One researcher locates friction between the African American community and largely white reform advocates in areas such as increasing financial oversight; "a school board selected by businessmen"; local, black superintendent candidate Manfred Byrd's being passed over for an outsider; and the mayor's "replacement of two African American board members with two white women." The community's an-gry response "set in motion a grass-roots electoral campaign that some identify as the impetus for Harold Washington's election as Chicago's first African American mayor."[32] It is possible to view these events as the latest chapters in black Chicago's long series of attempts, beginning in the 1860s, to secure a positive future for its children through quality education.

Washington's untimely death in 1987 opened the way for the election of current mayor Richard M. Daley. This in turn led to the second wave of reform, based in the 1995 state law that gave the mayor and his directly appointed team the authority "to determine which schools require intervention; to dismiss, lay off, or reassign any and all personnel in them; . . . to dissolve elected Local Schools Councils (LSC's) . . . to cut costs, privatize work usually performed by employees, and abrogate any collective bargaining agreements."[33]

These second wave changes signaled the new primacy of corporate management models over both traditional educational models and the 1988 decentralization, and of the mayor and his appointed superintendent over the drastically weakened teachers' and principals' unions.

Second wave reforms altered the context for teaching and learning and reduced the power of LSC's, but did not insure instructional success. In fact, they contained their own contradictions. Implementation questions abounded: how would rapidly changing structural, governance, staffing, and financial contexts affect the dynamics of teaching and learning? Let us listen further to Kato's experiences as a teacher under continuous waves of change.

### Teachers under Reform

It seems pretty clear that the schools were stuck and that the energy for reform came from outside the schools. Many teachers like me had been trying for years to change the system from within, but truly, nothing really happened until the parents and community really got angry about what was going on in the schools. Business people and education researchers had been looking seriously at the Chicago schools for many years before the 1987 strike. Education activists had been talking about restructuring the school system before the strike as well. How can we forget about U.S. Secretary of Education William Bennett's labeling Chicago schools as the "worst in the nation?" If that doesn't create energy for reform, I'm not sure what would.

Now, if we're actually talking about *implementation* of school reform rather than energy for it, that's a different story. The energy for that absolutely comes from the people who work inside the school.

Initially I think teachers were considered the "establishment" rather than change agents. There was a lot of talk about "clearing out the dead wood," because it was thought that many teachers were lazy and greedy. It didn't help that there were so many strikes in which the main focus was on salaries rather than improving educational conditions. During the strike of 1987, I really looked around for teacher groups who supported reform because I saw this as a great opportunity to change the school system, but I didn't find any. Instead, there were a lot of parent groups and community groups meeting.

After the strike, I didn't still feel that teachers had a place at the discussion table of how schools were going to be restructured. The Chicago teachers union certainly didn't have much say, and each new contract has gotten weaker and weaker. Although our salary has had incremental raises, when I went back to look at the school calendars for the last ten years, teachers are working eight full days more this year than in 1990—three of them teaching students.

Frankly, I felt that teachers ended up being the drones—doing all the work, getting none of the credit. When there was so much talk about site-based management, who did they think was going to develop curriculum, sit on committees, and work with parents and LSC's who had no educational background? In fact, by 1994, three quarters of the Chicago principals were new. Who was expected to show them how the school worked? Then, with two waves of early retirements in early 1990s, we lost 2,500 teachers—a tenth of our force. So many of the veterans who would have helped to shoulder a lot of this new work were gone and most of it fell to the ones I call "young veterans." Where there were no veteran teachers, brand new teachers were on principal evaluation committees and writing curriculum—kind of scary.

Under the first wave, you had a lot more freedom, but no support. You'd call down to the Board of Education, there wasn't anybody there. You want staff development, that's great, but you've got to find the agency yourself. For many teachers, the feeling was, "I used to spend ninety percent of my time worrying about instruction, and now I can spend only forty percent of my time because there are so many other things that I need to do." Teachers said, "We're better off, but we're exhausted." Plus, the first wave didn't reach instruction, it just seemed to take your attention and your energies away from instruction.

The second wave is actually affecting what's going on in classrooms. Schools are being put on probation based on their test scores, assigned external partners, and monitored. If there's a very good teacher who wants to do literature-based instruction in one of these schools that's on probation—they can't do it anymore. A lot of the instructional decisions are made as *de facto* consequences of mandates like, you're going to retain third, sixth, and eighth graders if they don't hit certain marks on the Iowa test scores; principal evaluations are going to be lower if your test scores are low. I've talked to teachers who say "We're not buying reading materials anymore, we're buying test-taking materials."

In the second wave, what gets to the public is an impression that things are really moving. When the state legislature gave the mayor the power, they gave him money too. New school buildings are getting built, old ones are being fixed. The schools are looking good. The test scores appear to be going up. Maybe it's because kids are doing the same grade three times, I don't know; but it appears they're going up. So the general impression is, schools are doing better. But it's not like it was under the first wave and the schools were doing better because the parents were involved on the local school council. A lot of councils can't get enough people to run. There's actually less and less parent involvement, truthfully. But the impression is that schools are doing better.

I think it's amazing that of all the educators who were superintendents of our school system, nobody seemed to touch instruction, and now we have a budget director in charge, and everybody is worried about instruction. Now, we have learning outcomes that are being held over our heads, bottom lines. If your test scores aren't high enough, then you can be told what kind of instruction to do, and even if you're a good teacher, if your school is being told that they have to do a certain kind of instruction, you have to buy into it. You used to be pressured into it because it was site-based. Pressure from your peers is really different from your principal saying, "No, I'm not going to buy these other materials. We have to do this test-taking. You have to spend time on that. I'm going to come into your room and check that you're doing that. You've got external partners coming here."

I think there's a lot more pressure on people. It's done in a very punitive way. I think it would be different if you were saying that we're putting more time and money into early childhood reading programs and reading recovery, but to cut that, and have everything be done in summer school programs and retentions, seems very after-the-fact. And I think part of it is, there's no vision for what good instruction is, except some kind of general, kind of simplistic ideas of, you know, these are the basics. It's not like they're reading current theory or visiting classrooms or anything like that.

## Second Reflection

Kato's account suggests the importance, at the implementation level, of two politically charged forces, *contradiction* and *resistance,* which help explain why systemic reform has not so far been more successful. At least three major contradictions impede successful implementation, one related to structure, one to leadership, and one to teaching. These contradictions directly relate to, in fact often create, the kinds of resistance that impede change.

The first contradiction, a structural one, I call *be democratic till we order you to stop.* As part of reform, decentralized structures like school-based management and small learning communities are mandated at the school level, but a centralized command-and-control management style governs the whole system. These two styles are frequently at odds; democratic activity does not flourish in a confined arena that exists only through the *noblesse oblige* of corporate authoritarianism. As governing styles, the two are based in widely differing visions of education. The first, if it is to be successful, requires a high degree of autonomy for teachers and parents, highly developed collaborative management skills on the part of principals, and a long period of relative stability to build trust. The second regards teachers as a means of productivity, seeks to dictate both curriculum and pedagogy, routinely changes course without warning, and treats principals as middle managers strictly accountable for a set of short-term performance goals (usually test scores). Reconciling the frequently contradictory demands of these two styles is a major, unacknowledged task facing current systemic reforms, a task in which leadership must come from top district personnel who make the rules, not from teachers and principals who react to them.

Let us consider initially only the first component of this contradiction, the mandate to decentralize, to adopt some form of school-based planning or school-based management (SBM). Under the best of circumstances, making SBM work is a challenging task. Here is Kato's account of her own experiences with SBM.

At my school, the old principal quit in 1990 because the teachers formed a fairly strong, united front. He didn't quite get that the rules of the game had changed with site-based management. Several teachers encouraged someone they knew and respected to apply for the interim principal position, and she got it. During her time with us, our school underwent a renaissance. We hired new personnel of a like mind—who believed in a student-centered curriculum, used writing process, incorporated a literature-based reading program, used a hands-on approach to science, problem-based math, and integrated the curriculum. We met before and after school and during the summer to write curriculum and develop alternative assessments. We organized staff development programs in writing after school for teachers who needed support.

The new principal believed in and practiced shared decision making, so we met with parents and community members in workshops to articulate a common vision for the school with both long-term and short-term goals. We hammered out school budgets that put our money where our mouths were. There was a lot of difficult conversation but everyone had a place at the table.

But I don't think our school was typical. The initial wave of school reform created tremendous chaos and stress because schools didn't have the old rules and structure to fall back on. Calls down to the central office often went unanswered because there wasn't anybody picking up the phone. Some schools were spending discretionary funds on cheerleader outfits while other schools were building up classroom libraries and buying science equipment for the first time in years. In other words, there was the freedom to do amazing and positive things as well as to spend money and energy foolishly. There were no checks and balances.

### Third Reflection

Research on SBM nationally accords with the Chicago experience described by Kato: results have been decidedly mixed.[34] The National School Boards Association concurs with Elmore that "in many instances, the idea that SBM involves the decentralization of authority and responsibility to schools is no more than 'a convenient fiction.'"[35] The Association particularly singles out communication as a key variable, calling the collection and distribution of useful information, "especially that pertaining to organizational performance and the flow of resources," as "the driving force behind school-based change."[36] When difficult conversations are part of school culture and shared planning and decision making are real, great progress can occur. But skilled leadership, a free flow of information, and a climate of trust are needed to maintain the delicate balance between authority and participation. In the pressured, punitive atmosphere of top-down change, administrators are tempted to treat questions about process as challenges to authority and to silence uncomfortable dialogue about difficult problems, both fatal mistakes.

SBM, difficult to accomplish on its own, is immensely more difficult if individual schools are unsupported, or worse, actively threatened by district-level behavior. The balance between central office and school is as delicate as that between principal's office and teachers. When central office policies are authoritarian or unresponsive—when at the other end of the phone there's either a threatening voice or no voice at all—communication and trust become scarce commodities, the delicate balances are jeopardized, and change loses its driving force.

A second, related contradiction I call *lead collaboratively or you're fired.* It can be seen as the expression of the first contradiction in the dimension of school leadership. In 1980 a corporate task force in Chicago concluded, in the words of one of its members, that decentralization was risky because "we didn't think that the principals had the tools to do the job," that principals needed significant training so that "if they were given the authority, they could have a chance to succeed."[37] But reform went forward, in Chicago and elsewhere, and during the 1990s the urban principal's job description shifted from "maintainer of the status quo" to "manager of change." As the leadership dimension changed, superintendents began seeking a new generation of principals. So far, they haven't found nearly enough of them. Turnover of existing principals is a continuing problem, and few solid training programs are in place to help principals respond to or even understand their new role as managers of change.

New principals are in short supply because, under current conditions, the urban principalship has become a job fewer and fewer people seek. Principals are expected to run their schools democratically and collaboratively while themselves being treated as interchangeable management parts in the command-and-control structure. They must demand more and better work from teachers, but their authority over curriculum and instruction has diminished, accountability has greatly increased, and job security is practically nil. Top administrators see clearly that principals are a key to successful implementation of change, but seem unwilling or unable to recognize the connection between the structural and political contradictions of reform and the growing crisis in the principalship.

The third contradiction I call, *do what you're told and teach those kids to think for themselves.* It is rooted in a schizophrenic vision of the teaching profession, at once demeaning and hopeful. On one level teachers are regarded as disaffected incompetents, with the poor test scores of urban students taken as prima facie evidence of their incompetence. This demeaning attitude is communicated by school systems and the media in a thousand ways, and it is difficult to find an urban teacher who has not felt deeply disrespected. On the other hand, in any proposed reform teachers are acknowledged to be key implementers and their professional development plays an important role. This implies that teachers are important and that continued professional growth is not just possible but a routine part of the profession.

Teachers are asked, on the one hand, to work longer, think harder, master new complex skills, and participate in the democratic governance of the school, and on the other, to submit to micro-management of their classrooms, deliver pre-packaged curriculum at a pre-set pace, and shut up and do what they're told or risk being fired. These inconsistencies raise a multitude of questions, not the least of which is, can teachers who are treated like assembly-line workers and made to feel like drones produce students with the high-level literacy, problem-solving, and reflective skills reformers claim they want? More likely, most teachers will just spend more time teaching to the new tests in the old way, reading scores will go up slightly for a time and then plateau, and little long-term change will occur. On the other hand, in schools or districts where high quality, well-planned professional development takes place over a significant period of time, real change begins to be possible. Here again, careful implementation is a key to success, and addressing contradictions and the resistance they engender is part of careful implementation.

This brings us to the question of resistance. Contradictions in structure, leadership, and attitude towards teachers create school-level resistance, overt or covert, to mandated change. If school-based decision making is perceived to be a sham because the real decisions are being made downtown, teachers respond in kind: pseudo-democracy invites pseudo-participation. If site-based management is really site-based punishment for failing to achieve unrealistic goals under impossible conditions, morale plummets. If questions are treated as threats and silent compliance as the only acceptable response, resistance goes underground and becomes sabotage, an art at which teachers are masters. Evans discusses a "culture of resistance"[38] in reforming schools, and Darling-Hammond has named silencing of resistance as a national problem, "Schools today largely function by submerging talk about those things that are likely to be most controversial—and thus . . . most important . . . Schools have tried to implement bureaucratic rules and procedures by burying the dialogue that would allow real problems to emerge."[39] Without such dialogue, and the school-level modifications it enables, it is difficult to see how reforms can have staying power.

To summarize: the merging of two systems, decentralization at the school level, and corporate hierarchy at the system level, inevitably results in contradictions. As implementation unfolds in schools, these contradictions engender resistance. If contradictions are not acknowledged and freely discussed so adjustments can be made, resistance hardens and may move from questioning to non-compliance to passive sabotage. Bureaucratic quashing of resistance is not a sustainable response because, as presently constituted, schools are inherently collaborative environments with multiple stakeholders: students, teachers, parents, principals, external partners, the district, the larger community. Finally, as Fullan reminds us, in recent years our knowledge of what makes "collaborative cultures really work, and what it takes to sustain them" has grown greatly, and one of the big things we know is that "breakthroughs occur when we begin to think of conflict, diversity and resistance as positive, absolutely essential forces for success."[40] So a legitimate question to pose to the new wave of corporate-style school leaders is, to what extent do your policies and mandates expect and plan for school- and community-level conflict, diversity, and resistance and treat them as essential forces for success?

In Chicago, as in other urban areas, the answer to this question has too often been to repress diversity in favor of superficial uniformity, to treat resistance as insubordination. Consider these three brief anecdotes from Kato, emblematic of the post-1995 era. One involves a principal, one a student, and one a teacher.

### Three Anecdotes

After 1995, when the state law was amended and the mayor was given full control over the Chicago school system, there was a big change. In many ways, it seems that we have gone back to the old centralized, bureaucratic, top-down system we had before 1988.

The first story is from a principal whose school was on probation and had to work with an external partner. When I spoke to him about becoming involved with the Chicago Area Writing Project so that we would provide support from a literacy coordinator who knew both reading and writing instruction, he said, "I know what good instruction looks like. We just can't do it until we get off of probation." So instead of reading books and writing stories, the students had to complete test prep exercises everyday. This was a pretty good principal and he knew better, but his hands were tied.

This second one is about a student, told to me by her teacher. When Superintendent Vallas began in the 1995–96 school year he instituted a "no social promotion" policy for eighth-grade students. If they didn't meet the cutoff score on the Iowa test, they would be retained. By the next school year, he expanded this policy to include the third- and eighth-grade students as well. Initially, he didn't make any contingency plans for kids who failed it a second and then a third time, although teachers could see the flaw in this horrific policy. Anyway, by 1999, the teacher told me that an eighth-grade student had pleaded with her to "make her special ed." The reason she said this was because only special education students and some bilingual students were exempt from the policy. She said if she weren't classified as special ed, she'd never get out of eighth grade.

The last story is about a teacher I interviewed for my dissertation. She also teaches in a school that has an external partner, and this partner checks on whether she is using the prescribed SRA reading kits every day. This teacher is a white suburban woman who really wanted to teach in the city with a diverse student and teaching population. She continually takes classes and workshops to improve her practice, but after nine years she's worried that she might have to leave the CPS. Here's a direct quote:

> I'm ashamed to say. . . . That I may not be able to teach in the city. I'm going to get emotional actually which is not good. That I may not be able to teach in the city for the rest of my career, you know? I can't work in a system that I don't think values teachers and I don't think values kids—forget teachers. That I don't think values kids.

This one bothers me the most because I hate to see good teachers leave the system. She was almost crying. She's done everything she was asked to do—be an activist, take classes, head committees, even argue with her principal—but what bothers her most is that she said she thinks she's being forced to teach poorly. She said she would be embarrassed to have me observe her classroom because of all the test preparation and SRA stuff she has to do.

Before school reform, good teachers had no support. I can deal with that. I'll buy my own books, supplies, and pay for my own courses. During the first wave of school reform, good teachers were overworked. I can deal with that as long as we have a say in the curriculum, books, schedule, budget, and personnel at our school. But during this second wave of school reform, good teachers are actually restricted in HOW and what they teach. The Board has prepared mini-standards for each subject in each grade, and teachers must cite each mini-standard for each lesson they write on the Board-prepared lesson plan books. This takes hours for some teachers. At some schools they must write each of these mini-standards on the board each day. In the meantime, the Board is preparing what is called "structured curriculum" in which each day's lesson for each grade for each subject is being written down. What is this nonsense? If someone needs verbatim instructions to teach, it's my suggestion they find another career!

## THE ROLE OF EXTERNAL PARTNERS

The notion that failing schools can be significantly improved by mandating rote teaching of inflexible, externally developed lessons is a fallacy, of course. But the frequent use of this strategy in Chicago and elsewhere attests to both the desperation and the lack of imagination of district leaders who just can't seem to figure out what else to do, and know that a "get tough," back-to-basics stance will at least enhance their standing in the press and with the public.

Increasingly, districts are contracting with "external partners" as part of their strategy for tackling such schools. Nationally, outside groups play a variety of roles, often in the implementation of exemplary programs under the sponsorship of two initiatives mentioned previously, the private Annenberg Challenge and the federal Comprehensive School Reform Demonstration Act (CSRD). Two of Kato's stories cited above mention external partners, which in Chicago are universities or outside agencies who are paid to provide support to the least successful schools.

Though school-college collaboration is an established field, the use of a broad range of external partners to help troubled schools on a contract basis is relatively recent. In addition to colleges and universities, partners include national and locally based exemplary program providers, non-profit and for-profit agencies, and community groups. Because they are becoming so common, understanding more about them and how they are viewed is important to developing a full picture of urban reform. I will here give three brief viewpoints, and in the next section we will take an extended look at such a partnership through the eyes of its director, Sharon Ransom.

Shipps, citing Wong et al.,[41] Cohen,[42] and Dantowitz[43] as well as her own research, warns that in Chicago "the expansion of privatization and outsourcing . . . since 1995 . . . raises concerns about accountability." A wide range of services are outsourced under the new management model, including "academic remediation . . . and training for new and continuing principals, . . ." She finds that though "individual schools have a great deal of accountability, . . . corporate entrepreneurs and private educational service providers are rapidly increasing the numbers of unaccountable private groups in control of school decisions" and concludes that, "Arguably, a great number of public decisions have been privatized, rather than democratized, in the current Chicago reform strategy."[44]

A second view, fanciful but pointed, was related to me by a woman I will call Paula Mast, a systemwide, K-12 professional development coordinator working out of Chicago's reconstituted central office. Paula's job is to contract with outside groups to provide services to schools. When I asked her to give me some insight into her role she said with a laugh:

Let me tell you a little fable about how things go here. A university tells us that they have a program that will teach any child to read, but it's expensive. So we pay them a lot of money and they tell us, just take these magic chairs and have the teachers put them in a circle every day and then have the children read. So we pick a group of schools where the students are reading way below grade level and we give all the teachers magic chairs and have them use them for a year. And at the end of the year, we test the kids and find out that they haven't made much improvement. So we go back to the university and say, these magic chairs you sold us don't work. We had the teachers put them in a circle every day for a year and the kids didn't learn to read any better than before. And they look us right in the eye and say, "Excuse us, but there's nothing wrong with our chairs. The stupid teachers arranged them in the wrong order!"

A third view, from Barbara Kato, notices that highly specific, top-down curricular mandates and one-size-fits-all external programs share a common philosophy: learning problems can be solved by making all schools the same. She argues that the opposite is true:

One of the problems I see, especially in Chicago, is that there's no understanding that learning is constructed. Instead, there's this really simplistic idea that if you put out these mandates, all schools are going to look exactly the same, they're going to function exactly the same. Or that a school, once you've done "school change," somehow is supposed to stay in a certain way. I guess that's what sells, the idea that "let's just get one model and every school's going to follow it" and then somehow, everything's going to work out fine. There's no idea that you can't replicate a school. Schools are really organic kinds of entities, nothing stays the same. You can change a principal, change a couple of teachers, and the programs don't work the same way they did.

Mandates aren't going to manifest themselves the same way in every school. At some schools, the local school council's working fine; at some schools, it's not. Some local school councils are dealing with parents who can't read, and you're acting like they should all be the same. In some of the places, especially with the standards that are set up, I think they're playing school. They don't know enough about instruction, or they don't want to accept it, and so they're giving third-grade kids who read at the first-grade level third-grade material, as though somehow, you know, it's actually going to work. And they want to be hard-nosed about it, and say, "You have to get up to these standards," but they don't understand what you need to do to get kids to those standards, and there's a feeling now that if we put more time into it, whether it's after-school programs or summer school, that somehow qualitatively, instruction has gotten better. And there's nobody that's judging that instruction is getting better. So instruction isn't getting any better. And we've got a lot of new teachers coming in, and there's not really good support. And I think that it's really simplistic, this cookie-cutter idea. Schools are not cookie-cutters. They're very, very different from each other.

These three viewpoints caution us that the dynamics of outside interventions are tricky and that bringing in an outside group or program to aid a failing school is no guarantee of success. On the other hand, interventions can bring new ideas and new resources, and well-designed, reflective professional development is always welcome. The participation of outside agencies, whether in the form of consulting, workshops, coaching, pre-packaged programs, or other means appears to have become a permanent feature of urban reform, and so we need to understand more about the way external partnerships function and what factors promote their success.

What if an external partner were to start with the philosophy that "schools are very, very different from each other" and build an intervention program from there? In the next section, we will get an inside view of such an approach.

## SHARON RANSOM: THE PERSPECTIVES
## OF AN INSIDER-OUTSIDER

Sharon Ransom's experiences in education provide her with multiple perspectives on Chicago's school reform. She began her career in Chicago in 1972 as a teacher of high school English and later of elementary Language Arts and Reading. For eight years she left the public schools to direct a program focusing on literacy training for adults in Chicago's steel mills. She returned to the schools as a writing specialist with $6^{th}$, $7^{th}$, and $8^{th}$ grade students. Earning a second master's degree, in urban education, gave her a chance to "think about classroom and school environments . . . what was happening and what was not happening . . . what was causing children and adults to have unpleasant experiences in schools." She became a curriculum director and then was responsible for coordinating professional development in reading and writing for "a small region of 20 Chicago schools." This led her to take an active role on the Illinois Language Arts Advisory Committee, the group that develops the state assessment. For two-and-a-half years, she also served on the sister committee developing the state language arts standards. In 1995 when the city put out a call for universities to become "external partners" to failing schools, she moved to Northeastern Illinois University to direct one such project. At the time of this interview, Sharon's project had an annual budget of over $2.5 million to work with eleven high schools and seven elementary schools in Chicago as well as one high school and four elementary schools in suburbs outside Chicago. Her team included forty-three full- and part-time coaches and consultants in curriculum areas such as math, literacy, and organizational development. She exemplifies a new type of role that has been created by urban school reform: the professional insider/outsider, experienced with classroom contexts as well as larger organizational structures, policy mandates as well as their implementation.

I was especially interested in Sharon's views because her program individualizes an intervention for each school rather than bringing in a pre-packaged answer or off-the-shelf solution and then lightly tailoring it to the local site. The latter model, which seeks to "go to scale" with "exemplary models," has not been conspicuously successful and is vulnerable to claims that "ambitious, large-scale school reform efforts, under current conditions, will be ineffective and transient."[45]

I began my conversation with Sharon by asking in what ways she viewed her program as exemplary, how she and her team went about intervening in a school that had been labeled "failing," and what they experienced once they began working there:

The approach that we take to school reform is a little bit different. We are the external partner for twenty-four schools, and for fourteen of those we are the CSRD partner. We think we are exemplary because we individualize what needs to be done in each school, so in a way, it's contradictory. When we enter a school, that's one of the first questions we ask: what's going on here? What are the programs? And it sounds strange, but we don't at any time tell them not to do what they're doing, but help them to coordinate and evaluate the productiveness of what they're doing. We work on the premise that each school is unique. They have different needs, each culture is different, the availability of time is different, so each school has a plan that is designed individually for them.

Our first goal is to build a relationship with the school and the teachers and we believe that they and the school hold a quite a few of the answers. My job is to facilitate them in discovering what they need to do and providing them support. Sometimes it might be support in resources, or support in mentoring or facilitating. We might provide professional development to the school's leadership or to the teachers.

We work in a school, minimum, two days a week, maximum, five days a week. We work in teams. There are always at least two people working in the same school, and the idea is that there is one person who is responsible for helping to facilitate the process throughout the school, the coordinator and troubleshooter. A coordinator could, in one school, also be a reading coach or writing coach, at another school, something else. We change roles, but there's one person who is designated to be the lead person.

All of these schools have been designated as low-performing schools in crisis because of their scores in reading and mathematics. But those are not necessarily their real problems, just some of the outcomes of the problems. In understanding that, we are quite often looking at a dual layer, because the schools, of course, are just overwhelmed by being told that it's reading and math, and they want some direct attention to that. But low scores often come from other problem areas in the school, things like organization of time, organization of resources, or relationships between administration and faculty members, or among staff members. We try to use a triage-like approach while we're making a diagnosis on the root of the problem.

The intervention model used by Ransom's programs recognizes that human relationships issues are often closely tied to root problems of school failure, and so the "diagnosis" pays close attention to human dimension of organization and instruction. I asked her, "What's on your mental checklist the first time you visit a new school? What are you looking for?"

The rapport between students and teachers, the rapport between administration and teachers, the rapport between administration and students . . . just the general organization and the relationships in the building. We have a protocol for entering a building. After we meet with the principal and leadership team, we meet with the full staff, and we do mini focus groups. About nine of our team members will go in and talk simultaneously with all the members in the school, and we ask them the question, what's needed to raise student achievement here at this school? The answer's here, and we're here to facilitate the process. We do that because we want to model for them that we're working in a team, because that's how we want them to work, and also that we're working with them in a very open environment, that everyone gets all the information. We bring the groups together, we debrief on what was shared, and then every teacher in the school gets a written report. And from that, we begin to do planning with our teams of teachers, administration, the leadership team, on developing a professional development plan for the school. We think that that goes a long way in our process because the first time that they interact with us, they interact with us one-on-one. And that's how we want to interact with them. That is, we are at that time attempting to build a relationship and model for them how we'd like the relationship to continue.

I next asked, "What kinds of conditions are you likely to find when you first enter a school?"

A lot of people are sleepwalking through their day. The behaviors are so rote, the school culture is so profound, that people have lost all sight of why they are doing things, how they are doing things, they're just doing them. There's a feeling of hopelessness and helplessness, and they're just moving, just doing, and that's it. In those buildings, people have not been attending to each other as human beings, they haven't been attending to the students as learners, each other as learners, as colleagues; there needs to be some attention paid to that to provide an environment in which learning can take place.

Often these schools are places for teachers and administrators to "hide out," because they won't get the demands from the community, they won't get the reprimands from Central Office. A big school serving a low-income, minority population can hide a large, a critical mass of people. If you understand about a culture of any organization, as soon as you get a large number, that becomes the characteristic of that particular organization.

In that kind of organizational culture, low expectations from teachers contribute a great deal to the lower performance of minority and second-language students. There's still a paternalistic presence: "These kids come from such poor backgrounds, we can't give them any more stresses, we can't do this, we can't do that . . ." and that's wrong. Or "these kids just don't have it, you know, their parents aren't worth much, so, there's only a certain level of expectations, or experiences that these children need to have." There is a belief that "we're doing all we can; the problem is the students."

That kind of attitude isn't always based on race or language, it can also be based on class. In some of the predominantly African American elementary schools, there can be up to 70 percent minority teachers. And that's why I said we get an issue of class. High school's a little different; there are fewer minority teachers. But in four of the high schools, 60 percent of the students are second-language learners. Two of the high schools have three or more languages. One has Polish, Spanish, and I think Urdu. And then another has ten different languages in the school. These schools are in a part of the city where new immigrants are constantly arriving. In Chicago, they're in the bilingual program for three years. It often seems that as soon as they've been here about three years they hit high school, so this is the first time they're really out of a bilingual program. Sometimes the elementary school finds a way to keep them in a bilingual program until they reach high school. So the challenges for those students are great because now they're in ESL *and* in high school, and it's too much all at once so it's devastating for them.

When I asked Ransom to be specific about ways her program helps schools to address these negative conditions, here's what she told me:

According to the teachers I'm working with, the thing that benefits them most about this reform process is the opportunity to learn new knowledge. One of the things that has struck me for the last three years is the lack of conceptual understanding about teaching and learning. In some schools we've been partnering with for three years, reform has allowed us to spend a large amount of time helping teachers understand instruction, especially in reading and writing.

This process has also helped us to identify talent within the schools. There's a lot of criticism about outsiders coming in, but we all know that quite often we "can't hear a prophet in our own land." In a number of schools, we've been able to identify and support people who had never taken a leadership role under the safety of co-facilitating with us and we hope when we move out of the school, we will have really helped to develop some leadership in the schools. We also have an adminis- trators' network. Our principals get together on a monthly basis and what we've seen is that this idea that it's okay to be on a learning curve yourself, when you're an administrator of a building, is quite fine. Our network gives principals some support and understanding and instruction in why things are going on in their buildings, and shares with them how to collaborate.

On a larger level, I think that as educators, this whole reform has helped us to look at the fact that we need to monitor our own profession. It is not all right if you're in a school and you know that the children in the class across the hall are not getting what they should receive—it affects us all. We have to, within our own buildings, do what it takes to make those changes. And I think those are the posi- tive things. That is not looking away from all the heart-wrenching stories we have about children who are emotionally distraught because they were held back, or teachers who were unjustly moved because the district had to re-engineer a build- ing or reconstitute a building. Because of the site-based management, in those com- munities where parents and community members did not have the knowledge and savvy to make the decisions, schools have suffered. They did not know how to choose a principal; they did not know how to make recommendations on how to use monies.

We are now at a point where a lot of that independence is being taken away from schools because of the greater number of mandates, and I do straddle the fence on this, because I have seen some schools that did not do well in that process, and they really do need some help, they need some guidelines, though there have been some schools that have really profited from that. Where does it balance out—you don't know. Those policies do have negative repercussions, but we also have to look at the fact, and we have to be honest about the fact, that there are some things that we have not been doing for years, and that reform has been an opportunity to begin to do them.

For me, personally it has been great to be able to work systematically in schools. This is the first time that the principals, the teachers, felt that this is important. It has helped us also to grow as professional developers, because you have to sup- port those teachers who told you, "Don't come into my classroom again," just like the teachers who welcome you with open arms, so we've grown, too. And I really have an understanding about how learning happens in those environments. It's been beneficial, I think, for both communities, the higher education community as well as the schools.

## CONCLUSIONS

### The Politics of "Two Reforms"

In the introduction to the second half of this book I described the "two reforms" phenomenon, the gap between the reform vision outlined in the superintendent's press conference and the frantic but halting pace of school- level change. I argued that achieving an understanding of the implementation-level realities of reform is essential to improvement, and that school-based practitioners—teachers, principals, coaches, insider/outsiders—are in the best position to provide this information, but to date their testimony has been neither actively sought nor highly valued.

Muncey and McQuillan cite political considerations among the main causes of the failure of reforms, because schools are ill-equipped to handle the politics of change.[46] In this chapter I have used testimony from practitioners to analyze political dimensions of the "two-reforms" phenomenon, placing particular emphasis on the equity implications of reform and on structural dilemmas that create school-level resistance.

It's much easier to reform the top half of large systems—curriculum, administrative structure, downtown personnel, goal statements—than the bottom half—the messy, human business of teaching and learning.[47] Because of this, much reform has concentrated on the top half, which is increasingly influenced by the leadership styles of corporate America. But so far school systems seem to be ignoring one of the hardest won lessons of the corporate makeovers of the 1980s and 1990s: in times of uncertainty and change, leaders must overcommunicate. The change message and its ramifications must be repeatedly and clearly communicated, not simply mandated, and employees (teachers and principals) must have multiple opportunities to discuss and adapt it at every level if change is to take hold.

To date, urban central offices have been very good at communicating reform goals to the media and the public. They have been less effective at communicating downward to teachers and principals. They have been even worse at seeking input from teachers and principals and supporting appropriate site-level modifications. The need for top-down control, or the appearance of control, has trumped the need for buy-in and collaboration from those charged with day-to-day implementation of the goals. One of the results has been what Golden calls "Potemkin schools" and Kato calls "playing school."

Reformers commonly invoke the business metaphor of "scaling up" to describe efforts to spread what they consider to be best practices and model programs. This convenient bit of jargon ignores the fact that many industrial and corporate workplaces today offer workers more input than do school systems. Auto workers participating in "quality teams" at the innovative Saturn plant in Tennessee or software engineering groups at high tech firms arguably exercise more control over their own productivity than do teachers. Instead, in the name of reform, education has often settled for a kind of participatory authoritarianism, creating highly visible structures of power sharing with little democratic substance.[48]

To achieve change, school systems need to provide a clear message that stays constant over at least three years. Schools need opportunities, and the necessary freedom, to understand and adapt this message to their individual circumstances, because "schools are not cookie cutters." Teachers must feel safe in exploring ways in which these goals relate to their particular situations. They need a stable and adequately resourced environment in which to begin changing, as well as occasions to reflect, adapt, and improve, and a fair and consistent monitoring of outcomes.

Instead, from the practitioners' point of view, the prevailing implementation mode is the mandating of multiple, mixed messages that change regularly, a chaotic, underresourced environment in which to implement them, and inconsistent accountability systems riddled with political and interpersonal loopholes.

This was brought home to me forcefully not long ago at a meeting in an East Coast city where I was serving as a consultant. The deputy superintendent had just completed an impressive Powerpoint presentation on the "thirteen highest priorities" for the system's high schools for the coming year. The priorities were admirable; they formed a best-practice "to do" list that any progressive educator could be proud of—high schools should be broken into small learning communities, teachers should regularly look at student work in groups, and so on.

The person next to me said quietly, "If there are thirteen of them, they can't all be priorities." Based on the school system's past history, both of us knew two things. Not only were there too many items on the list, but there was a good chance that a similar meeting a year from now would introduce a new list of priorities, even though no rational person could think that the items on this year's list could be accomplished in one year's time. To me it seemed probable that only the young or the foolish would take them at face value. Whether this attitude would constitute resistance to change or common sense was not for me to decide.

Overall, the situation was a veritable quagmire of "good intentions/bad design." There were too many priorities, and too many teachers and principals knew that they could go, in a very short time, from being priorities to being forgotten. There was no timetable for implementing them sequentially over a three-to-five-year period, no list of resources to be allocated to schools to support the changes, no evidence that district-level personnel had more than a superficial familiarity with the techniques being mandated or any sense of what it took to introduce them successfully. Yet the deputy superintendent was proceeding as if it were a foregone conclusion that high schools were going to implement all these changes at once, starting immediately, because it had been so declared.

I mention this incident because it is an "implementation dilemma," an incident that lets us see clearly the gap or mismatch that characterizes the "two reforms" phenomenon. When we acknowledge the existence of implementation dilemmas and ask what we can learn from them, they begin to cease being obstacles to reform and become sources of knowledge that can help us achieve it more quickly.

## The Politics of Implementation

Imagine a Goodyear blimp looking down on our cities, equipped with a camera able to capture not just visible realities, but also invisible ones like power, hierarchical structure, and human relationships. Now imagine that camera taking a wide-angle shot of the civic environment as a whole, then zooming to a mid-range shot of just the school system, then to a close-up of an individual school. In discussing the politics of implementation, these are the views I will take, using Chicago as a specific example but drawing generalizations that are nationally applicable.

### Wide-Angle/Conclusions about Political Relationships between Urban School Systems and the Wider Civic Community

*Urban school reform often presents itself as a strictly management-and-performance oriented, equity-neutral civic endeavor. This presentation is not accurate. Rather, equity tensions form a continuous subtext to systemic reforms, one that we ignore at our peril.*

In schools, the decades preceding current reforms were characterized by equity-based reforms focused on race, language-minority status, disability, and gender. Current reforms present themselves quite differently, emphasizing governance, school organization, curriculum, and testing. But systemic reforms have major consequences for equity.

Education is woven into the economic and political fabric of the wider community, and in politics it is always instructive to "follow the money." In 2000-2001 the Chicago Public Schools had an estimated budget of $3.5 billion dollars—a lot of money by anybody's standards. Approximately 90 percent of the system's students, and presumably their parents, were African American or Latino, as were 65 percent of its principals and 53 percent of its teachers.[49] Local School Councils consisted of six parent representatives: two community representatives, two teachers, the principal, and one student representative per high school. In mandating school-based LSC's, the "first wave" reforms of 1988 transferred decision making power over an enormous budget to a school-based political structure that favored Chicago's minority community. In the second wave (1995), the white, mainstream power structure regained decision making authority over the budget in an attempt "to reorganize the school system on the model of a corporation in the hopes that restructuring would then follow patterns more familiar to business."[50]

Whether these patterns will be more successful than previous models is not yet known, but the transfer of power the new structure represents highlights a general issue for urban school reform: how can the minority communities whose children comprise the vast majority of urban public school students gain significant, long-term input into their children's education? This question leads us to a second conclusion.

*Improvements in the social and economic conditions of minority communities will help improve schooling.* Two traditional roles for urban public schools have been assimilating newcomers into mainstream culture and providing them with academic bootstraps for economic advance. For some immigrants, notably European Catholics, the price asked for these advantages was too high to tolerate. Facing threats to faith and loss of ethnic identity, Catholics created their own alternative to public schools, the ethnically identified parish school. In time, their progress on the economic and political fronts helped change the relationship between Catholics and public schools. Their success suggests that we need to add a second pattern to our thinking about the relationship between non-mainstream communities and public schools. The traditional pattern still holds: public schools have been and will continue to be important avenues for social progress into the mainstream, as long as they are not forced to abandon equity goals in the name of standards-driven reform. But equally important are advances that raise the economic and social status of non-mainstream groups, advances that can't wait till we have "fixed" the public schools.

Economic and social gains don't just help group members, they also broaden the mainstream, making it more inclusive. And when economic and social status rise, performance in schools can be expected to rise as well. Some current research suggests that when government programs help parents obtain adequately paying jobs, test scores and school grades improve, as well as, in some cases, children's school behavior and overall health. Researchers observed these results with preschool-age and elementary-school-age children over a broad range of programs nationally. Merely providing or increasing work, without increasing income, did not lead to school gains.[51] One report called this research "the first concrete data to suggest that spending tax dollars to increase family income translates into school improvement."[52] Considering the amount of tax dollars being spent on school reform, these findings suggest a second way of attacking the problem of poorly performing urban schools—improving the condition of the families whose children attend them.

The relationship between economic opportunity and school performance can be clearly seen over the long term and with European immigrant groups, as in Perlmann's study of Providence, Rhode Island from 1880 to 1935.[53] Achieving similar progress today may be more difficult, because there are qualitative differences between the reception, however negative, accorded to European immigrant groups and the legal and attitudinal barriers faced by African Americans and today's non-white immigrants. The communities whose children form the vast majority of urban school students are the most vulnerable economically and, judging by voter turnout, least involved politically of all urban residents. If we are serious about school reform, it is vital to recognize that progress on social equity in all its forms—jobs, housing, health care, the criminal justice system—helps improve schooling. If the minimum wage rises, enabling an immigrant parent to work fifty hours a week rather than fifty-five, that frees up time to be spent with school-age children. If a work-based literacy program helps an African American parent gain a G.E.D., there will be positive consequences for the education of that parent's child. If a community-based well-baby clinic helps a mother deliver a healthy baby, that baby may not enter kindergarten as a special needs student. It's not just a question of schools helping communities rise, but of community health resulting in better schools.

Our thinking about school reform should explicitly embrace this two-way model, seeking improvement of the community through better schools and improvement of schools through a stronger community. From this perspective, it is legitimate to ask of civic and business leaders who are pushing for higher standards and tougher tests, "where do you stand on increasing the minimum wage? Where do you stand on public/private partnerships for workplace literacy programs? Where do you stand on community health programs?" Improvements in employment, health, and family literacy are also reforms that will help raise test scores.

Instead, systemic reform has often ignored such barriers to school improvement, focusing narrowly on test scores. If we are serious about urban reform, we have to ask if change plans have allocated time and resources to classroom management and motivation issues arising from conditions of poverty, to the needs of second-language learners, to the impact of high mobility and poor attendance. In many places, practitioners feel that the school system acts like these issues don't exist, sending the message that teachers and principals should ignore such obstacles and carry on as if they don't matter, when of course they do. The implication is that if you're a good teacher you'll implement new curricula and pedagogies and prepare students for new, high-stakes tests, regardless of the conditions you teach in or the support you receive, and if your students don't succeed, you're just not a good enough teacher.

### Mid-Range/The Conclusions about the Structure of Systemic Reform at the District Level

1. *The current systemic reform model is beset by structural contradictions that create resistance to successful implementation.*

In most cases, reform's authors have relied on mandates and have not acknowledged these contradictions, nor have they sought ways to turn inevitable resistance into positive energy for change. I have named three contradictions which I believe are national in scope, and which are illustrated with particular clarity in the two waves of Chicago reform: "be democratic till we order you to stop," "lead collaboratively or you're fired," and "do what you're told and teach those kids to think for themselves."

Other contradictions of this type are unique to particular local reforms, but the principle is the same. Identifying and addressing such contradictions and creating techniques for making the resistance they engender a positive force for change should be part of the role played by district level and superintendent's office staff. This raises the issue of equal accountability.

2. *There is a need for accountability throughout the hierarchy of systemic reform, not just at the school level.* One of the hallmarks of systemic reform has been the call for accountability. This is fine as long as it applies in some way to all levels of the system. District and central office administrators need to be accountable to schools as much as schools are to them. Outside partners need to be accountable to someone, either at the school level or the district level. In too many city school systems, accountability pressure goes in only one direction, from the top down. At the bottom of the structure, principals, teachers, and students are pushed out of shape by the pressure. Many good teachers will recognize part of themselves in the demoralized teacher who said, " I can't work in a system that I don't think values teachers and . . . kids—forget teachers. That I don't think values kids."

Meanwhile, those who are calling for school-level accountability may be getting a free ride—no one is saying what they should be accountable for or how it should be measured. But if those in the middle and upper levels are insulated by power or political position, accountability becomes an exercise in authoritarian exploitation of the weaker elements in the system by the stronger. This is unlikely to lead to lasting change.

### Close-up/Conclusions about Reform at the Building Level

*Districts need to work closely with principals, researchers and professional development providers to understand the new demands reform places on principals and to construct support programs that will give principals the skills to meet these demands.*

In 1990, a group of prominent researchers in school leadership concluded:

The demands for leadership mount, yet there is limited guidance from theory, research, or training about what constitutes good leadership, how it might be cultivated, and what we might expect of it in the future. To move forward, we need . . . research that is rooted in problems of practice. We need to augment faith in the scientific method with faith in the wisdom of practice. We need to expand concern with leaders to include an equal interest in those whom they try to lead.[54]

In 2000, the Annenberg Institute for School Reform at Brown University, tapped into the wisdom of practice by bringing together "a group of visionary school and district leaders from across the nation" to discuss leadership challenges, including these questions:

How do traditional school and district organizations need to be changed to remove any roadblocks to improved student achievement?

Where will sufficient numbers of strong, effective leaders for our nation's schools and districts come from?

What kinds of preparation do educators need in order to assume these leadership roles?[55]

For urban school systems these are urgent questions, particularly with respect to principals. Systemic reform has made principals the front-line managers of change, demanding that they raise test scores in response to high-stakes testing and threatening their jobs if they fail. At the same time, aware of "best practice" literature on school change, systems demand that principals implement participatory decision making, work with an expanded range of outside partners, create effective staff development programs, and reach out to communities which, in many cases, have been alienated for decades from their schools. It is little wonder that the number of applicants for the principalship is down, that good principals once found are hard to keep, or that effective training is in short supply.

In Washington State, a statewide, K-12 look at the effects on principals of a 1993 "performance-based" reform law found that 91 percent were involved in decentralized decision making and 79 percent in creating school/business partnerships. Principals were working more hours, spending more time on management and less on leadership, and experiencing increased frustration. New, reform-related responsibilities were being "layered" on top of each other, while there was no relief from traditional duties like building maintenance, staff supervision, and discipline. Principals felt that mandated decentralization came "without clear guidelines about which responsibilities rest with the principal and which remain with the district," and that their roles were becoming increasingly ambiguous and complex because of the paradox of "decentralization of responsibility, coexisting with centralization of authority." Although they welcomed reform-based changes, principals felt more frustrated, less secure, and less enthusiastic about their jobs. The researchers concluded that many principals in Washington were "reaching the limit of the number of hours they can, or are willing to devote to the job."[56]

Washington's reform initiative is fairly typical of those found around the country, as are its effects on principals. However, particularly in urban centers, school districts as well as individual schools have significant particularities, and one-size-fits-all training approaches will work no better for principals than they do for teachers. Obviously, training programs need to know and advocate practices that have been proven to work, but the questions are, proven to work where? and under what conditions?, must always be asked.

As a complement to nationally recognized best practices, home-grown solutions must be identified and supported. This involves recognizing that knowledge can be developed within the school system, not just outside it, which involves honoring some aspects of local practice. This prospect is anathema in some circles, because it challenges a basic premise of many people's thinking, that the local system is bankrupt and the local practitioner totally incompetent.

But in any city, local principals have a good part of the knowledge necessary for understanding the changing role of the principalship, and this knowledge must be tapped and shared. To do this, educational leadership programs are increasingly employing "case story" approaches.

In the belief that "the story form is a sense-making tool for educators," Ackerman et al. ask administrators to write and share "brief stories of their own experiences" according to a formal, four-step method that they describe as a blend of "aspects of the conventional case study method with the traditions, artistry, and imagination of storytelling."[57] Faculty at UCLA have reported success with a similar approach.[58] These uses of practitioner inquiry methods with administrators are hopeful signs, as are techniques like the administrators' network mentioned by Sharon Ransom, which validates the idea that principals can be on a learning curve too.

Using such techniques to explore the new world of the principalship, and blending that knowledge with current "best practice" thinking, districts can develop local approaches to training and supporting principals. The kinds of collaborations now common between universities, individual schools, and community groups suggest a structure in which such a venture can be undertaken, for the task is complex and it is doubtful whether either the school system, the university, or community groups can succeed by tackling it alone.

*Districts need to recognize and resolve contradictions, at the building level, that undermine effective staff development for teachers.* Creating staff development programs that actually change what teachers do in the classroom is one of the central problems facing reform. Unfortunately, research suggests that much of the training traditionally provided by school systems has not been very effective.[59]

Batton and Vereline's study[60] of two underperforming New York City schools reminds us that a great deal of time, money, and effort can be sunk into professional development with negligible results. In contrast are Elmore's studies of the same city's Community District Two and Meier's account[61] of the development of New York's Central Park East. These suggest that a well-designed, thoughtfully executed, long-term approach to staff development at either the district or school level can make a tremendous difference to the quality of teaching and learning in urban settings. In their comments both Kato and Ransom emphasize the need for, and the value teachers place on, opportunities to learn new knowledge that will help them better understand instruction and deepen their conceptual grasp of teaching and learning.

How can professional development foster deeper learning? For Simon Hole and Grace McEntee, two teachers with long experience in reform, reflection is at the heart of successful teaching practice, "(t)he life force of teaching is thinking and wondering. . . . During these times of reflection, we realize when something needs to change."[62] If promoting reflective practice is a key to improving teaching, what effect has systemic reform had on reflection?

In most urban reforms, changes are mandated, not discovered, and reflective practice is increasingly devalued, its place taken by teaching to the test and close adherence to a prescribed curriculum. Thus actions at the system level contradict what is needed for success at the building level. Some systems have begun to recognize this contradiction and are trying to change course despite mounting pressure from state-mandated high-stakes tests. In Boston, the system's own study concluded that "(t)he district's ability to dramatically improve student performance in reading and math depends on whether it can redefine the nature and quality of its professional development, moving away from teaching "to improve scores" and toward teaching "to improve student learning."[63]

If Boston can confront this issue, other systems can too. Arguing for reflective staff development is not arguing against reform; it is arguing for the deep level of change that is the only hope of bringing needed improvements to urban classrooms.

District-level support for programs that include reflection and theory as well as best-practice strategies is critical. Only with district direction can teachers understand the links between the systemwide change plan and the professional development they are receiving. In many places, no such links exist because the reform message degrades as it goes down the levels from central office to classroom. The further down the school hierarchy the message travels, the less sense it makes to those who are hearing it. Goals that seem clear and shiny in public pronouncements become fuzzy and dim by the time they reach teachers.

The fuzziness comes chiefly from the difference between ends and means. To implement classroom level change, teachers must concern themselves with both what to do (goals) and how to do it (means for implementation). The latter must be accomplished in the situation they're in, with the students they have in front of them. From the teacher's viewpoint, reform communication can seem one-way (from the top down), and heavily tilted towards goals (assessment rubrics, testing benchmarks) and away from implementation (strategies for putting the goals into practice in ways that will work in *my* teaching situation, with *my* students). From this perspective, the message about change that gets received at the school level is frequently much different than the one central office thinks it is sending. This causes problems because no matter how many standards are developed and how many exemplary programs are initiated, unless something changes in what goes on between teacher and student when the classroom door is closed, little has really been accomplished.

## NOTES

1. Wayne Urban and Jennings Wagoner, *American Education: A History,* 2nd ed. (Boston: McGraw Hill, 2000): 42.

2. *The American Heritage Dictionary of the English Language,* 4th ed., s. v. "politics."

3. Chicago Public School Website, "CPS at a Glance," 2000, <*http:// www.cps.k12.il.us/* > (27 August 2000).

4. Dorothy Shipps. "The Invisible Hand: Big Business and Chicago School Reform," *Teachers College Record* 99, no. 1 (1997): 105.

5. For a detailed, regularly updated chronology see the *Catalyst* "Chicago School Reform Timeline" at *www.catalyst-chicago.org.*

6. Robert C. Johnston, "Chicago Schools' Chief Executive Will Step Down," *Education Week,* 13 June 2001, 3.

7. David Tyack, *The One Best System: A History of American Urban Education* (Cambridge: Harvard University Press, 1974).

8. Nicholas Lemann, *The Promised Land: The Great Black Migration and How It Changed America* (New York: David McKay, 1992).

9. Tyack.

10. Mary J. Herrick, *The Chicago Schools: A Social and Political History* (Beverly Hills: Sage Publications, 1971).

11. James Sanders, *The Education of an Urban Minority: Catholics in Chicago, 1833-1965* (New York: Oxford University Press, 1977): 47.

12. Ibid.

13. James Crawford, *Bilingual Education: History, Politics, Theory, and Practice,* 3rd ed. (Los Angeles: Bilingual Education Services, 1995); Charles Albert Ferguson, Shirley Brice Heath, and David Hwang, *Language in the USA* (New York: Cambridge University Press, 1981).

14. Herrick.

15. Crawford, 25.
16. Tyack, 171.
17. Lemann, 70.
18. Lemann, 91.
19. Alfred G. Hess, Jr., "Renegotiating a Multicultural Society: Participation in Desegregation Planning in Chicago," *Journal of Negro Education* 53, no. 2 (1984): 135.
20. Lemann, 234.
21. Hess, 135.
22. Hess, 135.
23. Maribeth Vander Weele, *Reclaiming Our Schools: The Struggle for Chicago School Reform* (Chicago: Loyola University, 1994).
24. Sanders, 212.
25. Hess, 143.
26. Julia Wrigley, "Chicago School Reform: Business Control or Open Democracy?" *Teachers College Record* 99, no. 1 (1997): 161.
27. Rosalind Rossi, "School Program Sends Principals Back to Class," *Chicago Sun-Times,* 6 December 1995, News section, 2.
28. Chicago Public School Website, "Fact Sheet," 2000, *http://www.cps.k12.il.us/* (27 August 2000).
29. Michael B. Katz, Michelle Fine, and Elaine Simon, "Poking Around: Outsiders View Chicago School Reform," *Teachers College Record* 99, no. 1 (1997): 117–57.
30. Initial interview with Barbara Kato conducted February 6, 1999, New York, NY; follow-up on January, 27, 2000, Chicago, IL.
31. Barbara J. Kato, "For Better and for Worse: Veteran Teachers Trying to Teach Well under Eleven Years of Chicago School Reform," (Ed. D. diss., Roosevelt University, 2000): iii.
32. Shipps, 90.
33. Shipps, 73.
34. Ann Lieberman, ed., *The Work of Restructuring Schools: Building from the Ground Up.* (New York: Teachers College, 1995).
35. Darrel W. Drury, *Reinventing School-Based Management* (Alexandria, VA: National School Boards Association, 1999): 9.
36. Ibid., 45.
37. Shipps, 90.
38. Robert Evans, "The Culture of Resistance," in *The Jossey-Bass Reader on School Reform* (San Francisco: Jossey-Bass, 2001), 510–21.
39. Linda Darling-Hammond, "Reframing the School Reform Agenda: Developing Capacity for School Transformation," *Phi Delta Kappan* 74 (1993): 760.
40. Michael Fullan, *Change Forces: The Sequel* (Philadelphia: Falmer Press, 1999), ix.
41. K. Wong, R. Drebeen, L. Lynn, and G. Sunderman, *Integrated Governance as a School Reform Strategy in the Chicago Public Schools* (Chicago: University of Chicago, 1997).
42. David Cohen, "Reforming School Politics," *Harvard Educational Review* 48 (1978): 429–47.

43. B. Dantowitz, "Schools Need Businesslike Approach," *Chicago Sun-Times,* 7 July 1994, 16.

44. Shipps, 105.

45. Richard F. Elmore, "Getting to Scale with Good Educational Practice," *Working Together Toward Reform* (Cambridge: Harvard Educational Review, 1996), 1.

46. Donna E. Muncey and Patrick J. McQuillan, "Education Reform as Revitalization Movement," *American Journal of Education* 101 (1993): 393–431; "Preliminary Findings from a Five-Year Study of the Coalition of Essential Schools," *Phi Delta Kappan* 74 (1993): 86–9.

47. James Hoffman, "When Bad Things Happen to Good Ideas in Literacy Education: Professional Dilemmas, Personal Decisions, and Political Traps," *The Reading Teacher* 52, no. 2 (1998): 108.

48. Gary Anderson, "Toward Authentic Participation: Deconstructing the Discourses of Participatory Reforms in Education," *American Educational Research Journal* 35 (1998): 571–603. "Participatory authoritarianism" is a term I learned from my colleague Martha Montero-Sieburth.

49. CPS Website, 5 January 2001.

50. Shipps, 107.

51. Pamela Morris, Aletha Huston, Greg Duncan, Danielle Crosby, and Johannes Bos, "Executive Summary," *How Welfare and Work Policies Affect Children: A Synthesis of Research* (New York: Manpower Demonstration Research Corporation, 2001).

52. "Welfare Reforms Found to Lift Children's School Grades," *Quincy, MA. Patriot Ledger,* 23 January 2001, 4.

53. Joel Perlmann, *Ethnic Differences: Schooling and Social Structure among the Irish, Italians, Jews, and Blacks in an American City, 1880–1935* (New York: Cambridge University, 1988).

54. Lee G. Bolman, Susan Moore Johnson, Jerome T. Murphy, and Carol H. Weiss, *Re-Thinking School Leadership: An Agenda for Research and Reform* (Cambridge : Harvard Graduate School of Education, 1990).

55. Mary Neuman and Warren Simmons, "Leadership for Student Learning," *Phi Delta Kappan* 82 (2000): 8.

56. Bradley S. Portin and Jianping Shen, "The Changing Principalship: Its Current Status, Variability, and Impact," *The Journal of Leadership Studies* 5, no. 3 (1998): 93–113.

57. Richard Ackerman, Patricia Maslin-Ostrowski, and Chuck Christensen, "Case Stories: Telling Tales About School," *Educational Leadership* 53, no. 6 (1996): 21.

58. UCLA Graduate School of Education and Information Studies, *Center X Quarterly* 8, no. 2 (1996).

59. Michael Fullan and Matthew Miles, "Getting Reform Right: What Works and What Doesn't," *Phi Delta Kappan* 73 (1992): 745–52; Edward Miller, "Idealists and Cynics: The Micropolitics of Systemic School Reform," *The Harvard Education Letter* XII, no. 4 (1996): 1-3; David Tyack and Walter Tobin, "The 'Grammar' of Schooling: Why Has It Been So Hard to Change?" *American Educational Research Journal* 31, no. 3 (1994): 453–79.

60. Barbara Batton and Linda Vereline, *Literacy Practices at C. E. S. 28 and C. J. H. S. 117* (New York: Institute for Literacy Studies, 1997).

61. Deborah Meier, *The Power of Their Ideas: Lessons for America from a Small School in Harlem* (Boston: Beacon Press, 1995).

62. Simon Hole and Grace Hall McEntee, "Reflection Is at the Heart of Practice," *Educational Leadership* 56, no. 8 (1999): 34.

63. "Executive Summary," *Professional Development Spending in the Boston Public Schools* (Boston: Boston Plan for Excellence and the Boston Public Schools, 1999), 8.

*Chapter 6*

# San Francisco and Oakland: Language Issues and Urban Reform

## INTRODUCTION

Culture and language are inseparable, core elements of individual and group identity. Evidence of this fact is all around us, from the on-going split in Canada between English- and French-speakers to continuing political battles in the United States around English-only legislation.

The educational ramifications of language use are many, and in parts of this chapter I will engage in technical discussions of language policy and programs. Such discussions are meant to elucidate, not obscure, the essential, powerful reality underlying linguistic issues in schooling: language is part of cultural identity and cultural identity is part of language. Threats to language are felt as threats to self, to family, and to group; advocacy for language is felt as support for culture, family, and self. And for any student, anywhere, whether the school is felt as a threatening or a supportive environment has a strong effect on whether that student succeeds or fails.

Improving schooling for linguistic minority students is one of the most urgent issues facing urban reform. In many cities, such students form a third or more of the entire school population. In individual schools these figures can be much higher, in some cases approaching one hundred percent. Yet systemic reformers have advanced few programs or strategies specifically tailored to the needs of linguistic minority students or their teachers. More often, in the face of research evidence to the contrary, reformers have taken the position that whatever is good for native English speakers will be good for linguistic minority students too.

Even under the best conditions, the presence of large numbers of linguistic minority students places additional demands on already overtaxed urban systems at every level. Students have to create an identity and gain an education while living in two cultures simultaneously, home and school. Schools, carriers of mainstream culture and values, are forced to confront the role their institutional stance plays in the success or failure of these students. School systems must manage the increased cost and complexity associated with serving many language groups.

But linguistic minority students seldom find themselves in the "best conditions." Often they are concentrated in the schools with the biggest gaps between "should" and "is"—the most underresourced schools in the system. Dropout rates, particularly for Latino students, are high, and academic performance is often low.[1] Clearly, if systemic reform is to live up to its claim of improving schooling for all, this is an area in which much work still needs to be done. To begin to understand the effects systemic reform has had on language minority students and their teachers, we must look at both large cultural patterns and specific local conditions.

At the local level, the San Francisco and Oakland Unified School Districts are rich sites for looking at reform in schools with large linguistic minority populations. These districts are linguistically diverse, educating significant numbers of native speakers of Arabic, Cantonese, Filipino, Khmer, Korean, Lao, Mandarin, Mien, Russian, Spanish, and Vietnamese. More than one-third of the total student population in each district is classified Limited English Proficient and an additional percentage as Fluent English Proficient. In addition, both districts have active reform agendas and have recently hired new superintendents to carry them out.

At the national level, mainstream American attitudes towards other countries and cultures are changing in unpredictable ways. On the one hand, domestic attitudes in areas like trade, politics, and health have become increasingly affected by developments elsewhere in the world. The election of a new president in Mexico or the rapid spread of AIDS in Africa is now seen as directly affecting the United States. One the other hand, our language attitudes and policies are increasingly at odds with those of the rest of the world. At times U.S. attitudes are tinged with a regression towards nativism that is reminiscent of the late nineteenth century, also an era of record-breaking immigration.

To examine systematically both larger issues and school-based realities, in this chapter I will progress by stages from the largest level, global attitudes, to the smallest, the individual classroom. I begin with sections on the global and national contexts for the schooling of language minority students. I proceed to a brief historical consideration of multiculturalism and education in San Francisco and Oakland, two urban systems with high numbers of such students. I then take a close look at some current realities of linguistic diversity and systemic reform in the two cities and discuss language minority issues in the wake of Proposition 227, the 1998 California English-Only law.

This analysis is supported by extensive comments from San Francisco and Oakland teachers who work in linguistically diverse schools undergoing reform. A set of conclusions completes the chapter.

Throughout the discussion I use three terms that will benefit from definition here: "minority language," "majority language," and "mainstream"/ "mainstreaming." A *minority language* is "a language of low prestige or low in power," and also a "language spoken by a minority of the population in the country."[2] These characteristics are usually found together, but not always. After the Norman Conquest, French was a minority language in Britain in the second sense but not the first, because a small minority of French-speaking nobles held power over the land. For linguistic minorities in U.S. schools, both definitions apply.

A *majority language* is "a high status language usually (but not always) spoken by a majority of the population of the country."[3] Typically, the majority language is that spoken by a society's dominant or *mainstream* population.

Culturally, the *mainstream* refers to "the prevalent attitudes, values, and practices of a society or group."[4] Bartolomé describes the American cultural mainstream as a "macroculture that has its roots in Western European traditions. More specifically, . . . the culture and traditions of white, Anglo-Saxon Protestants (WASP)." Although the cultural mainstream in the United States is now more diverse, traditional WASP "bodies of knowledge, language use, values, norms, and beliefs"[5] remain culturally dominant in the middle class. Educationally, for linguistic minority students, *mainstreaming* occurs when students no longer receive special language support such as ESL classes and take their subjects in English.

## LANGUAGE DIVERSITY AND GLOBALIZATION: "EMBRACING CONTRARIES"

In urban America today language minority communities, like the school systems that serve them, are characterized by contradiction. This is particularly true where immigrants are concerned, and our country is in the midst of the largest immigrant influx in its history.

Miami's exile Cuban community, for example, has been staunchly opposed to the Castro regime from the Bay of Pigs invasion of 1961 to the Elian Gonzalez controversy of 2000. Yet the same community adds from 700 million to one billion dollars annually to Cuba's economy in the form of remittances to the families they left behind.[6] The flood of dollars from Miami has created its own unofficial economy in Cuba, becoming the island's de facto second currency and undermining the effects of the U.S. embargo which the leadership of Miami's Cuban community so steadfastly supports.

Contradictions are also evident in the attitudes our educational system displays towards language. In their curricular guidelines, state and federal governments advocate the academic value and economic importance of learning a second language. Four-year colleges commonly require entering students to have passed two years of a foreign language in high school, and some states have now instituted a language requirement for all high school students, college-bound or not. At the middle school and elementary levels, foreign language classes are increasingly common. Reasons cited for such decisions usually include reference to "global competitiveness" or the need for American students to hold jobs in "the global economy." Also cited are the values associated with understanding other peoples and cultures.

But when immigrant students enter a school in possession of a language other than English, they meet attitudes that are anything but welcoming. Their familiarity with another language is seen as a liability, not an asset. Often, they are pressured to drop their native language as soon as possible and become proficient only in English. In many cases, schools take away students' first languages, give them an imperfect command of English, then demand, at the high school level, that they learn a "foreign" or "world" language to graduate.

Because of such contradictions, it may be that our ability to understand the realities facing urban second-language learners and their teachers depends on our skill at "embracing contraries." This is a term that Peter Elbow uses to describe "a larger and more inclusive model of thinking" that finds a "paradoxical coherence" in combining seemingly opposite conceptual models, "structured logical thinking" and "intuitive, unstructured thinking."[7] Such contraries are regular features of the everyday life of second-language communities in their encounters with schools.

One important contrary is that, *the global is the local.* Globalization is often thought of in terms of two images: global village and global marketplace. The global village is shorthand for the notion of the "shrinking" of the globe by technological advances such as jet planes, internet communications, and cell phones. Global marketplace reminds us that in a world where the Chrysler Corporation has become Daimler-Chrysler and most of the clothes at Wal-Mart are made in China, the context for both producers and consumers is clearly global.

What has not been so clearly recognized is that connections between the global and the local greatly affect schools in which there are large numbers of non-English speaking students. Immigrants come to the United States for the same reasons they always have: to escape political and economic crisis at home, to build a better life here. But the world is much smaller than it was in the nineteenth century; contact with home may be no more than a cell phone call away, and trade developments like NAFTA promote freer movement of both labor and capital. A viewpoint that sees the educational effects of globalization solely in terms of preparing native-English speaking American students for jobs overseas misses a key reality: the United States itself is changing as part of a rapidly changing world.

Globally, linguistic diversity is more common than not. America's aggressive monolingualism is the exception, not the rule. Italy, for example, which most of us view as a homogeneous country with a single language, has thirteen cultural and linguistic minorities.[8] Speakers of these languages are not immigrants but "historical minorities" who have for hundreds of years lived on what is now Italian territory. More importantly, Italians of all educational levels and regions move back and forth between "standard Italian" and their local dialect or second language. A government survey conducted in the late 1980s showed that for a large majority of the population (62 percent), "dialects or non-Italian tongues remain the parlance of choice at home and with friends. . . ."[9]

In Spain, the language we call Spanish is referred to as "Castellano," a recognition that it is a local dialect raised to the level of a national language when Ferdinand and Isabela, King and Queen of Castile, unified Spain in 1492. Three regional languages are also widely used: Catalan, Gallego, and Basque (Euskera).

In much of Africa the situation is even more complex. Students come to school from dozens of tribal language groups, and many African nations have chosen to conduct schooling in a former colonizer's language such as English, French, or Portuguese. They do this to provide a unifying element to the educational system, to avoid favoring one tribal group over another, and to expose students to a broader "world" language. This does not mean, however, that students stop speaking the tribal language. They are expected to be able to function competently in two, or often three languages. They may have a native oral language which is tribal, a first written language such as English, Arabic, or Swahili that is the language of instruction in their school, and a school-learned "foreign language" that is part of the curriculum.

In Asia, India's one billion people share two official languages, English and Hindi, but fourteen other languages are recognized by the constitution, including Bengali, Urdu, and Sanskrit. Many other countries have more than one official language. In Switzerland, of course, there is no "Swiss" language; German, French, and Italian share co-equal status, each dominant in a certain part of the country. In Ireland both Irish (Gaelic) and English are official. In Peru, both Spanish and Quechua, the indigenous language of the Incas, have legal status. In Tanzania both Swahili and English are official, with English the primary language of higher education. Arabic is also widely spoken in Tanzania, as are many tribal languages. Literacy, which stands at 68 percent of the population, is defined as being able to read and write in English, Swahili, or Arabic.[10]

To our immediate north and south, language diversity is also the rule. Canada conducts schooling in English for most of the country, in French and English in Quebec, and in English and tribal languages for some indigenous populations. We think of Mexico as a Spanish-speaking country, but it is also home to hundreds of thousands of indigenous people whose languages originated long before Spanish. These include Nahuatl (the language of the Aztecs), Mayan, Otomi, Tzetzal, and over 100 others. Schooling is conducted in both Spanish and indigenous languages.

On U.S. soil, Puerto Rico conducts schooling in Spanish, but English is a mandatory subject from the first grade, and a stated goal of the Puerto Rican Department of Education is to develop "bilingual citizens" by "responding to the need for the mastery of the two languages."[11]

It is for reasons like these that what used to be called "English as a Second Language" (ESL) is now called instruction for "English Language Learners" (ELL) or, in California, EL ("English Learners"). For many foreign students English is not a second, but a third or even fourth language. Acceptance of language diversity is part of the globalization process, but one the United States and its schools have been reluctant to embrace. As the global increasingly becomes the local in urban schools, this reluctance creates a growing barrier to the school success of language minority students.

One standard linguistics textbook reminds its readers that "Speakers of different languages have always been in contact with each other. But at no other time in history have there been such intensive contacts between language communities as in the last few centuries."[12] As cross-language contacts increase, bilingualism and multilingualism[13] become increasingly common. More than half the population of Europe now speaks a second language.

Globally, the prominent exceptions to this rule are the United States and Japan. In the United States,

bilingualism is mostly relegated to immigrant communities, who are expected to learn English, the dominant language, on arrival. Frequently, these immigrants are also under pressure to lose their native language . . . which often occurs within one or two generations. The adaptation is one-sided in contrast to what is found in most other areas of the globe, where neighboring communities learn each other's languages with little ado.[14]

Even in the United States, attitudes towards language were once much more open than they are today. During the great immigration of the nineteenth and early twentieth centuries, "Language variety was accepted as the norm and encouraged through religion, newspapers in different languages, and in both private and public schooling."[15] It was not until World War I that language attitudes began to become more restrictive.

In sheer numbers, our current wave of immigration has now surpassed the classic "immigrant era." But faster travel and communications keep immigrants in closer contact than ever with the lands and people they left behind. On our streets, in workplaces, and in urban schools, the global has become the local. At the same time, American commerce and technology have steadily extended their reach to new markets in Europe, Asia, Africa, and Latin America. The local has become the global. As the twenty-first century unfolds, one of the tests of our schools will be their ability to embrace this "contrary," to succeed in the increasingly important language dimension of education.

Success will mean not just creating strong "world language" programs in well-funded suburban schools, but recognizing and capitalizing on the opportunities created by multilingual urban student populations. Though Spanish speakers form the majority of English Language Learners, the spectrum of language groups in our schools is truly global. In Chicago, Sharon Ransom has described reforming schools with high populations of speakers of Polish and Urdu. In San Francisco there are speakers of Cantonese and Mandarin, as well as Tagalog (the main language of the Philippines), Laotian, Russian, Vietnamese and Arabic.

When global becomes local, the consciousness of and attitudes toward language diversity displayed by schools become crucial factors in the success of their students. As the Oakland, California school department highlighted in the much-publicized but little understand "Ebonics" controversy, such consciousness and attitudes are equally important to native speakers of non-standard English such as many African American students.[16]

What attitude has systemic reform taken so far to language diversity? To date, there has been little consciousness of its importance, or rather, the consciousness has been that of the dominant, mainstream society: lose your native language, learn English as fast as you can so you can score well on standardized tests.

When immigrant students from Mexico, Africa, and elsewhere enter U.S. schools, they experience a devaluing of their language and culture that arises directly from this attitude. This also holds true for students from Puerto Rico and the Philippines, who are strictly speaking migrants rather than immigrants, and for students from the non-English speaking or non-standard English speaking communities commonly found in U.S. cities, such as South Central Los Angeles or many parts of Detroit. This devaluing takes many forms but it is felt by students as an attack on their own and their family's worth and identity, and students who feel attacked by their own school find it difficult to learn.

In order to understand how such attitudes, and the programs and actions they engender, negatively affect immigrants and other non-standard speakers, it will be helpful to examine the troubled relationships that have historically existed between the San Francisco and Oakland school systems and the linguistic and racial minority populations of those cities. Further, such an examination will bring to light another set of antagonisms: tensions between and among non-mainstream groups as each attempts to secure for its children the scarce resource of a good education. The brief multicultural history that forms the next section was researched and written by Julie Kalnin of the University of Minnesota, Carol Tateishi, director of the Bay Area Writing Project at the University of California, Berkeley, and Alex Casareno of the University of Portland. Their account tracks multicultural issues in Bay Area schools , but stops just prior to passage of the landmark "English Only" ballot initiative, Proposition 227, that since 1998 has transformed the educational landscape for linguistic minority students in California. The passage and consequences of Proposition 227 will be discussed as part of my own in-depth look at schools undergoing reform that immediately follows their brief history.

## DIVERSE COMMUNITIES, DISTINCT PURPOSES: EDUCATION AND MULTICULTURALISM IN SAN FRANCISCO AND OAKLAND—JULIE KALNIN, CAROL TATEISHI, AND ALEX CASARENO

While San Francisco and Oakland share a pluralistic past, they differ demographically. As different ethnic groups entered the area and their numbers swelled, they have pursued educational resources not as allies with other groups but as factions, focused on the needs of their own children. After their independent fights to end legal segregation in the nineteenth century, factionalization among ethnic groups again emerged during conflicts over school integration in the mid-twentieth century. Debates about language policies for non-English speaking immigrants, which began in the 1960s, continue today.

### Asian Exclusion in San Francisco

In contrast to patterns of discrimination elsewhere, Asian immigrants bore the brunt of early discrimination in schooling in the Bay Area. While Oakland remained homogeneously white and European until the 1940s, the 1849 Gold Rush brought immigrants from around the world to San Francisco, including, for the first time in U.S. history, large numbers of Chinese, and later, Japanese immigrants.

African Americans, in the 1850s only one-tenth the size of the Chinese population, were considered less threatening and therefore earned legal access to the schools more quickly. The first African American school, sponsored by African American churches, opened in San Francisco in 1854. Three years later, when California limited educational funding to white students only, San Francisco became the first city to appropriate funds to

educate non-white students.[17] In 1874, California's first school desegregation case supported maintenance of segregated schools;[18] however, the San
Francisco Board of Education, as Oakland had done ten years before,
opened its school doors to black students.[19]

By contrast, the Asian community met with harsh resistance in its fight
for access to schools. In 1871, although the United States had a treaty with
China promising that Chinese children could attend public schools, San
Francisco's superintendent used a loophole in state law to close the ten-year-
old public school for Chinese students. It was not reopened for fifteen years.
School-age Chinese, if they were educated at all, attended private Chinese
schools. The curriculum in these low-cost institutions was designed with
the assumption that the children would one day live and work in China.[20]

Soon after the 1880 California decision declaring segregation illegal,
Joseph and Mary Tape, natives of China, challenged the district because
they were not allowed to enroll their American-born daughter Mamie in
their neighborhood school. They won their suit in Municipal Court (*Tape
v. Hurley*), but the San Francisco superintendent used his influence to have
a bill brought in the legislature reinstating the right of school districts
to establish separate schools for "Mongolians and Indians."[21] The
district hastily reestablished the Chinese school, which Mamie was forced
to attend.

Discrimination against the Chinese ebbed when immigration was curtailed in the late 1800s, but by the early 1900s, Japanese immigration had
grown significantly, and the Japanese became the new "Asian threat." In
1905, the San Francisco school board voted to create a segregated Japanese school but lacked the funds to establish it. When ordered to send their
children to the Chinese school, Japanese parents refused. They notified
government officials and newspapers in Japan that their children were being deprived of an education, and sued the district (*Aoki v. Deane*), pro-
voking an international incident. Ultimately, President Theodore Roosevelt
brought the entire San Francisco Board of Education to Washington for
mediation. The board agreed to drop its policy of segregation against the
93 Japanese students—not even one half of one percent of San Francisco's
28,000 student population—in exchange for Roosevelt's promise to limit
Japanese immigration.[22]

World War II created a second "Gold Rush." High-paying defense jobs
in shipbuilding stimulated population growth and for the first time brought
a significant number of African Americans to the Bay Area. The propor-
tional increase was particularly dramatic in industrial Oakland, which recorded a 341 percent gain in its African American population between 1940
and 1945.[23] Violence against African Americans increased, and they were
increasingly isolated in residentially segregated neighborhoods.[24] These segregated neighborhoods, combined with white flight from the cities, created
segregated neighborhood schools in both Oakland and San Francisco.

### Desegregation in San Francisco and Oakland

In San Francisco, the NAACP repeatedly sought and won the power of the courts to redress segregation. In 1971, under court order, the board adopted the Horseshoe Plan to bus children within seven ethnically balanced zones. The plan's implementation unveiled factionalism among ethnic communities. Many white parents placed their children in private schools or left the city; the elementary school population dropped by 16 percent.[25] One group of Chinese parents organized a school boycott to oppose busing their children out of Chinatown. A small number of Chinese physicians signed hundreds of transfer applications for children slated to be bused, claiming that busing posed a health risk. When the district approved these applications, the boycott ended and Chinatown's schools were effectively resegregated.[26]

While a socioeconomically diverse group of African Americans had united to fight for integration, when it came to implementation, middle-class African American parents were reluctant to bus their children into poverty-stricken areas. Other African American groups protested that their children were being bused into a predominantly Latino area where the schools were old, while Latino students were attending newly built schools in an African American neighborhood. African American parents also began actively seeking transfers to neighborhood schools where community organizations were establishing special programs. Latino community members formed the Mission Coalition and sued the district, claiming particular discrimination in predominantly Latino schools.[27] Resistance from all of these communities meant that ethnic balance never made it past the blueprints.

For many years San Francisco operated under a 1983 consent decree, the result of an NAACP suit brought on behalf of African Americans and Latinos. Schools had to enroll at least four major ethnic groups, and no single group could exceed 45 percent of the total school population. The consent decree also brought $34 million—out of a total budget of $530 million—in state funding to the schools to reduce class size and offer specialized instruction for Latino and African American students. Academic high schools were established in both African American and Latino neighborhoods. The Chinese community contested the decree in 1994, claiming it denied Chinese students an equal opportunity to attend Lowell High School, the city's preeminent academic high school. The suit argued that the desegregation plan was equivalent to an ethnic quota scheme;[28] but in 1997, the court ruled against the Chinese community, upholding integration. Legal action continued, and in 1999 the court ordered the district to stop using race as a factor in student assignments. The court upheld this order in 2001, though it did agree that the schools could continue to receive $37 million a year in desegregation funding, provided it was used to strengthen education for underperforming students of all races.

In Oakland, desegregation meant politicization. Oakland's desegregation movement flared into action in 1961 around the newly built Skyline High, located in the affluent and predominantly white Oakland hills. Oakland's policy had been to foster heterogeneous school populations by drawing attendance zones that stretched from the poorer, eastern flatlands to the affluent, western hills. Skyline's attendance zone, a thinly veiled attempt to slow white flight, was a long, narrow rectangle, stretching from north to south along the hills. The NAACP, Congress of Racial Equality (CORE), and other African American civil rights groups focused on changing Skyline's attendance boundaries. In 1964, the board, under pressure from state education officials, voted to expand Skyline's attendance zone to include several, mostly black, junior high schools as feeders.[29]

During the next six years, other small and discrete desegregation projects were undertaken, but because of the large non-white population in Oakland, none attempted to achieve integration on a district level. In the face of disparities in funding for predominantly white schools and predominantly non-white schools, priorities shifted from desegregation to political participation. In 1966, the impetus for local control of schools, particularly over the use of federal funds, briefly unified twenty-one disparate political organizations, representing both African Americans and Latinos.[30] When the board refused to endorse local control, the coalition initiated a three-day student boycott that revealed the power of community organizers.

Ethnically based political organizations next concentrated their efforts on the selection of the district's superintendent. When Marcus Foster was hired in 1970, Oakland became the first major urban school district to hire an African American superintendent.[31] Foster quickly reallocated money from white schools to non-white schools and successfully balanced the competing desires of Oakland's diverse communities.[32] For example, Latinos found, for the first time, an ear receptive to their demands for bilingual education. Foster's assassination in 1973 by the Symbionese Liberation Army (SLA), a radical political group also known for its abduction of Patty Hearst, marked the tragic end of his efforts to respond to all of the district's constituencies. Today, African Americans continue to have the dominant voice in Oakland. As its Latino and Asian populations grow, however, the question of factionalism in Oakland arises anew.

### Beyond 2000: Language Issues

Since the 1970s, unprecedented levels of immigration into California and a shift in the ethnic origins of immigrants have raised tensions about language education. Thirty years ago, most immigrants came from Europe, while today, the Americas and Asia are the primary areas of origin. Currently, the Bay Area is among the most ethnically and linguistically diverse regions in California, and San Francisco has the state's second highest concentration of students classified as Limited English Proficient.

In the heat of the 1960s battle for school integration in San Francisco, Chinese parents had begun lobbying for children who were not proficient speakers of English. Of the nearly 3,000 Chinese-speaking students, about 63 percent received no special instruction in English or Chinese.[33] Increasing numbers of Chinese secondary students dropped out. Between 1964 and 1969, the juvenile delinquency rate for Chinese rose by 600 percent.[34] While the Board acknowledged students' needs, members argued that because non-English proficient students were provided with the same education as other students, the district had fulfilled its legal obligation.

Failing to find recourse through political pressure, the Chinese community filed suit (*Lau v. Nichols*). In 1974, after four years of litigation, the U.S. Supreme Court delivered a unanimous decision: "There is no equality of treatment merely by providing students with the same facilities, textbooks, teachers and curriculum; for students who do not understand English are effectively foreclosed from any meaningful education."[35] No more important decision on education has been handed down since *Brown v. Board of Education*. Many districts around the United States including Oakland have since been brought to court by groups within the Latino community for failing to adhere to the *Lau* decision.

Today, San Francisco provides bilingual and English as a second language (ESL) programs to almost one-third of its students. In a period of scarce educational resources, *Lau v. Nichols* and the federal and state funds it directs toward these students sometimes create inter-ethnic controversy, because bilingual and ESL programs can make racial integration more difficult. San Francisco attempted to respond both to its consent decree and *Lau v. Nichols* by putting monolingual English speakers (in a 2:1 black/white ratio) into bilingual classes when those classes were not fully enrolled.[36] In 1995, under pressure from the African American community, San Francisco discontinued this practice.

As its student population has changed, Oakland too has struggled with federal and state guidelines. The appropriation of federal dollars for language instruction created tension when African American children were also in need of additional resources. In 1997, Oakland's School Board issued a resolution asserting Ebonics to be the primary language of many of its African American students. Criticized, among other reasons, as a ploy for obtaining bilingual funds, the proposal immediately created a national furor. U.S. Education Secretary, Richard Riley, condemned the proposal, stating that Ebonics did not constitute a language and that no bilingual funds would be appropriated for speakers of non-standard English dialects.

In an amended proposal, the Oakland board faced these criticisms head on, recommiting to appropriate funding for this effort. The proposal asserted the district's interest in equal opportunity for all limited English proficient students and recognized "the English language acquisition and improvement skills of African American students are as fundamental as is application of bilingual or second-language learner principles for others whose primary languages are other than English."[37] Inservice programs to train teachers to draw upon Ebonics as they taught standard English began in 1997.

As the Ebonics debate illustrates, questions of quality and equality are as complex today in these school districts as they were when achieving physical integration was the predominant goal. As ethnic factions become more entrenched, addressing the needs of multicultural populations requires districts to attend simultaneously to the particular needs of individual groups and to the welfare of the school community in general. Accepting and responding to diversity thus poses a dilemma for Bay Area schools that will not be easily resolved.

## REFORM AND LINGUISTIC DIVERSITY IN SAN FRANCISCO AND OAKLAND

Turning again to my own analysis, at least four lessons can be carried forward from this brief history that will help us analyze current reform efforts in San Francisco and Oakland. First, two levels of ongoing struggle are visible around issues of educational equity. In the big picture and over the long term, the struggle for educational resources can be seen as a bipolar one between dominant and subordinate (in terms of power) or mainstream and non-mainstream (in terms of culture) groups. This tension is clearly seen in examples like the Lau decision and the desegregation of Oakland. But at the local level and in the short term, the struggle often presents itself as an inter-ethnic one in which non-dominant groups are pitted against each other in a zero-sum contest created by the mainstream culture's unwillingness to provide adequate resources to schools whose primary clientele is non-mainstream groups. This phenomenon is evident in the San Francisco consent decree and the Oakland Ebonics controversy.

Second, the vigorous, long-lasting, and committed nature of these struggles gives the lie to the notion that minority communities do not value education. Many educators and policymakers, particularly those who are members of mainstream culture, are unfamiliar with or choose to discount the effects of this history of discrimination. Once one is familiar with the obstacles minority parents have faced and continue to face, it is impossible not to be convinced of their lasting commitment to improving their children's lives through education, or their firm belief that education will help their communities take their rightful place in the overall picture of American society.

Third, both levels of struggle are important contextual elements in today's urban schools, not just in the Bay Area but nationally. These local histories of tension affect the day-to-day life of schools by conditioning the attitudes, relationships, and beliefs of those who work in them, of parents whose children attend them, and of the communities whose taxes support them. Such considerations are particularly important given the widespread adoption of "exemplary" national models with no local roots as a basic strategy for urban reform. Yet few "systemic" reforms include such considerations in their planning processes, preferring the easier road of a one-size fits-all, we-know-what's-best-for-you approach.

Finally, the multicultural history also makes it clear that language diversity in the Bay Area is part of a larger pattern of racial/ethnic diversity. This pattern includes native-born minority communities such as African Americans, long-established, multi-generational immigrant communities such as Mexican Americans and Chinese Americans, and more recent arrivals such as Laotians and Russians. Before looking specifically at language-minority students, therefore, we first need to see the broader picture of these school systems as a whole.

### The Nature of Diversity in San Francisco and Oakland

Unlike Chicago, no single racial/ethnic/linguistic group forms a majority in either Bay Area city. In San Francisco, Asians make up 43 percent of the student population, with the rapidly growing Latino population at 22 percent, African Americans at 16 percent, and "white non-Hispanics" at 12 percent. In Oakland, African Americans represent a plurality at 48 percent of the student population, with Latinos second at 27 percent. Tables 6.1 and 6.2 show the complete racial/ethnic breakdown for the two districts for 1999–2000; racial/ethnic designations are those used by the state of California to collect data ("Fil" = Filipino, W/nH = white/non-Hispanic).

Racial/ethnic figures provide an important part of the demographic context for understanding language issues. But by lumping together groups that are culturally and linguistically dissimilar, broad racial/ethnic categories mask distinctions that have important implications for teaching and learning. A category like Asian, for instance, includes speakers of Mandarin, Cantonese, Laotian, Korean, and Vietnamese. Categories like Asian and Hispanic also group recent immigrants who may have no English proficiency with native-born students who may have grown up speaking English and have no command whatsoever of another language. Therefore we also must consider the language backgrounds and proficiencies of these students.

Table 6.1
Oakland Unified, 1999–2000 Total Enrollment: 55,051[38]

| Af-Am | His/Lat | Asian | W/nonH | Other |
|-------|---------|-------|--------|-------|
| 48.4% | 26.6% | 16.3% | 5.6% | 3.1% |

Enrollment percent by racial/ethnic group.

**Table 6.2**
**San Francisco Unified 1999–2000 Total Enrollment: 60,896**[39]

| Af-Am | His/Lat | Asian | W/nonH | Fil | Other |
|-------|---------|-------|--------|-----|-------|
| 15.6% | 21.5% | 42.8% | 11.9% | 6.9% | 2.3% |

Enrollment percent by racial/ethnic group.

In San Francisco, according to the language census taken by the state in spring, 1998, 31 percent of the system's students were "Limited English Proficient." There were nine languages with 200 or more speakers in the system, including Spanish (6,860), Cantonese (6,653), Filipino (992), Vietnamese (649), Russian (642), Mandarin (420), Khmer (253), Arabic (214), and Korean (200). In Oakland, 33 percent of the students were classified "Limited English Proficient" and six language groups had over 200 speakers, including Spanish (9,847), Cantonese (2,750), Khmer (1,219), Mien (917), Lao (247), and Arabic (233). In both systems an additional percentage of non-native English speakers was classified "Fluent English Proficient."[40]

This rich diversity has had important implications for policy in the Bay Area. In Chicago, a significant part of the reform story has to do with the tension between large minority communities and the dominant mainstream political and business culture. In Oakland and San Francisco such tensions are not absent, but the broad diversity of the school populations lets us see a new tension that is also part of the reform story: inter-ethnic rivalry among non-mainstream groups over the scarce resource of a quality education. The Oakland school board's 1996 Ebonics resolution, as well as San Francisco's battles over the Desegregation Consent Decree, reflect tensions between the Latino and African American communities in particular.

### Proposition 227 and Its Effects

In Oakland and San Francisco, Proposition 227 has had a major impact by severely restricting the conditions under which schools can support English Learners (EL). In the past, many students who lacked English proficiency had the support of Transitional Bilingual Education (TBE) programs in which subject-matter instruction was conducted in their native language while they improved their English skills. Community advocates and many local school systems valued the programs for the social, cultural, and academic support they provided to students. But from the state's point of view, TBE programs were wasteful and inefficient because their primary purpose was to teach students enough English to get them into the mainstream, and this was not happening fast enough.

Differences of opinion about purposes and outcomes set the stage for a statewide confrontation in the late 1990s between opponents of TBE and its supporters, who included language minority communities and urban school systems. In this dispute, the passage of Proposition 227 in 1998 was a clear message that the opponents had won. Bilingual programs could continue only if parents signed waivers specifically requesting bilingual education. Most LEP students are now assigned to English-only subject matter classes while receiving support through English Language Development (ELD) classes taught by mainstream teachers with little training or experience in working with such students.

The passage of Proposition 227 had a particular symbolic resonance in the Bay Area because, in *Lau v. Nichols* (1974), San Francisco had virtually given birth to Transitional Bilingual Education in the United States. The court-approved solutions in the case, usually referred to as " Lau remedies," became the basis of federal bilingual education policy for the next ten years.

By the mid-1980s, Californians were realizing the speed with which their public school system was becoming "majority minority," meaning that white, English speaking students represented less than 50 percent of the total statewide student population, Advocates for language minority students increased their efforts, and so did opponents. When former California governor Ronald Reagan became president the stakes became national. The Reagan administration withdrew the Lau remedies and left policy in this area up to the states. This set the stage for a shift in attitudes towards the rights of language minorities which led directly to Proposition 227 and similar legislation in other states, such as Arizona.[41]

Proposition 227 is playing out in urban school systems in interesting ways. In July 1998, for example, Oakland declared that recent standardized test results "vindicated its position on bilingual education" by showing that "bilingual students in Oakland who become proficient in the English language exceed the national average in their academic performance . . . and even do better than their English-only counterparts."[42] To achieve such results, Oakland had been keeping students in bilingual programs for much longer than the law prescribed. In doing this, they had the support of an international body of research showing that it takes much longer than three years for students to make a successful transition to academic proficiency from one language to another. However, the state took a contrary view, pressuring Oakland to move students into the mainstream more quickly or risk losing millions of dollars of state and federal aid for bilingual education. In spring, 2000 the state withheld $5 million dollars, citing statistics that showed "fewer than 1 percent of the 7,000 least-fluent students were being shifted into mainstream English classes annually, compared with a state average of 7 percent." According to accounts of the controversy, "Another 21,000 immigrant students in mainstream classes weren't receiving specialized instruction and were falling behind, promoting accusations from the U.S. Office of Civil Rights that they were being denied an equal education."[43] Oakland immediately instituted staff development programs and other measures to speed up the rate at which students were moving into the mainstream and to give teachers and administrators new skills for dealing with ELD instruction. In January 2001 the state restored funding on a partial basis, with a promise of full funding if Oakland passed a review of its programs later in the spring.

### Systemic Reform in San Francisco and Oakland[44]

In August 2000, San Francisco hired Arlene Ackerman as Superintendent to manage a complex array of reforms. Some initiatives are district-authored, for example, a new "Standards, Testing, Accountability, Reflection, and Support System" to evaluate teachers. Others arise from the community's historic use of federal courts to force the school system to address equity issues. Still others, like the "reconstitution" of schools that have performed poorly on California's test-driven Academic Performance Index (API), are responses to state mandates.

In Oakland, the reform landscape is even more complex. Superintendent Dennis Chaconas was hired in spring 2000 to implement a comprehensive, long-term School Site Empowerment Initiative adopted by the school board in February 1999. However, after reviewing a state audit highly critical of the school system (of which the bilingual issue cited above was a part), he declared that "virtually all systems in the Oakland Unified School District have broken down," and that Oakland was "operating in a permanent crisis mode, unable to move beyond day-to-day survival to address the fundamental structural and cultural problems creating the crises." He then announced his own "unflinching review of all personnel, programs, and processes," and declared a need for "revolutionary change."[45]

His reform plan, introduced in January, 2001, centered on "the three R's": Renaissance ("Redesign schools and district operations to create personalized learning environments."), Renewal ("Engage the community at the site level to support teaching and learning."), and Results ("Use student data to improve teaching and learning").[46]

It was not immediately clear how these "revolutionary" reforms related to the Board's 1999 initiative. The Board's plan had established "uniform curriculum standards, graduation standards, and student assessments" and mandated districtwide implementation of best practice "comprehensive school site empowerment policies" that included "site flexibility . . . including adoption of innovative, research-based school reform models such as Comer, Small Autonomous Schools, and Success For All"; ongoing professional development for principals; "collaborative decision making" by mandated "school site councils/management teams"; principals as "instructional leaders," which will necessitate making "the principalship a highly desirable administrative position in the District"; *parent involvement; site-community partnerships; central office restructuring*," which includes "shared decision making with site leadership"; and *broad accountability*: "All staff at all levels must be held accountable."[47]

Finally, in both San Francisco and Oakland the reform universe includes powerful forces beyond the district's control. Many schools, targeted as underperforming by the API or other measures, have been flooded with reform initiatives. These include state-sponsored "whole school change" interventions under California's Instructional Intervention in Under-performing Schools Program (II/USP), federal CSRD and Title I programs administered through the state and the district, and a host of privately spon-sored Annenberg Challenge programs. The latter originate from the local representative of the Challenge, the Bay Area School Reform Collabora-tive (BASRC-pronounced "basrac").

In addition, like other California school districts with large EL popula-tions, San Francisco and Oakland are deeply affected by instructional changes mandated under Proposition 227. The proposition pushes most EL students into the mainstream, where they are supported by English Lan-guage Development (ELD) classes taught by regular education teachers, not EL specialists. Commonly these classrooms use reform-mandated reading programs and materials developed for native English speakers, not second-language learners.

Mandates cover not just the curriculum and instructional methods, but also the time spent on various aspects of the curriculum and the way stu-dents are grouped. Mandated professional development has been provided to help teachers cope with the changes. Teachers have been stripped of any control over basic instructional decisions in their own classrooms. The same can be said of principals in their own buildings.

In order to understand why this has happened, it is necessary to look at the political context for educational change in California. By "political context" I mean the power relationships between mainstream and non-mainstream groups in relation to education. This topic is worth a detailed look for at least two reasons. First, since trends seem to start first in Cali-fornia and move eastward, the Proposition 227 context may soon be a national one. Second, the Proposition 227 context deals with the relation-ship between bilingual education and mainstream education, and there may be no segment of American schooling that is more widely misunderstood than bilingual education.

### Language Minority Issues in the Wake of Proposition 227

In 1999, after a hard-fought battle, California's "English-Only" propo-nents won a clear political victory with the passage of a ballot proposition virtually eliminating bilingual education. Proposition 227 is important not because it is a well-crafted piece of legislation—it is not—but because it enacts into a law a belief system about immigration and language learning that is both controversial and shared by voters in other states; Arizona, for instance, passed similar legislation soon after 227.

The California proposition mandates that almost all EL students be instructed in English-only settings. The only exception is a waiver process by which groups of parents can request that a local school system provide bilingual instruction in a given language. Under this provision some bilingual programs survive, chiefly to serve the more organized language minority communities in big cities.

As a result of Proposition 227, Section 300 of the California *Education Code* now advances these reasons for English-only education: "Immigrant parents are eager to have their children acquire a good knowledge of English, thereby allowing them to fully participate in the American Dream of economic and social advancement," and the state has a moral and constitutional duty to provide the state's children with "the skills necessary to become productive members of our society;" chief among these is English literacy. However, currently the public schools of California "do a poor job of educating immigrant children, wasting financial resources on costly experimental language programs whose failure over the past two decades is demonstrated by the current high dropout rates and low English literacy levels of many immigrant children." But "young immigrant children can easily acquire full fluency in a new language, such as English, if they are heavily exposed to that language in the classroom at an early age."

The law describes the means to achieve this in the following terms: "all children (shall) be placed in English language classrooms. Children who are English learners shall be educated through sheltered English immersion during a temporary transition period not normally intended to exceed one year. . . . Local schools shall be encouraged to mix together in the same classroom English learners from different native-language groups but with the same degree of English proficiency."[48]

A clue to the extent to which political and educational beliefs have been conflated in the law can be seen in the reference to "failed" and "costly" "experimental language programs." The debate preceding the vote on 227 made it clear that this was a reference not just to bilingual education, but to whole language as well. By the late 1990s, whole language programs had became a volatile political battleground and negative articles about them appeared in even such unlikely places as the front page of the California-based *Investor's Business Daily*.

In this climate it is perhaps not surprising that the passage of 227 was followed by an announcement from Hewlett-Packard heir David Packard that he would fund the adoption of a phonics-based basal reading series, Open Court, in some of the state's urban school systems with large second-language populations. California has a statewide textbook adoption law and Open Court was not on the approved list. Accepting Packard's largesse, which included staff development for teachers in the use of the new system, required an end run around the normal adoption process. Currently Oakland, Los Angeles, and a number of other school systems have accepted Packard's offer and not only mandate Open Court in the early elementary grades, but also strictly monitor its use through classroom visits.

In effect, a civic-minded, activist multi-millionaire's largesse has taken decisions on curriculum and instruction out of the hands of public officials charged with making them. This was able to happen because the political feeling against immigrants, bilingual education, and whole language is so strong, and because resource-starved urban school systems feel, as an Oakland teacher I interviewed put it, "if we can't get the money any other way, we have to go for (it)."

The battle over language issues in California is far from over. Critics of Proposition 227 have their own viewpoints on both its philosophy and its implementation. They point out, for example, that many members of racial and linguistic minority communities believe in an American Dream that allows them to retain their racial, cultural, and linguistic heritage rather than rejecting it for a white, middle class dream of "Americanness."

They also point out that immigrants arrive at all ages and with varied histories of schooling. In addition to the young children cited in the law, there are thirteen-year-olds from Cambodia who have grown up in refugee camps and sixteen-year-olds from El Salvador and Guatemala whose schooling has been interrupted by years of civil war. Bilingual programs provide such students with more than just a native language base from which to start learning English. They provide a culturally sheltering environment, a "safe place" from which to face the overwhelming speed and confusion of American life, and the complexity and strangeness of the American public school. Forcing such students immediately into the mainstream seems as likely to drive them out of school altogether as it is to insure that they will quickly become proficient in English.

Critics of the law also question the causal connection between "costly experimental language programs" and high dropout rates for immigrant children, citing multiple social and economic causes for such an effect. They also remind us that there is strong research support for the belief that the proposed curricular solution—all English all the time—is, of all possible approaches, the one least likely to achieve the stated goal.

Long-term research by Thomas and Collier in particular finds that for language minority students three important program components that promote academic success are: "(1) Cognitively complex academic instruction through students' first language for as long as possible and through second language for part of the school day; (2) use of current approaches to teaching the academic curriculum through both L1 and L2, through active, discovery, cognitively complex learning; (3) changes in the sociocultural context of schooling, e. g., integration with English speakers, in a support- ive, affirming context for all; an additive bilingual context . . . and the trans- formation of majority and minority relations in school to a positive school climate for all students, in a safe school environment."[49]

Phonics-based instruction in a basal reader series developed for native English speakers and delivered by mainstream teachers with little or no training in working with language minority students does not fulfill any of these conditions. So from a research perspective it is highly unlikely that Proposition 227 will achieve its stated educational goal of ensuring strong English literacy skills for immigrant students.

Critics would argue that its unstated, political goal—making clear to all that despite rapidly mounting legal and illegal immigration the white, English-speaking majority is still in charge in California—was achieved with passage of the bill. Negative educational consequences for immigrant chil- dren only add injury to this insult.

On the other hand, it must be admitted that many TBE programs do not fulfill Thomas and Collier's conditions either. Their research compares "well-implemented, mature" examples of five types of programs for lan- guage minority students. Only two types, Two-way Bilingual Immersion and Late-Exit Bilingual Immersion plus content ESL, showed results in which students met or exceeded the average performance of native English speak- ers. In three types of programs, Early Exit Bilingual plus content ESL, Early- Exit Bilingual plus traditional ESL, and ESL pullout with traditional instruction, the academic performance of linguistic minority students fell well below the performance of native-English speakers. The program type that most closely resembles the instruction mandated by Proposition 227, traditional ESL instruction, produced by far the worst academic results. In simple terms, California has gone from allowing instruction that fulfills some of the three conditions some of the time, to mandating instruction that almost never meets any of them.

This conclusion may require some explanation. In the schools of Cali- fornia and Oakland, as in urban school systems across the United States, most bilingual programs mandate some English grammar instruction every day and a "three-years-and-out" timetable, meaning that after three years the students are supposed to be mainstreamed. Thomas and Collier refer to this model as "Early-Exit Bilingual Education plus traditional ESL." It is called Early Exit because a growing body of research shows that, depend- ing on how old immigrant students are when they arrive and how much formal schooling they have had in their native language (known as L1), they need from five to seven or more years to achieve academic proficiency in English (L2).[50]

Academic proficiency is defined as a level of English which will allow them to perform on a par with native English-speaking classmates on tasks like reading a Dickens novel or a Chemistry textbook, writing a research paper, or answering an essay test question. Most TBE laws mandate that students leave bilingual programs after three years—well before they are academically proficient in English, a set-up for failure in the mainstream. Bilingual teachers know this and often find ways to keep students in TBE longer than the three years provided by law. In addition, in urban areas some bilingual teachers feel their students are physically safer in the bilingual classroom than in mainstream classrooms. When they keep students out of the mainstream, however, they violate the letter of TBE laws and open school systems to the kind of censure cited earlier from the state toward Oakland.

Like other programs in underresourced schools, TBE programs are of varying quality. In many cities, it is hard to find enough qualified L1 personnel to teach in bilingual programs. Thus content area subjects may be taught using techniques that are traditional rather than progressive by current American standards, and English instruction may be provided by an L1 speaker whose own English is less than perfect. In a description that could apply to TBE programs in many mainland cities, the Puerto Rico Department of Education concluded "poor academic achievement in English has been promoted through the use of deficient teaching methods such as memorization and repetition without comprehension," and found that, in Puerto Rico, "The reality is that almost 50 percent of English teachers do not hold an English teaching certificate."[51]

In addition to legitimate criticism, bilingual programs face politically based criticism that is far from legitimate. It is always easy to make bilingual education look bad, for example, by comparing the test scores of language minority students in an underfunded, poorly administered TBE program to the test scores of majority students in a well-funded, well-run mainstream program. Drawing conclusions on this basis is like looking at reading scores from some of the lowest performing mainstream classrooms in New York City and concluding that requiring twelve years of English for all students should be abandoned because it clearly doesn't work.

But when like is compared to like, the most common type of bilingual program in the United States (Early-Exit TBE combined with ESL instruction) falls in the middle range. Students make more progress than they do with ESL instruction alone, but not as much as with Late-Exit TBE or Two-way bilingual immersion.

I have gone into these matters in some detail because, in my experience, few educators really understand either the political or educational underpinnings of bilingual education, and because the complex range of program options outlined in Thomas and Collier represents the real world in which the teachers heard in this chapter live their professional lives. It is time now to turn to their voices.

## LANGUAGE DIVERSITY AND REFORM: SAN FRANCISCO AND OAKLAND TEACHERS SHARE THEIR EXPERIENCES

One common claim of reform advocates is that "raising the bar"—creating common learning standards, enforcing them with high-stakes tests, and punishing students, teachers, and administrators who do not measure up—will diminish the minority/white "achievement gap" by forcing improvement in the lowest-performing schools at the bottom of urban systems. Because such schools commonly have very high percentages of poor African American students and students whose home language is not English, issues of status and power around income and language inevitably come into play.

This is especially true when, as is the case in most urban systems, poorly performing schools are subjected to "intervention," put on "probation," or "reconstituted." These are some of the terms used in various parts of the country to describe the process of dismantling a failing school and starting over again, often from the ground up, with new administrators, new staff, and new programs.

The viewpoints on failing schools held by publicity-savvy district superintendents, state legislators, and private reformers receive regular public attention. To get another point of view, I spoke to teachers in reconstituted or low-performing schools with high second-language populations. The teacher's perspective is certainly not the only significant one in a situation like this, but it is the one we've heard least and one from which I believe we can learn a great deal.

In urban schools politicized by reform, practitioners do not easily open up to outsiders. Veteran teachers and principals have been tested and researched almost beyond endurance, and if someone they don't know walks through the door and says "I'd like you to be honest with me about what's really going on here," the reception can be frigid. Long-term research on such settings can be equally frustrating because staffing, administration, curriculum, and students often change radically from one year to the next.

To gather teachers' perspectives I worked through an established, teacher-centered network they trusted, the Bay Area Writing Project at the University of California Berkeley. I administered questionnaires and conducted interviews and focus groups with nine well-trained, committed, veteran teachers in Oakland and San Francisco who work at low-performing schools. I concentrated on issues that cut across both systems, asking them to discuss their experiences with reform and the effects, as they see them, of language issues on reform. In order to gather responses that were as honest as possible, I agreed not to use any information that could identify them or their schools.

I chose teachers whose subject areas were literacy-related rather than quantitative because I wanted insight into language issues. Four were English ESL or reading/literacy teachers. One taught kindergarten full time and college part time; one taught fourth grade, one social studies. One had recently taken a job as an elementary curriculum specialist for a national reform group after more than twenty years in an elementary classroom.

All held or had held leadership posts related to reform in their schools. These included the positions of literacy coach, coordinator of an accreditation self-study, and teacher-research group leader. Almost all worked in schools where BASRC was active; several were members of their school's BASRC leadership team.

As a group, they had current or recent experience in eight schools (4 elementary, 1 middle, and 3 high—two were from the same school). The youngest had been teaching for six years, the most senior for thirty years; on average they had been teaching sixteen years. Eight were female, one was male. Two were white, three were Asian, one was African American, three were Hispanic.

Their schools were characterized by high percentages of EL students and low standardized test scores. In Oakland and San Francisco as a whole, about one-third of the student body is designated Limited English Proficient (LEP). In the schools I was gathering information about, EL students ranged from 50 percent to 100 percent of the school population; the average of EL learners in the classrooms of the nine teachers was 70 percent. The vast majority of the non-EL students were African American.

In California, all schools are rated yearly on an Academic Performance Index (API) based on student performance on standardized tests. Every school in the state is ranked by a raw score and placed in a decile, or increment of ten percent, that ranges from 1 (lowest) to 10 (highest). Each decile contains 10 percent of all the schools in the state. Seven of the eight schools where these teachers worked were rated three, two, or one in 1999, meaning that 70 to 90 percent of California's schools had better scores. The single exception, a school with an almost exclusively African American student population, had received a rating of five in 1999 but was still scheduled for intervention because it hadn't met its state-set "growth target" of five-percent improvement.

My questions invited a teacher's-eye view, asking for information on the school contexts for reform and the effects of reform on language-minority students. The themes that emerged when teachers answered these questions were nearly identical for both cities. They included an institutional setting characterized by frequent administrative change, frantic pressure to improve test scores, and a smorgasbord of external, grant-funded programs that were embraced not for their programmatic content but because they brought additional resources to the school. Outside programs, usually sponsored by either BASRC or the state, proved to be teachers' most common way of experiencing instructional reform.

Teachers welcomed and valued them, but were also resentful and keenly aware that grant-funded, short-term reforms were an inadequate remedy for years of systemic public neglect and underfunding of their schools. As one put it,

These grants . . . if we're not going to get the money any other way, we have to go for them. I mean, we went for a "digital high school" grant this year. The digital divide is just horrendous, our students have very little access. And we got the grant, so now we're going to have to jump through hoops to keep it. And I know BASRC is looking at getting more funding. If they do, we will jump through the next hoop they throw out to us because we will need the money. And I will resent it every step of the way, but I know we'll do it, because it's the only way we can provide any opportunities whatsoever to our kids.

Another said:

Teachers who are industrious and caring, they're grasping at these reform things because there's not enough in the schools, and basically the lowest income areas, the kids that need the most from the schools, absolutely get the least.

## LONG STORIES SHORT: ADMINISTRATIVE CHAOS, TEST-SCORE MANIA, AND ATTEMPTS AT AUTHENTIC CHANGE IN THREE SCHOOLS

The first step in considering the relationship between language and reform is to examine the school contexts in which learning takes place for EL students. Language issues are imbedded in the day-to-day life of the school, whether a school's leadership focuses on them or not (and as we will hear, language concerns are often last on the priority list). To frame my discussion, from the accounts of the nine teachers I have selected three illustrative stories of the unfolding of reform.

The first is from a teacher I'll call Jill Reddy, a social studies teacher and BASRC leadership team member at a school I'll call Woodward High.

### Jill Reddy: "tremendous political pressure to change, change, change."

We started in the late 1980s by changing our teaching schedule by adding minutes onto the day Monday and Tuesday. We started a Wednesday morning meeting, and as soon as we did that we had time to talk to each other about how the kids were doing terribly at school. And it led to a 1274 grant, a California State reform effort.

And we used that money to move ourselves into what we called smaller learning communities.

So we changed our school into six smaller groups and we based them on careers, in part just because the outside community liked that. We started with one state-funded academy, the media academy. It was followed in the early '90s by an architecture academy. Then we had these little career courses which we helped bolster with the 1274 grant. When that was up in 1996 we applied for BASRC funding, which we got in 1998.

Meanwhile the district in the fall of 1998 blessed us with academy status for all our little houses. And by doing that they actually gave us a partial budget, which was helpful. And we now have four funded academies at the school. So if you think about the fact that we went from one to four, we have a lot more money on campus for our smaller learning communities than we used to. That's a significant change.

I've always felt that it was no way to fund a public school, having to write these constant grants. So as an individual person who's been involved in the writing of the grants, I think it's ridiculous. On the other hand, I feel like we can't function without them. And that's a societal question. Because, you know, our smaller learning communities make a difference when they're functioning. We have about 200 kids in each academy. And I would say we have two very functional academies, one pre-functional academy, one that's now getting the state pressure because they've just gotten state funding, and then two that are not functioning.

Three years ago they added a grade to our school. They just built portables and they absolutely jammed the school. We had about 1500, 1600 kids on campus and overnight it turned into 2200. We now have between five and seven roving teachers every year, which translates to a lot of classrooms being used so teachers don't have their classrooms during their conference periods. The hallways are very, very crowded.

I've been at this school for fifteen years. We've had seven principals. And it looks like we're going to lose our seventh, who I feel understands what we're trying to do, understands the curriculum. We have a new superintendent under tremendous political pressure to change, change, change. I don't think the superintendent's going to last. If they make a change, that will be the eighth leader in sixteen years. I have come to believe that you cannot really make progress with no stability at the top.

Jill's account is interesting in several respects. It presents a picture of a core of activist teachers and administrators attempting to move an under-resourced school forward over a ten-year period by incremental implementation of three related "best practice" reforms that have become very common in urban high schools. These are: breaking a large school down into small learning communities (SLC's), using school-to-career principles as the basis for curriculum and pedagogy in those communities, and revising the school schedule so teachers have common planning time. Federal Perkins Act funding has supported such changes in many places, and at Woodward and elsewhere schools have been opportunistic in combining short-term local, state, and federal funding initiatives, including Annenberg

Challenge funding, to help them move towards a long-term goal: full implementation of SLC's.

At times the district has supported Woodward's work, and this has made a huge difference. But district level priorities keep changing. The current principal has also helped the school make progress; but Jill fears he will soon be gone. The larger picture is one of rapid administrative turnover and frequent top-level policy change that has frustrated rather than aided school-level efforts. The addition of a raft of new students to the school with no planning or adequate resources for integrating them has further retarded the school's progress. The bottom line is that constant "change, change, change" has upset the balance between stability and growth that is an essential element in any successful reform. If reform is good, more reform is *not* always better.

The second story, in some ways different and in some ways quite similar, is from Clara Farina, a young English/ESL teacher at Sifton High School.

### Clara Farina: "So you see what I'm saying? Like every time you turn around."

I've been at my school for three years, I came in after the school was reconstituted. Reconstitution is in response to a law to equalize education for students. When a school has low enough test scores consistently for a couple of years and a high number of minority students, the district will come in and the school gets extra funding and you have one year to bring up your test scores. And if you don't bring them up, then you get reconstituted. Basically every person at the school gets fired and has to reapply for a job at the school.

So anyhow, at our school about 50 percent of the teachers were hired back, re-hired to the school, which is a pretty—that's a high percentage. Because most of the time it's like 95 percent of the school is new after reconstitution. So I came in at that time.

Since that time there's been constant reform and it's going one way or the other way like crazy since I've been there. The first year I was there it was just upheaval because there was so much political activity going on, because 50 percent of the staff was new. Most of the teachers had been teaching there for at least 20 years and then half of them were gone. So all these new people come in and the people that had been there were just like, you don't even know what's going on here and you don't know what you're getting yourself in for.

There was a lot of fighting, I want to say, between the staff. A lot of pressure from outside and inside; it was everywhere, even from the students. The administration was all new, trying to change things and say, you can't do things how you did them in the past. But still, test scores didn't go up in that year despite the efforts.

Then the next year we had a visit from the state regarding the ESL and bilingual compliance. And that was also the year that 227 came in. We had a lot of students who were still designated as bilingual ESL students who had been in the country for like twelve years of school, or had been in school for nine years, because they hadn't met the exit criteria.

So we had to move all those kids to mainstream. And again that year we had about 50 percent staff turnover and things were still going crazy. And then suddenly somebody realized about midway through that year that our school was going to be visited by the state for accreditation.

I was the coordinator of that accreditation project. Normally, I guess, schools will take about a year and a half to get ready for that. Well, we never got the information that we were going to be visited by the state until about April of last year. So that whole process has to happen in half the time. It's self-study and the process is valuable but it's got so much paperwork and so many steps that ideally it would be great, but teachers are completely overwhelmed, especially in a school where you keep on getting new students thrown at you, because somebody's quitting tomorrow, you know. Teachers coming and going.

And then the state came out with this other project called the Immediate Intervention Underperforming Schools Program and our school ranked in the bottom of the state because of our test scores, again. So then in the fall of this past year we got cited for that program, which is another reform effort.

So you see what I'm saying? Like every time you turn around. And then about March of this year we got word that another high school was going to be moved to our school. But the parents from that school were like, we don't want to go to there. But then the other day in the newspaper I read that, unbeknownst to any staff, students, or administrators at our school, supposedly, the first school isn't going to move in with us, but a second high school, that's a charter school, is. So they came and they measured the school. Architects came and they measured the school, but without telling teachers. A couple teachers were like, God, they came into my room and they were like, "yeah, we're going to be doing some work around here, we just need to measure your classroom." Well as it turns out, they were making plans for the charter high to move into our school. And they were going to set up doors so there's a separate school within our school.

Now as far as space goes, it would be possible to do that. But in terms of reform, it will hurt us, and we are actually making some small progress at our school, on test scores and other things. But it's small, and it's not enough for the state. So anyhow, it seems like our school just gets dumped on, and efforts to do reform aren't necessarily respected and given the time that they need to actually start self-perpetuating.

Clara's account gives us a window on a school that has hit bottom and is trying hard to climb back to respectability. Unfortunately, Sifton seems to be firmly mired in a morass of local, state, and federal intervention programs, institutional manifestations of the familiar "quagmire of good intentions."

In "reconstituted" schools like Sifton, teaching and learning often proceed in an environment of constant "churning" in the name of reform. To those above or outside the school, this furious activity may seem a sign of progress. To those inside, it is clear that little lasting improvement is being made.

What happens when teachers and administrators take reform's promise of site-based autonomy seriously, when they reject outside programs and continual churning in favor of long-term, school-generated efforts at improvement? In our third story, Rita Ramirez, a Spanish bilingual teacher and member of the BASRC leadership team at Rivera Elementary School, describes how such a change can occur.

### Rita Ramirez: "Thank you for the money but you need to understand . . ."

I'm a kindergarten teacher. I have a Spanish bilingual class. And we are a leadership school under BASRC.

Our school is one of the few schools in San Francisco that was reconstituted twice. And I think that the story of reform in our school, it's very much described as led by our two administrators. That worries me. I am afraid that when they retire, then we will not be able to sustain it. And for some people and at times for me, that is a problem. But the rest of the time it is such a relief to have somebody who you can trust that their eyes are on the right place and that they're doing things for children, protecting you from all the other stuff. They take care of all this, you take care of the children and the teaching, and that's excellent.

What happened after the second reconstitution of the school was that these two women, my two co-principals who have worked together as professors at a local college and directors of clinical schools, they went to the superintendent and said, okay, we have a proposal for you. We want to take one of your bottom schools, urban schools with children in low socioeconomic levels, and we will put in a program to train teachers for an urban setting. We want to take teacher candidates and put them in a school, not give them the classes at the college and send them to their student teaching, but have them be part of the school for the whole year.

So now we're linked to the college and we have a cohort of thirty student-teachers who are interns in our classrooms in the morning—each of us gets two of them—and in the afternoon the professors from the college teach their courses in a room that is dedicated for that up on the third floor.

We also teach at the college. It puts us in the role of being teachers for our children, teachers for our student-teachers and mentor-teachers within the classroom, and then also professors in the afternoon, or in the evening in many cases. So that's a lot. But it also brings the strength of those student-teachers to the school.

This partnership made BASRC notice us, and I found that BASRC was very personality driven. The people that were our contact people were in love with our school because we were the school that had the highest gains in test scores for four years in a row. So we were their, "Oh, look at them," school and we were in all the national papers and everything.

Then we changed to another test and our test scores plateaued and then slipped down a little bit. And when that happened, all of a sudden the same things that we were doing before were not good.

So this year BASRC gave us a terrible evaluation on our rubric. Our leadership status went from cream of the crop to the dungeon overnight. And we were very, very upset because that happened at the same time that, even though we had made all this progress, the state department selected us as one of the underperforming schools because we were still below where they thought we should be.

When the outside evaluator went to talk to the BASRC contact person for our school she asked her a couple questions about the school and the BASRC person couldn't answer them, and the evaluator said, well, "Have you ever been to the school?" And the woman flatly said, "No, I've never been there." And then the question is, how can you have thrown all these dollars at that school without even having been there? As long as we did what they told us and made them look good that's what they wanted.

But there's new personnel there now, they're saying accountability and meaning it, where before they just looked at the rubric but there wasn't really any accountability. This year when we got a poor evaluation on our rubric, I was very upset at BASRC. Their whole approach was, well the state department says you're lacking, then you're lacking. And I felt that instead of offering help, they kicked us while we were down. After the rubric, you do a report of accountability, and a group of teachers and other people, not BASRC personnel but other people, read and score your report of progress, and score you on the rubric. Well, that document was put together by the principal in one week because the rest of us were dealing with another, state-mandated report and couldn't do anything else really. She couldn't sleep for I don't know how long, trying to put it together. And she was all stressed out. So it didn't work out. They scored us very low and then they said, "We will come and visit the school." It turned out that the team leader had no idea what our program was. Once she walked through the building she said "Give me the rubric back" because she saw what the reality of the building was. Well the BASRC people told her no, right there in front of us. And it was a big thing, because right there they said, "No, no, no. They stay where they stay in the rubric. They already got their score."

So I really minded. I said, "Well, wait a second. So what was the whole point of this visit? Why were we preparing for this visit? If you were never going to change our score, why do all this? So I felt that their tactics had changed, that they want things done a certain way and they want it now. What is going to happen is that we have said no. Under the state's process we have the time, we're forced to look at ourselves and we're forced to write a plan. That was what we should have done under BASRC, all of us together. BASRC didn't supervise us and now the state is making us do it and sitting down with us and saying, "No, no, no. You will have these timetables, and this is the problem here and this is what we're going to do about it."

So we are saying to BASRC, "You know what? Thank you for the money but you need to understand that now you either stand behind us and support us or you get out of our way. But you will not be pushing us in your direction because we cannot afford it." We now have the opportunity to do what we should have done, which is work collaboratively, all of us, on one plan.

Two lessons stand out from Rita's narrative, both related to the negative effects of using standardized basic skills tests as the sole criterion for judging a school's effectiveness. First, there is ample evidence in Rita's account that important positive changes were happening at the school that had nothing to do with test scores. The partnership with a local college, for example, had significantly improved the climate for teaching and learning. It had also added to the pool of adults in the building working with children, and had introduced prospective teachers to the San Francisco public schools in a positive way. This type of innovation is particularly important in urban communities, where finding and keeping the next generation of teachers is an urgent problem.

Second, after four years and using a new test, the school's scores leveled off, a phenomenon that should be familiar to anyone at all experienced in this type of testing. Yet in the eyes of the BASRC partner, the school fell from exemplar to failure based solely on the fact that scores were no longer shooting up. The partner had no real understanding of what was going on at the school, but was willing to tout the school as a national model based on a single number—the test score. When that indicator changed, the partner's attitude towards the school changed too.

From Rita's point of view, the process dictated by the state for improving the school was better than, and the opposite of, the process advocated by the Annenberg partner. In Rita's words, "you will not be pushing us in your direction because we cannot afford it," meaning that the school could no longer afford an approach to change dictated by someone unfamiliar with the school in which test scores are the only measures that count.

### What the Teachers Said about Reform's Effects on Instruction

In talking about ELD, EL, or bilingual instruction in schools, we are always also talking about issues of power, culture, and identity, for such issues are imbedded in instruction. There can be no completely decontextualized instruction because there is no such thing as decontextualized language. According to Lilia Bartolomé, who has done extensive research in this area:

The very real pedagogical entrapment experienced by linguistic-minority and other working-class students contradicts much of the "common-sense" presumption that in school settings, teachers actually teach students more "academic" ways of communicating and students simply fail to acquire these more advanced communication skills . . . there is . . . a tendency to glorify and romanticize a particular type of academic language discourse that is inaccurately referred to . . . as "decontextualized" language . . . language production for meaningful communication cannot be achieved outside the cultural context that gives the produced language meaning in the first place.[52]

Because purely technical discussions of instruction for language minority students touch only part of the actual teaching context, I will frame my discussion of reform's instructional effects broadly. I will consider three important contexts: (1) the context of whole-school change, as described in the three stories above; (2) the attitudinal context set by mandated testing and mandated movement of EL students into English-only classrooms; and (3) the pedagogical context of what happens in both English-only classrooms and in bilingual programs.

### The Whole-School Change Context

The three stories above illustrate the diverse, sometimes contradictory welter of attitudes and programs that can descend on an urban school targeted for reform. The stories show how essential good leadership is for sustaining change, how rare such leadership is, and how at risk even the best principals can be when test scores are the only measures used to judge progress.

The kinds of culture and climate issues described in the stories are directly connected to classroom instruction. The way individual teachers perceive their students, the kinds of instruction they feel permitted to use, the materials they are given to teach with—all of these are heavily influenced by reform-driven changes like outside partnerships, mandated curriculum, and "best practice" staff development. Whole-school change initiatives reduce teacher autonomy—a good thing, in the eyes of many reform advocates—but in so doing place a heavy responsibility on their district and state level authors to dictate changes that are all moving in the same direction, that share a common philosophy.

Because, as we have seen in the last chapter, the politics of reform has been as influential as its pedagogy, this philosophical consistency has seldom occurred. Instead, teachers and principals have been stripped of autonomy, been given back a kind of pseudo-autonomy, and then made to sort through a shower of instructional mandates and exemplary programs that are frequently contradictory. Nowhere is this more true than in the area of instruction for language minority students. In the name of making ELL instruction simpler and more effective, reform-introduced contradictions are often making an already difficult area of teaching even harder.

In the whole-school change context, two responses are common: ELL needs get ignored because other needs are so urgent, or they are dealt with inappropriately by uncritically applying mainstream solutions to this quite different population. Consider this exchange at a focus group that included both mainstream and bilingual teachers:

*Carmen:* "Our kids don't have a loud voice. The rest of the kids have so many problems that our ELD kids, they're just not center stage in any way, shape or form."

*Jill:* "In schools that have reform initiatives, unless the preponderance of the community is second-language learners, the needs of the second language learners get sidetracked by the overwhelming needs of the entire school. The school where I am now, the Spanish bilingual program is one-third of the school, and it will get even smaller now, I know that. I see the needs of the ELD students, but I have done very little as part of a BASRC leadership team that responded specifically to the needs of the second language learners. Our team has responded to the overwhelming needs of the school. We pick a program. We went with staff development as the answer to our needs, something like reading recovery based training for teachers. But what do I know about the services they have for Spanish bilingual children? I didn't even ask the question. And when I saw that, I just went like, oh Jesus, you know, I feel like a wreck. But it's true because you're looking for what's best. The part cannot be better than the whole, so you have to improve the whole before your part."

*Betsy:* "At our school, more than 50 percent of students are not native speakers of English. And we have a similar problem. For example, we have this new ninth grade team program—anybody that is going to teach ninth grade will teach only four classes. All the classes are going to be limited to twenty so four teachers are going to handle eighty kids. Well I'm the head of the ESL/ bilingual program. So how are we going to parallel this with the ESL kids? What are we going to do with our kids? And then overwhelmingly the response was, we can't possibly do that for the ESL kids right away, because the other kids have too many other issues and too many levels."

*Rita:* "Sometimes what's good for the goose is assumed good for the gander, and it isn't necessarily so. And we just import solutions from one program to the other program, without having the time to really sit down and look at them . . . somebody makes the solution, then they say to the teachers in the bilingual program, you're going to have to do the same thing, without really listening to their voices and their solutions and that's another form of disrespect. If you as a teacher over there wouldn't like me telling you how to do your job, how to group your children, then don't do it to me. And that causes a breakdown in communication and isolation of the teachers that are working with the second-language learners."

### The Attitudinal Context Set by Mandated Testing and Mandated Movement of ELL Students into English-Only Classrooms

Two of the core beliefs of the current school reform movement are that home and school should work together and that students learn faster and better when teachers use "best practice" instructional techniques. For language minority students, these core beliefs can be directly at odds with two other core elements of reform—hyperemphasis on mandated standardized tests given solely in English, and movement of large numbers of EL students into the mainstream with little more than short-term, emergency staff development to prepare teachers to work with them.

At the school and classroom levels, the negative social attitudes transmitted by these mandates undermine attempts to bring home and school together and to institute best practice pedagogy. Adhering to the mandates can place schools and individual teachers in the position of insulting the home and actually separating the children from their parents and grandparents through language. Parents may feel that they're losing their children, and that the school's instructional and testing policies are a primary agent in this loss.

Instructionally, there is a similar contradiction. What we know about best practice for language learning generally and EL learners in particular is at odds with the pedagogy promoted by an English-only, test- and standards-driven environment.

This point was made very strongly by the Oakland and San Francisco teachers to whom I talked. They felt frustrated and trapped by the ways in which English-only laws and standardized testing were changing the relationship between language minority parents and their schools. These teachers understood that a message has been sent by California's political majority and has been received, loud and clear, by the parents of language minority students. The message, in the words of Jill Reddy, is "Your language is worthless."

Jill described her school's efforts to get Latino parents to school for an important meeting, and the parents' consternation when they found that only a handful of the school's English-speaking parents were in attendance. The Latino parents demanded to know, "where are the rest of the English-speaking parents, because whatever we say here has no value without them being here, because (the school) won't believe us." The Latino parents were sure that their voices alone would count for nothing. Jill was bitterly disappointed, but also recognized that, given the political climate, the Latino parents' position made perfect sense:

Oh man, that to me was like a stab. It was a huge stab. But it was real. That's how they feel. That's what they believe, that's what they've lived, that's what we're told. I mean, the laws are saying it, right? Your language is worthless.

One of the teachers I spoke with taught in a school with a majority Latino population and many Latino role models among teachers and administrators. The school also had significant populations of Chinese students and several other language groups. She felt that the Latino students were having problems with the home/school split, but their majority status in the school at least gave them a platform from which to discuss it. The other groups, however, were too ashamed to even name the problem:

The Latino kids at our school right now are having a big problem with the split, the conflict between their home and their public lives, whereas there are a lot of other kids that are just totally embarrassed to bring their parents around. They don't want you to call their parents, they don't want any kind of involvement.

Stories like these remind us that, in poor communities especially, schools are powerful mainstream institutions. Through the attitudes they display towards language, they can promote English as a complement to immigrant students' home languages and cultures, or use English to drive a wedge between generations, forcing students to choose between the values of their parents and grandparents and academic and economic success in contemporary American terms. Consider this exchange that began when Carmen described a policy at her school in which, to promote English learning, language minority students were told that their parents must speak only English to them while helping them with their homework. The policy rose directly from the unthinking use, with language minority students, of an "exemplary" reading program that had been developed for native English speakers:

*Carmen:* "These (teachers) should have known better, and here they were saying how they were encouraging the parents to read to the children and they were complaining about the parents not reading to the children. But their reading program required parents to read to the children in English. So, *hello!* And to speak to the children in English.

And . . . they were making these parents feel guilty because the parents were not speaking English to the children. And I thought we had left that way back there. And I had to say, hey, then you're limiting the conversation to what the parents can say in English, not to all that the parents could teach the children if they could do it, if you encouraged it. So they were like giving brownie points to the parents for speaking English to their children."

*Rita:* "Well, research shows they need to keep the home language alive. They need to encourage higher levels of comprehension. They need to encourage getting a book and having sustained silent reading at home, a book that really is of the child's interest."

*Jill:* "But it's so powerful in our culture to not respect what a language brings. So if a child can speak to their grandparents, then they have access to their grandparents' whole lives—all their stories and their history. We don't respect that in this culture. That's not part of the culture of power. I had a very poignant discussion with one of my students who's a junior in high school—very strong student, very strong English skills—who told me that she didn't talk to her parents very much. Basically they don't communicate very much because her Vietnamese is not very good. And her parents don't speak English. I thought that was tragic. I couldn't imagine having a sixteen-year-old daughter and not conversing with that child."

This exchange reminds us that schooling has more purposes than just high test scores. For immigrant students, achieving success can be a devil's bargain. If separation from home and family is the price of academic success, is the school doing its job? If building strong ties between home and school is a basic tenet of reform, can reform be achieved through policies whose basic message is "your parents' language is worthless"?

As one of the teachers pointed out, such policies ignore the fact that "the home language is a learning language." Parents can help their children learn math, chemistry, history, and other subjects perfectly well by working with them in Spanish, Arabic, or Cantonese. When schools dismiss the home language as a powerful learning language, they change the way students look at their parents and grandparents and leave children stranded between two worlds. Accepting the home language as a learning language can help children bridge those worlds. But schools in urban areas too often assume that parents' low economic status automatically translates to low status for the language they speak. Thus teachers may proudly sponsor "fun, food, and festivals" multicultural celebrations while never considering their attitudes towards minority languages as learning languages. Consider this discussion between Carmen and Rita:

*Carmen:* "Spanish is still not considered an academic language and is still not considered a language of money. So you might feel very proud of your culture and your language but—"

*Rita:* "It has nothing to do with school."

*Carmen:* "Exactly. (In the classroom) I can have Our Lady of Guadalupe here and the Aztec calendar there, and that doesn't mean much because Spanish is not a language associated with (learning). On the contrary, in order to succeed in academia you have to divorce yourself from your Latino heritage, and identifying yourself very much as a Latino means that you are gang bang. And you see that dichotomy in the kids."

It's a small step from "your language is worthless" to "you are worthless." Valuing home languages as learning languages when language minority students are pushed into the mainstream can help send a different message: "Your language is worth something, your family is worth something, you are worth something. Your family can use your home language to help you learn better in school."

### The Pedagogical Context of English-Only Classrooms and Bilingual Programs

The quickest way to get a handle on language-related pedagogical issues in relation to reform may be to look at how schools handle expository writing. For both English-only advocates and language minority communities, expository writing tasks carry symbolic value as markers of mainstream culture. In the words of a bilingual teacher from San Francisco: "When you talk about the language of power, the expository essay is definitely a form of that power. And certain cultures think linearly and in outlines, but other cultures think in different ways."

Both mainstream and bilingual teachers consistently mentioned pedagogical innovation around expository writing as a positive focus for instruction in their schools. Experimentation in this area included related "best practice" innovations like alternative assessment, cross-curricular planning, and effective parent outreach. Teachers saw activities in this area as direct counterweights to the negative effects of standardized tests and Proposition 227. They also identified professional development and other supports (e.g., time, money, materials) from agencies such as BASRC and the California Department of Education as essential to their efforts to reform their schools' practices in this area.

Shirley describes a three-year process in her school that includes all of these elements:

I wanted to tell you about our alternative assessments at our school. We use SAT nine data as one set of data, but we've come up with our own assessments that in the long run are supposed to inform teaching. One assessment that we've come up with—and this is our third year doing it—is the interdisciplinary senior project. And for this each senior is required to write a seven-to-ten-page paper on an international debatable topic, with thesis, evidence, parenthetical citations. It's a formal research paper. And several subject matter classes get involved in shaping this and supporting kids through this, and then the idea is that the entire faculty gets trained in the rubric and the scoring of this. And for two years we were given enough professional development that we were able to get the whole faculty involved, in scoring these senior projects.

After we looked at the data on the senior projects during that first year, we said, well, a lot of kids complained that suddenly in the twelfth grade year they were required to write this huge thing, they were unprepared, they needed earlier notification. So then the second year we said, well maybe let's institute something in the sophomore year. So another tenth grade teacher and I did a sophomore project. . . . So going into this coming year, the last year of BASRC, we have a sophomore project in place, still to be tweaked and refined, and then we have a senior project in place still to be tweaked and refined. We had a parent night where we talked about nothing but data. We showed parents the data from the senior project the last year and how things went. And the data collector disaggregated the information and we tried to focus on who's scoring low and who's scoring high and tried to have a conversation around that.

Another assessment that we have for our own data is the schoolwide writing sample. Ninth, tenth and eleventh graders are required to take a writing sample twice a year, once in November and once in April. And here again, this is just our school thing. They take this test pretty cold in October and November. Well, every year we decide on what kind of essay we want to focus on, so we make a decision as to what kind of essay. The last two years it's been the reflective essay. So this is announced in the beginning of the year. And then for the rest of the year teachers are encouraged to teach reflective writing in their subject matter.

I asked Shirley, "As a teacher, what information do you get from these projects and alternative assessments that you don't get from standardized tests?"

Number one, kids are more invested in these two assessments. . . . And also I think the teachers definitely were looking at college skills, so this paper is not just a report of information, but it's really critical thinking, critical analysis. . . . So it promotes a higher level of thinking and it definitely gives lower grade teachers things to work toward, and we realized this year that we need to definitely embed bits and pieces of it into the lower grade levels. So definitely it informs teaching, and that's what I like about it.

So we look at the scores and we say, well, how did the kids do and why did some of the kids not perform so well? Number one, they needed more training in maybe paraphrasing information. They needed more help in thesis formation or gathering evidence. So these are bits and pieces that could be embedded into instruction at the lower levels. So I like that.

Then we set up a parents' night to explain the data, and parents came. We had a good many Latino parents come. We wanted them to come, we wanted African American parents to come. We provided Cantonese translation and Spanish translation. Some of the folks had to work really hard all night long just translating things.

These school-developed rubrics seemed to be powerful tools both in ELD instruction and in native language instruction in bilingual programs. One high school teacher described a program similar to the one outlined above, and then mentioned that students who had not yet reached academic levels of English proficiency were allowed to complete their research projects in Spanish, and this had made a tremendous difference in keeping them engaged.

The importance of rubrics developed on-site and assessment results that help teachers improve their teaching was mentioned by Jill as well:

About the looking at student work. We've had senior projects at Woodward since 1993, and what finally brought up the quality was looking at—with the whole staff—looking at taped examples and throwing out a rubric. And everybody argued about where they fell. And what came out was a much better rubric, and then the rubric went out to the students. You know, it's just the simple, basic process of making it very clear about what was good and what wasn't. And we've seen a real upping of the quality of the senior projects.

But I think that looking at student work and trying to really make it clear to the students what's expected is the whole thing, that's the name of the game. None of that's reflected in standardized test scores, including essay writing. I mean, I feel passionately that my students need to be able to write expository writing. That's one of my jobs as a social studies teacher in high school. They have to be able to back up and be persuasive. They have to be able to back up their opinions with facts. That's not reflected on a standardized test.

We've been able to make these things happen because of the BASRC money. Without funds, once again, you can't have teachers come in on a Saturday or do extended hours and collect these papers. The funding is crucial.

At the elementary level, a San Francisco teacher in a largely bilingual school had high praise for a model called the Authentic Language Assessment System (ALAS):

ALAS has made us talk together as a group, and I think that's the value of teaching right there, is that collaborative working, that coming together and talking about our children and looking at their progress.

I mean, the focus of this particular work is on writing, and we came up with a 14-point rubric that the teachers made up, and it's a developmental rubric that flows with the child wherever he or she may be, actually from pre-K to five. It's the one piece that we have formed a common language around as a staff. Our principal has made us come back around the table and look at each other once a month. "Here are my writing samples, let me see yours."

Similar praise was given to alternative assessment efforts in reading. Rita and Carmen described the effects of the state's "results assessment initiative" and contrasted its usefulness to the non-useful STAR test, also required by the state:

*Carmen:* "You know, the state department sponsored this results assessment initiative, training for elementary school teachers, during the summer, in a package of assessment tools for the different grade levels."

*Rita:* "For reading."

*Carmen:* "For reading, right. And it was just amazing, because each one of the grade levels had a different set of assessments. And the data that was collected from there was put into a website. And then you got this fancy, multi-colored printout—these are the children that have met the benchmark by the middle of the year, these are the children that have not. What was amazing was that we had been trying to push for a common assessment plan at the school and because of the competing prima donnas every person was—you know, some people wanted to do it and some people didn't want to do it because they didn't want to compromise. And having a common assessment pool was so valuable when you sat down and you said, okay, let's look at these kids. Who and where are the problems?

So we realized fluency was a problem. Children were reading well but they were reading too slowly and we know if there's slow reading, comprehension is compromised. So we were then looking at other things that we can do and having activities in the classroom that were really tailored to the needs of the groups of children that presented a particular profile or a particular need. So that was like really, really valuable to have those other assessment tools. And it provides information that absolutely the STAR test cannot give you, because the STAR test, like by the fourth grade, if the kid is reading way below, then how much below the 50th percentile can you be? So you got the three questions that are very easy in that section, everything else you have wrong, and pretty much you were overwhelmed by it, while these other tests are really informative tests."

*Rita:* "Right."

*Carmen:* "Not to rank you, but to tell me what it is that you need help with. And they can be scored and they can be presented and they can be reported and they can be reliable. So I do not understand how if we can come up with a group of assessments that can really inform practice and that really responds to what we're trying to teach, if there are things like that and it was so easily—not easily, but if it was put in place in a couple years and it can get improved, then why the STAR test? It has nothing to do with our standards. The STAR test has no correlation to our curriculum."

## CONCLUSIONS

Linguistic minority students are one of the fastest-growing populations in urban schools today, and finding better ways to meet their needs is one of the great challenges facing urban reform. Unfortunately, reform has too often dealt with these students in one of two ways—by ignoring them, or by applying solutions appropriate to mainstream students and blaming linguistic minority students and their teachers when the solutions don't work.

In this chapter I have taken a close-up look at conditions in San Francisco and Oakland to give a local face to this national problem. In these cities roughly half the students have a home language other than English; the global has truly become the local. I have presented teachers' accounts of their schools in some detail, because I believe the conditions and attitudes they describe are typical nationally. In the wake of Proposition 227, language issues are highly visible in California: attitudes have hardened and battle lines have been drawn. But there are cities and schools throughout the United States with conditions and attitudes similar to those described here.

I have argued that the responses which systemic reformers have made to language minority issues are often both ineffective and contradictory, and that improving current conditions will require acknowledging and resolving reform-authored paradoxes. One way to do this is to begin from a stance that involves what Elbow calls "embracing contraries" and Fullan calls "incorporating resistance." In this concluding section I will identify three such paradoxes and suggest ways of resolving them.

### Paradox One

*Reformers commonly mandate solutions for "whole school change" and systemwide reform which use research-based "best practice" strategies. Yet few professionals in key reform positions are knowledgeable about comparable research and "best practice" strategies for language minority students.*

One of reform's goals is to bring best practices to failing schools. Much effort is devoted to identifying and disseminating optimal techniques for both teaching and school management. Yet an entire body of research on best practice has been largely ignored because it looks at pedagogy within a wider cultural framework that includes consideration of power relationships between dominant and subordinate groups. This growing body of work, largely produced by minority scholars, is especially compelling in the area of language and literacy. Scholars such as Au, Bartolomé, Cummins, Delpit, Gee, Leistyna, Macedo, Moll, Montero-Sieburth, Nieto,[53] and many others have made substantial contributions. Because the orientation of these scholars is sociocultural rather than systemic, their contributions have been largely ignored by the mainstream policymakers and implementers of urban reform.

Many systemic reform advocates are uncomfortable with such approaches because they consider them too "political." But as we have seen in the previous chapter, few areas of American civic life have a longer political history than schooling. This research may be being ignored because it raises uncomfortable questions about reform's good intentions, suggesting darker motives than civic virtue for the close involvement of corporate chiefs and other establishment figures in the control of urban schooling. Bartolomé, for example, points out that,

The solution to current underachievement of students from subordinated cultures is often reduced to finding the 'right' teaching methods, strategies, or prepackaged curricula . . . it is erroneous to assume that blind replication of instructional programs or teacher mastery of particular teaching methods, in and of themselves, will guarantee successful student learning, especially when we are discussing populations that historically have been mistreated and miseducated by the schools.[54]

Even on a technical level, reform advocates have paid little heed to research approaches and best practice solutions developed specifically for linguistic minority students. Typically, reform planners can cite the research on whole school change, small learning communities, school to career curriculums, school site decision making, parent outreach, and Success for All-type reading programs. But few have any knowledge of, for example, Krashen's Monitor Model, Cummins' work on additive and subtractive bilingualism and empowerment pedagogy,[55] Bartolomé's studies of the teaching of academic discourse,[56] Montero-Sieburth and Villaruel's work on the social and educational contexts for Latino academic achievement,[57] Thomas and Collier's studies of the comparative success of various program models for ELL students,[58] and Hakuta, August and Beatty's work on bilingual education.[59] If we are serious about reforming schools with high linguistic minority populations, knowledge of the second set of approaches must become as common as knowledge of the first.

As a start, districts should routinely include bilingual educators and other language minority teachers and advocates in all reform conversations and planning processes, at every level, and take their knowledge and input seriously, even if it seems to be slowing down implementation and leading to conclusions contrary to the prevailing way of doing things. In my experience, such inclusion, and serious attention to the resulting input, is the exception rather than the rule.

Further, if they are going to mandate changes that directly affect this population, reform planners have an educational and moral obligation to become familiar with best practice in this field, even if some of its approaches and implications make them uncomfortable. In this area as well, such familiarity has been the exception. Instead, research and best practice strategies for linguistic minority students have been ghettoized in reform thinking in the same way linguistic minority students are ghettoized in reforming schools.

### Paradox Two

*Districts are acutely aware of the key role principals play in the success or failure of reform. To improve principals' performance, many districts have instituted strict accountability standards and created "best practice" administrative development programs. Yet few districts have held middle and upper management accountable for the effects which their own attitudes and policies have had on principals, or asked what middle and upper management can learn from principals about school leadership under reform.*

The importance of strong, stable school leadership was strongly confirmed by the Bay Area teachers I interviewed. Unfortunately, so was the difficulty of finding and keeping such leadership. As teachers of and advocates for linguistic minority students, they recognized the vital role strong school leaders could play in setting a climate and supporting programs that enabled their students to succeed.

The typical experience of these teachers was the "revolving door" principalship, and they took it as an article of faith that if a good principal did show up, the district was bound to move him or her before long. What surprised me, as conversation progressed, was the extent to which the minority teachers were both attracted and repelled by the idea of becoming principals themselves.

Senior teachers are a primary pool from which new principals are drawn. Teachers are acute observers of the principalship, because their principal has an enormous and direct effect on their lives. The observations of teachers I interviewed help explain why fewer and fewer qualified applicants are seeking principalships under reform. One discussion between Ana, Betsy, and Carmen started with them comparing various principals they had experienced:

*Betsy:* "One principal hired me and he left that year. He was a sweetheart and he had the school for a long time. Then we had one principal who lasted nothing, he was awful. Then we had another principal who lasted a few years but did not have good leadership and there were big problems, and then there was another principal and another principal, so I was there for at least six principals in something like ten years."

*Ana:* "I was trying to think when you were saying that. I would say we had six principals—three interim and three regular—in the fifteen years I've been at the site."

*Carmen:* "I've never experienced a principal to stay longer than three years."

*Ana:* "We've had long and short. Right now we're going through the very short period. So this new guy coming in, he's from out of district so I'm holding my breath because the last guy who left with a bloody nose and nervous breakdown was from another district and just from that alone it's like, oh my God, out-of-district guy, we're going to really have to break him in."

Betsy, Ana, and Carmen seemed so hardened to principals' comings and goings that I asked, "Did any of you ever have the desire to be an administrator yourself?" Their responses surprised me, and suggest that the enormous demands and pressures urban districts now place on principals have a great deal to do with the shrinking pool of strong candidates, particularly female and minority candidates:

*Ana:* "You know, I interviewed last year for principal at our site because I was really pressed by my school community to do it. I had just finished my Master's program. I thought, what the hell, why not? I was real cocky. I did it, I interviewed. And after I interviewed I left there hyperventilating. I thought, oh my God. I can't breathe, I can't sleep. I couldn't even eat. That's a big sign for me that something's really wrong. I called after a week, I called downtown. I said, "You know, I withdraw myself. I can't." And I was told that I had been given the position. They were going to give it to me with no experience of administration, nothing. But just because of the committee, the parents, the teachers calling in to get me on there. I couldn't do it. And then I felt like a total shit after that.

I withdrew myself, because seeing all the principals that we've had and seeing how large our school is—well, more than 500 students K-5. The women principals that we've had, one divorced while in administration. I'm married still, two kids, young kids. And the other one was divorced and her kids were already adults. So basically the school becomes their family, right? And I still have my young family and I didn't want to have them orphaned. That was a real big issue for me. I felt I would have had to choose one way or the other, my school or my family."

*Betsy:* "I completely agree with that, because I've thought very seriously about being a principal, but my kids are eleven and twelve, and I just keep making the decision to be with them, I don't want to be gone all the time."

*Ana:* "That's right. If they were older, it'd be different."

*Carmen:* "But I also want to say something about this because when you talk about the district, one of the things I see with the principals, I mean they're going to yank a good principal from our school. I mean, I expect it. If they don't, it will be a miracle. And these principals, the most intelligent, in my opinion, the most caring, the most compassionate and politically savvy people, they don't want to live like that. And you know, (names a principal) do you know him?"

*Others:* "Mm-hm [affirmative]."

*Carmen:* "In a long conversation I had with him he came across as an excellent principal. He said the district made his life so miserable. They pulled him from a very successful school to try to rescue another one. And that's the other thing, is that if a principal is really good in one community then the district has got to grab that person because there's such a scarcity of people that are effective and they stick them into a new place. And so their stress level, it never changes unless they choose not to do that job anymore."

### Paradox Three

*In order to create lasting change, districts must institute complex, long-term practices like "looking at student work," project-based learning, and alternative assessment. But reform itself helps create chaotic, rapidly changing, mandate-governed school environments that make sustaining instructional change difficult.*

Urban school reform is complex, multi-layered, and often self-contradictory. Reform mandates high-stakes, English-only standardized tests and prescribes, for linguistic minority students, reading programs developed for native English speakers. Such mandates are philosophically at odds with equity-based initiatives. Both approaches come under the general heading of reform, and share, at least in the eyes of their authors, the common goal of reducing the achievement gap between minority students and their mainstream counterparts. How can they be reconciled, particularly in difficult urban settings like those described in this chapter?

I would argue that districts must change their approach to reform in three important ways. First, they must promote stability as an essential element of reform, something they have been loath to do because of the political pressure for "change, change, change." Second, they must promote a positive, open climate for language diversity at both the system and the school levels. An open climate would permit, not discourage, school-level autonomy in areas like using the home language as a learning language and allowing some work in the native language by students who are at pre-academic levels of English literacy. Third, and perhaps most important, districts should recognize that, in the face of rapid administrative turnover and rapidly shifting policies, veteran teachers are the most stable element in schools and thus to be valued.

As a group, teachers are not a bunch of incompetents and they are not the enemy. Obviously there are poor teachers and burned-out teachers as well as superior and energetic teachers. But in the conditions that currently prevail, even if districts could wave a magic wand and bring in the smart, committed, low-salaried recruits they claim to want, how different from today's teachers would those recruits look after five years in schools like Woodward and Sifton? Districts must begin to value their teachers as the one stable, long-term element in otherwise chaotic schools, and build on teacher expertise to make long-term change. This particularly goes for experienced, successful teachers of minority students who at present, like their students, "don't have a loud voice" and are "not center stage in any way, shape, or form."

The teaching ranks for the immediate future will continue to be filled by middle class, English-speaking professionals whose primary experience base and cultural orientation are mainstream. In urban areas, where classrooms are made up almost exclusively of non-mainstream students, cultural mismatch between student and teacher is an everyday fact. Veteran minority teachers and experienced, "culturally responsive" white teachers possess a knowledge base that even the brightest, most idealistic new teachers typically lack. As English-only laws, testing mandates, and curriculum policies proliferate, tapping this knowledge is essential if the rapidly growing number of linguistic minority students is to have any chance of succeeding.

## NOTES

1. "Status Dropout Rates, by Race/Ethnicity, Table 23-2," *Digest of Education Statistics* (Washington, DC: U.S. Department of Education, 1999).

2. Colin Baker and Sylvia Prys Jones, "Bilingual Education in the United States," in *Encyclopedia of Bilingualism and Bilingual Education* (Philadelphia: Multilingual Matters, 1998): 704.

3. Ibid., 703.

4. *The American Heritage Dictionary of the English Language,* 4th ed., s.v. "mainstream."

5. Lilia I. Bartolomé, "Beyond the Methods Fetish: Towards a Humanizing Pedagogy;" in *Breaking Free: The Transformative Power of Critical Pedagogy,* ed. Pepi Leistyna, Arlie Woodrum, and Stephen A. Sherblom (Cambridge, MA: Harvard Educational Review, 1996): 231.

6. Public Affairs Office, U.S. Interests Section, Havana, Cuba, *ormhav@usia.gov* (27 January 2001), email to author (checkj@aol.com). Based on estimates by Cuban economist Pedro Monreal and international banking sources; "Family remittances revisited," *Cubanalysis #32,* <*http://www.CUBANALYS@aol.com*> (30 January 2001). Based on data from the Economic Committee for Latin America of the United Nations (CEPAL) and the Anuario Estadistico de Cuba, 1996, 1998.

7. Peter Elbow, *Embracing Contraries: Explorations in Learning and Teaching* (New York: Oxford University, 1986): 4, 142.

8. Albanian, Catalan, Franco-Provencal, French, Friulian, German, Greek, Ladino, Occitanian, Romany, Sardinian, Croat, and Slovenian.

9. Patricia Corbett, "Foreign Affars: Babel All'italiana," *The Atlantic Monthly,* May 1994.

10. "Tanzania," *The World Factbook,* <*http://www.cia.gov*> (19 January, 2001).

11. *Proyecto para formar un ciudadano bilingüe/Project for the development of a bilingual citizen* (Santurce: Puerto Rico Department of Education, 1997): 3.

12. Edward Finegan and Niko Besnier, *Language: Its Structure and Use (*New York: Harcourt Brace Jovanovich, 1989): 312.

13. Members of a community acquiring more than one language natively.

14. Finegan and Besnier, 312.

15. Baker and Jones, 545.

16. See Robin Tolmach Lakoff, "Ebonics—It's Chronic," in *The Language War* (Berkeley: University of California, 2000): 227–51.

17. Rudolph M. Lapp, *Blacks in Gold Rush California* (New Haven: Yale University Press, 1977).

18. *Ward v. Flood,* 48 California 42–26, 1874.

19. Charles Wollenberg, *All Deliberate Speed: Segregation and Exclusion in California Schools, 1855–1975* (Berkeley: University of California, 1976).

20. Wollenberg.

21. Wollenberg, 42.

22. Wollenberg.

23. Albert S. Broussard, *Black San Francisco: The Struggle for Racial Equality in the West, 1900–1954* (Lawrence: University of Kansas, 1993).

24. Broussard; David L. Kirp, *Just Schools: The Idea of Racial Equality in American Education* (Berkeley: University of California, 1982).

25. Doris Renee Fine, *Civil Rights, Uncivil Schools: Disarray and Demoralization in the Public Schools of San Francisco* (Ph. D. diss., University of California, 1983).

26. Ibid.

27. Ibid.

28. Nanette Asimov, "Single Standard for Admissions at Lowell High Exceptions for Income, not Race," *San Francisco Chronicle,* 28 February 1996, A1.

29. Kirp.

30. Ibid.

31. Jesse J. McCorry, *Marcus Foster and the Oakland Public Schools: Leadership in an Urban Bureaucracy* (Berkeley: University of California, 1978).

32. Ibid.

33. Margaret C. Wang, L. C. Rigsby, and Maynard C. Reynolds, eds., *School-Community Connections: Exploring Issues for Research & Practice* (San Francisco: Jossey-Bass, 1995).

34. Ibid.

35. Ibid., 61.

36. Venise Wagner, "S. F. to Dump Its Bilingual Classroom Integration," *San Francisco Examiner,* 16 April 1995, sec. A.

37. Oakland Unified School District Web Site, "School Committee Resolutions," <*http://ousd.k12.ca.us/Amend Res9697-006.html*> (23 January 2001).

38. "Data Quest," California Dept. of Education Web Site, <*http://www.cde.ca.gov/*> (25 January 2001).

39. "Quick Facts about SFUSD/Statistical Information/Demographics," San Francisco Public Schools Web Site, <*http://storm.sfusd.edu/apps/newweb/index.cfm?*> (21 December 2001).

40. "Data Quest," "California Language Census," California Department of Education Web Site, <*http://www.cde.ca.gov/*> (25 January 2001).

41. Baker and Jones, 545–49.

42. "Oakland Test Scores Support Benefits of Bilingual Education," Oakland Public Schools Office of Public Information, 15 July 1998, <*http://www.ousd.k12.ca.us/*> (8 February 2001).

43. Meredith May, "Oakland Speeds Shift to English," *San Francisco Chronicle*, 1 February 2001, A13.

44. Reform legislation, policies, and personnel change so quickly that no school system profile remains current for long. These descriptions reflect conditions up to and including the 2000–2001 school year.

45. *Entry Plan for Superintendent Dennis Chaconas*, Oakland Unified School District Web Site, <*http://www.ousd.k12.ca.us/*> (8 February 2001).

46. Dennis Chaconas, Superintendent's Report, Oakland Board of Education Meeting, 10 January 2001.

47. *School Site Empowerment Initiative*, Oakland Board of Education Resolution 9899–0071, unanimously adopted 10 February 1999.

48. *Educating English Learners for the Twenty-first Century: The Report of the Proposition 227 Task Force* (Sacramento: California Department of Education, 1999): 38.

49. Wayne P. Thomas and Virginia Collier, *School Effectiveness for Language Minority Students* (Washington, DC: National Clearinghouse for Bilingual Education, 1997).

50. Wayne P. Thomas and Virginia Collier. *Promoting Academic Success for E. S. C. Students: Understanding Second Language Acquisition for Schools* (Woodside: Bastos, 1998); Carlos J. Ovando and Virginia Collier, *Bilingual and ESL Classrooms: Teaching in Multicultural Contexts*, 2nd ed. (Burr Ridge: McGraw-Hill, 1997).

51. *Proyecto para formar un ciudadano bilingüe/Project for the development of a bilingual citizen*, 7–8.

52. Lilia Bartolomé, *The Misteaching of Academic Discourses: The Politics of Language in the Classroom* (Boulder: Westview, 1998).

53. Katherine H. Au, "Participant Structures in a Reading Lesson with Hawaiian Children," *Anthropology and Education Quarterly* 11, no. 2 (1980): 91–115; Lisa Delpit, *Other People's Children* (New York: New Press, 1995); James Gee, *Sociolinguistics and Literacies: Ideology in Discourses* (London: Falmer Press, 1990); Donaldo Macedo, Literacy for Stupidification: The Pedagogy of Big Lies," in *Breaking Free: The Transformative Power of Critical Pedagogy*, ed. Pepi Leistyna, Arlie Woodrum, and Stephen A. Sherblom (Cambridge, MA: Harvard Educational Review, 1996); Luis C. Moll, "Some Key Issues in Teaching Latino Students,"

*Language Arts* 65, (1988): 465–72; Sonia Nieto, *Affirming Diversity: The Sociopolitical Context of Multicultural Education* (New York: Longman, 1992).

54. Bartolomé (1996), 230.

55. Jim Cummins, *Negotiating Identities: Education for Empowerment in a Diverse Society* (Ontario: California Institute for Bilingual Education, 1996).

56. Bartolomé (1998).

57. Martha Montero-Sieburth and Francisco A. Villaruel, eds., *Making Invisible Latino Adolescents Visible: A Critical Approach to Latino Diversity* (New York: Falmer, 2000).

58. Thomas and Collier (1998); Thomas and Collier (1997).

59. Kenji Hakuta and Alexandra Beatty, *Testing English-Language Learners in U.S. Schools: Report and Workshop Summary* (Washington, DC: National Academy Press, 2000); Diane August and Kenji Hakuta, *Improving Schooling for Language Minority Children: A Research Agenda* (Washington, DC: National Academy Press, 1997).

*Chapter 7*

# Boston: Three Cultures of Reform

We are always on shaky ground when considering cultural differences. Although it is important to examine how culture may influence learning and therefore achievement in school, the danger lies in overgeneralizing its effects.

—Sonia Nieto[1]

The school reform movement will not foreground issues of race in trying to change schools. Instead, the theory is, "what's good for the goose is good for the gander"—what works for white kids must work for black kids.

—Theresa Perry[2]

## INTRODUCTION

What is culture? In conversation, we use expressions like "drug culture" and "corporate culture," to describe realities of everyday life. Academically, scholars have created more than 160 definitions of culture,[3] including "the totality of socially transmitted behavior patterns, arts, beliefs, institutions, and all other products of human work and thought,"[4] and "a shared organization of ideas that includes the intellectual, moral, and aesthetic standards prevalent in a community. . . ."[5]

Why so many definitions? Cultural influences are pervasive and rapidly changing; definitions help us analyze cultural forces in action and trace their many effects. However, definitions are not enough. Cultural anthropologist Robert LeVine argues that our understanding of a culture relies chiefly on the research methods we use to learn about it, that "formal definitions do little to clarify the nature of culture; clarification is only possible through ethnography."[6]

It is important to know, then, that many current methods for looking at schooling come directly out of culture-investigating disciplines like anthropology and sociology. It is now common for individual teachers or whole faculties to adopt a "multicultural" approach to curriculum or study their own "school culture." Researchers can take a "socio-cultural approach" to school-based problems or look at teaching and administration in terms of a wider "culture of practice." Culture-based approaches have proven especially useful for understanding complex relationships within *urban* schools, which are more "culturally diverse" than ever before.

In my experience, at least three types of cultural influence typically affect urban schools: the influence of ethnic and racial identity, the influence of a building's unique "school culture," and the influence of a distinct "culture of reform" at the level of district, state, and national policy. In this chapter I will build my analysis of the Boston Public Schools around these three cultural influences.

By the first I mean the ethnically or racially centered beliefs, attitudes, and practices of "minority" school populations in relation to those of the mainstream culture represented by the public school, its teachers and administrators. By the second—school culture—I mean a pervasive system of hidden and overt operational rules that create a climate unique to each school. By the third—a culture of reform—I mean the beliefs, practices, and effects of systemic reform at the policy level, particularly in relation to "minority" students.

These three mini-cultures are like powerful trains centered on the same station, the school. If the trains acknowledge each other and operate in harmony, the station becomes a busy, productive place, a center of life in its community. But if each operates as if the other two do not exist, sooner or later the inevitable occurs: a train wreck.

Unfortunately, at the school level these cultures often operate not just independently, but in opposition to each other. The resulting cultural train wrecks have disabled many urban schools. The shiny new Reform Special, manned by an ambitious downtown crew and travelling at full speed, may have run headlong into the School Culture Slow Freight, a lumbering milk train with a crew that has been plying this particular stretch of track for years. Or the Cultural Resistance Ghost Train, running with its lights out and on its own timetable, may have collided with the Reform Express, whose crew never saw it coming because they refused to believe it existed.

Other schools, perhaps the victims of train wrecks in previous years, disable themselves in less confrontational ways, choosing neither harmony nor collision. Instead, all three trains creep at a snail's pace, their engineers constantly scanning the track for signs of trouble. The dreaded wreck is avoided but the school is much less busy and productive than it could and should be.

Boston is filled with powerful trains and interesting stations. For over two hundred years, the city's schools have reflected cultural battles waged in the larger society. In recent decades, in the wake of federal desegregation decisions, Boston gained notoriety as the site of racial clashes over court-ordered busing. During the 1980s and 1990s whites virtually abandoned the public schools and immigration from the Caribbean, Latin America, and Asia rapidly increased. In less than twenty years the system morphed from a polarized, black-white battleground into a multicultural, multilingual mosaic where 85 percent of the students are "minorities."

This chapter will open with a brief multicultural history of Boston's schools. I will then examine each of the three mini-cultures that interact at the school level: the culture formed by the ethnic and racial identities of the teachers, learners, and administrators; the unique "school culture" which influences the terms of interaction; and the "culture of reform" that sets the policy parameters in which interactions occur. The chapter will close with a short set of conclusions about culture and reform.

Throughout, I will explore the impact, on the three cultures of reform, of corporate models and influences. As Kaplan points out, "accountability, standards, and high-stakes testing are at the heart of the corporate vision of school reform. Without this trio, education's business "collaborators" clearly believe, there can be no measurable or significant change."[7] Boston is a particularly fruitful place to study such influences because the city's corporate community enjoys a long-standing, vigorous, and high-level relationship with the public schools.

## DOUBLE SEEING:
## PAST AND PRESENT IN BOSTON'S SCHOOLS

> The past isn't history. It isn't even past.
>
> —William Faulkner

### Introduction

In 1903, in *The Souls of Black Folk*, Massachusetts native and Harvard graduate W.E.B. Du Bois wrote prophetically that "The problem of the Twentieth Century is the problem of the color line." Here he also introduced a concept, *double-consciousness*, which has become seminal for the understanding of American race relations. For Du Bois, the experience of the black American in a white world was characterized not by a unitary "true self-consciousness," but by a duality or "two-ness" which "only lets him see himself through the revelations" of the white world. The essence of double-consciousness was "a sense of always looking at one's self through the eyes of others. . . . One ever feels his two-ness—an American, a Negro; two souls, two thoughts, two unreconciled strivings; two warring ideals in one dark body, whose dogged strength alone keeps it from being torn asunder."[8]

Working collaboratively with the Boston Public Schools over more than twenty years, I have often used a slightly different form of "two-ness," a technique I call "double-seeing." While focusing on the surface of today, I am always aware of the past, shallow or deeper, shining through, shaping and molding the present. I feel that if I see just the present, I see only part of what is really there. In our schools the present and the past, particularly in cultural terms, are in continual, dynamic interaction with each other. To relate present effects to their true causes, present realities to their shaping antecedents, I must practice double sight, viewing the past and present simultaneously, concentrating on the present but always being aware of the past shining through.

### The Burden of the Past

In Boston the past casts a long shadow. From colonial times, political activism has been a Boston avocation, and much of it has involved schooling. The oldest school district in the United States, Boston boasts the nation's first school, Boston Latin (1635), as well as the oldest continuously operating public elementary school, the Mather School (1639) and the earliest school law, a 1647 Massachusetts statute ordering towns with fifty or more children to hire teachers and establish schools based on the town's religious calling.

As the colony grew into a trading and financial center the original, religiously centered notion of schooling began to evolve. Between the Revolutionary War and the Civil War, complex issues of race, class, ethnicity, and religion began to play themselves out through education. At the very time the U.S. Constitution was being drafted in Philadelphia, the Massachusetts legislature received, and denied, a petition for African American access to the public school system. A petition for separate black schools eleven years later met a similar fate. In 1834 the Abiel Smith School, named after the white businessman who endowed it, was built for black children. Throughout the 1840s William C. Nell's Equal School Association boycotted the Smith School and called for "the day when color of skin would be no barrier to equal school rights."

The activities of Nell's group led directly to the filing of Boston's first school desegregation litigation, the Roberts case. On April 8, 1850 the Massachusetts Supreme Court ruled against Roberts because he had not proved that Smith School instruction was inferior to that of other public schools in Boston. Nell and his group then filed bills in the state legislature to end public school segregation; a first bill failed in 1851, but an amended version passed in 1855. In 1855 the legislature passed a bill ending school desegregation, and black children in Boston began attending the public schools.[9]

School battles were also being contested along religious and ethnic lines. In the 1820s and 1830s Boston was notorious for violent nativist feeling against the Irish Catholic immigrants whose children were appearing in the rigidly Congregationalist public schools in ever-increasing numbers. At the same time that the Abiel Smith school was being built, years of bloody Catholic-Protestant battles came to a head when a nativist mob burned to the ground Mount Benedict, a residential girls school and Ursuline convent in Boston's Charlestown section.[10]

These nineteenth century events presaged modern developments in at least three ways. First, the convent burning showed that schools could be a lightning rod for complex religious, class, and ethnic tensions in the larger society—a lesson that was re-learned by the city during the desegregation controversy of the 1970s.

Second, the convent burning and similar violence in Philadelphia and New York led the American Catholic hierarchy to conclude that it could not entrust the education of Catholic youth to the public schools, leading to the establishment of a parallel parochial system. As a memorial, scorched bricks from the Ursuline convent were used in the entry arch to the Cathedral of the Holy Cross in Boston's South End, completed in 1875.[11] By 1884, thirty-five Boston parishes had their own schools.[12] Ninety years later, Boston's parochial schools were to play a role in the politics of school desegregation. Today, some 18 percent of Boston's school-age population attends parochial or private schools.[13]

Third, pressure for school desegregation and anti-Catholic, anti-immigrant violence formed an important part of the context for Horace Mann's decision, in 1837, to resign as President of the Massachusetts Senate and begin his crusade to create public schools as we know them today—free, tax-supported Common Schools operated under civil rather than religious authority. As the twenty-first century begins, Boston and its schools continue many of these same struggles around race, class, religion, and access.

### Desegregation and After

The 1954 landmark desegregation decision in *Brown v. Board of Education of Topeka* caused communities around the country to look more closely at the racial situation in their schools. Boston was no exception. Its black population had grown rapidly after World War II, and the combination of segregated housing and neighborhood schools produced the predictable result. By 1960, 80 percent of Boston's black elementary students attended majority-black schools, which typically meant receiving a substandard education: larger classes in poorly maintained buildings, secondhand books, inadequate materials, and less-qualified teachers. Black parents pressured the Boston School Committee to remedy the situation, but an open-enrollment policy adopted in 1961 did little to change the pattern.

Angry at the lack of effective local response, black parents followed the path pioneered by William Nell over 100 years before and successfully pressured the Massachusetts Legislature to pass the Racial Imbalance Act of 1965, a ground-breaking law which defined any school with a nonwhite enrollment of more than 50 percent as "imbalanced." Strong sanctions could be used against school systems that did not take steps to correct racial imbalance, including denial of all state school aid. But the Act did not require integration of schools, prohibited involuntary transportation of students within a district, and failed to clearly define compliance, so there were many loopholes which school committees, particularly Boston's, could use to avoid desegregation.

By 1971, segregation in Boston had actually increased. According to a report issued by the U.S. Commission on Civil Rights in 1975, black students represented one-third of a total enrollment of 96,000, and over 60 percent of them attended schools that were more than 70 percent black.[14] Boston's black parents turned to the Federal government. In March, 1972 the local chapter of the NAACP filed suit in Federal district court, alleging, "governmental discrimination in creating and maintaining a segregated public school system."[15] The class action suit was brought on behalf of fifteen black parents and forty-three children, with the lead plaintiff a mother of three, Tallulah Morgan. Defendants were the Boston School Committee and its chairman, James Hennigan; thus the suit's legal name of *Morgan v. Hennigan.*

On June 21, 1974, 124 years after the Roberts case, twenty years after the Brown decision, and nine years after passage of the Racial Imbalance Act, Federal District Judge W. Arthur Garrity ruled in *Morgan v. Hennigan* that "school authorities had knowingly carried out a systematic program of segregation . . . and intentionally brought about or maintained a dual school system."[16]

In the wake of this decision, Boston began a long and acrimonious struggle to achieve racial integration by court-ordered busing. Attempts to bus black students from the Roxbury neighborhood into schools in predominantly Irish South Boston turned the city into a "war zone." Boston became nationally known "through televised images and front-page newspaper photographs featuring riot police, state troopers patrolling school corridors, rooftop police snipers, and legions of blacks and whites screaming racist chants at one another."[17] In 1976 the Pulitzer Prize for photography was awarded for a now-historic photo of a black passerby, Ted Landsmark, being clubbed with an American flag by white extremists during an anti-busing rally. The strife generated by the conflict was poignantly chronicled in the best seller *Common Ground,* which used, as one of its three profiles of families affected by desegregation, an Irish Catholic family from Charlestown.[18]

The upheaval surrounding desegregation caused many parents, both white and black, to remove their children from the Boston Public Schools, a withdrawal that continues to the present. In the year before desegregation, 60 percent of Boston's public school students were white. Seven years later, 35 percent were white; by 1987 the figure was down to 26 percent.[19] In 1999–2000 it was 15 percent,[20] and many of these were concentrated in the city's exam schools. The school system is acutely conscious of this issue. Its web site has a section detailing "Students Who Don't Attend the BPS"—a full 25 percent of Boston's school age population. In addition to 14,400 students who attend parochial and private schools, some 2,400 Boston students attend charter schools and 3,000 Boston minority students are bused to suburban public schools each day as part of a state-supported, voluntary, urban-suburban desegregation program. In 1999–2000 the racial breakdown of the 21,000 students not attending the Boston public schools was: 47 percent white, 41 percent black, 9 percent Hispanic, and 3 percent Asian. In comparison, of the roughly 63,000 students who did attend, 49 percent were black, 27 percent Hispanic, and 9 percent Asian.[21]

In contrast, in the same year, 61 percent of Boston's teachers were white, 26 percent were black, 9 percent Hispanic, and 4 percent Asian.[22] In the city as a whole, a little over 60 percent of the total population was white, 25 percent was black, and 11 percent was Hispanic. This distribution is changing rapidly, with Boston's Hispanic population, and to a lesser extent its black and Asian populations, growing much faster than its white population.[23]

It is difficult for outsiders to comprehend how deeply desegregation-related laws and decrees have affected schooling in Boston. Take, for example, the process by which parents choose a school for their child. Beginning in 1974 the process was governed by court-ordered busing to achieve racial balance. In 1987, thirteen years after his original decree, Judge Garrity ruled that the School Committee could adopt a new student assignment plan as long as it did not resegregate the schools. In 2001 the school department described its school assignment process in these words:

BPS elementary and middle schools are organized in three geographic zones. Students are assigned to schools in their zone of residence, based on choice and availability of seats. All high schools are citywide. The School Committee voted in 1999 to drop race-based assignments, a policy that had been in place since 1974. The 1999 plan sets aside 50 percent of a school's seats for walkers and gives priority for remaining seats to applicants who do not live in the "walk zone" of any school.[24]

In another example, consider these events from one five-month period in the mid-1990s:

- On April 12, 1996 Judge Garrity, still monitoring compliance with his 1974 decision, questioned whether Boston was setting aside enough seats for minority students at the examination high schools.

- On April 17, Massachusetts Governor William Weld announced he would press for legislation to repeal the Racial Imbalance Act of 1965.

- On May 15, after widespread protests from parents and educators, the Massachusetts Board of Education backed down on its Weld-inspired plan to ask the legislature to abandon the state's commitment to racially balanced schools.

- Later in May officials in Cambridge, MA announced that they would make the city the first in the nation to desegregate schools not just by race but by income level.

- On August 22, Judge Garrity ruled in favor of a suit brought by a white father alleging that his daughter had been illegally denied a place at Boston Latin School, even though her examination scores qualified her for entrance, because a racial quota system was in place. Garrity ordered the school to admit Julie A. McGlaughlin to the incoming class.

In the late 1990s the school department described itself in these words:

Some of the district's features match the urban stereotype: a recent history of court involvement and white flight, budget cuts and labor turmoil; poverty at 63 percent; dropout rates above 30 percent for most of the past decade; disproportionate numbers of students assigned to remedial and special needs classes; above 30 percent coming from homes where English is not the native language; student achievement levels hovering stubbornly slightly above or below the national averages on standardized tests despite repeated efforts for improvement. . . . Other features of the district contradict the stereotype: We have reversed enrollment trends in the city so that we are growing and our private school competitors are shrinking. We are not isolated from the community. The Boston Compact involving 350 businesses and 27 colleges and universities is a vital force in the district.[25]

### Ethnic Diversity, Poverty, and Language Minorities

The 1980s saw the withdrawal of middle-class students both white and black and the arrival of increasing numbers of non-English speaking students from Latin America, the Caribbean, Asia, and Africa. Boston evolved from a biracial school system to a multiethnic, multilinguistic one attended primarily by poor children of many backgrounds.

The politics of poverty continues to play a large role in schooling. In 1996 twenty-five percent of Boston's children under the age of eighteen were living in poverty.[26] In 1997 "78 out of 125 regular schools qualified as 'concentration of poverty' schools under Title I rules that called for a 75 percent concentration of low income students," and 27 percent of students lived in public housing.[27] In 1999–2000, 71 percent of Boston's students qualified for free or reduced meals.[28]

Second-language issues, almost unknown in the desegregation era, are rapidly becoming a major concern. During the 2000–2001 school year more than a third of all Boston students (34%) needed second-language services.[29] In 1990–2000, bilingual programs were offered to 9,300 students (15% of all students) in nine languages—Cape Verdean, Chinese (both Mandarin and Cantonese), Greek, Haitian Creole, Somali, Spanish, Portuguese, and Vietnamese. Spanish-speakers made up 61 percent of the total bilingual population. In addition, a "multilingual" program provided English as a Second Language Instruction (but no native language instruction), to low-incidence language populations such as Korean, Indonesian, Laotian, Portuguese, Russian, and Polish. Thousands of additional English Language Learners were in regular education classes, many with ELL support.

In October, 2001 students with disabilities (including identified special needs) formed 20% of the student population (the statewide average is 17%).[30] Taken together, SPED/disabled and bilingual/LEP students, who face special learning challenges, particularly in regard to English-based standardized tests, make up over 45 percent of the entire student population of the Boston Public Schools.

### Leadership, Systemic Reform, and Student Achievement

In 2000–2001 Boston had 131 public schools, some 63,000 students, and a budget of roughly $672 million ($575 M from city coffers and $97 M from other sources). The schools were governed by a seven-member, mayorally appointed school committee. Voters chose this format by referendum in 1991 and again in 1996 over the previous thirteen-member elected school committee.[31]

Like many urban systems, Boston suffered for many years from a revolving door superintendency and frequent changes in direction: in the twelve years between 1983 and 1995 the city had six superintendents. Since October 1995 the district has been headed by Thomas Payzant, a career educator who is a former head of the San Diego public schools and assistant U.S. Secretary of Education. Payzant has toughened appointment and evaluation standards for principals, overseen curriculum changes, and created opportunities for a number of national school reform groups to work in Boston. He has also collaborated closely with city's business and philanthropic community, particularly through reform advocacy groups such as the Boston Plan for Excellence (BPE), the Annenberg Challenge, and the Boston Compact. These groups have had a major role in Boston's school reform by shaping policy, by working directly with the schools, and by donating tens of millions of dollars to the school change effort. Payzant has called the Annenberg Challenge, whose programs touch every school in Boston, "crucial, not just for funds but also for ideas, encouragement, discussion, and constructive critique of our day-to-day work."[32]

The Superintendent's major task has been to implement a systemwide reform plan adopted by the school committee in 1999, to "improve teaching and learning to enable all students to achieve high standards of performance." Other priorities of the plan call for the system to:

- Implement a new student Promotion Policy, with strict requirements for coursework, attendance and achievement, to end social promotions;
- Develop summer and transition services for students who are falling behind;
- Close the achievement gap among racial groups by SY2003;
- Begin restructuring high schools to improve student achievement;
- Focus on literacy so all students are reading at grade level by grade 3;
- Improve instructional practice through schoolwide professional development.[33]

To date it is not clear to what extent this ambitious plan is succeeding. In recent years the high school dropout rate has hovered between 25 percent and 30 percent. There is concern that, if the state continues its present intention of using tenth grade Massachusetts Comprehensive Assessment System (MCAS) test scores as the sole criterion for graduation, dropouts will soar even higher.[34]

In June, 2001, over the vocal opposition of black and Hispanic community leaders, the mayor urged extension of Payzant's contract to 2005. Opponents, who included a city councilor and a former president of the School Committee, favored delaying reappointment pending further test results. Many Boston tenth graders failed the MCAS tests and may be denied diplomas in 2003. Speaking for the group, Councilor Chuck Turner said, "We can't tell our children that performance is the key to their success in school and then not hold the superintendent to that same standard."[35] Payzant was re-appointed in December 2001.

As the consequences of poor student performance grow more serious, many in the community argue that reforms have concentrated on peripheral aspects of education and ignored high class sizes, poor learning conditions and a basic lack of educational materials. A columnist for the city's major newspaper summed up the situation:

In some Massachusetts schools, money surges into children's hands. In this capital city on a hill, money surges into marathons, ballparks, designer hotels, and politicians' campaign accounts. But there is not enough money to make sure all of the children in Boston's public schools have all the basic tools they need to learn.

That is the simple truth, even if the city's political, business, and media elite prefer to blame the victims for the system's failure to provide enough money for adequate student supplies, especially books.[36]

## EFFECTS OF RACIAL AND ETHNIC IDENTITY ON
## TEACHING AND LEARNING

Raising student performance on standardized tests is the central measurable goal of current reforms. In urban school systems where "minority" students comprise up to 95 percent of the total population, accomplishing this goal necessarily involves addressing the "achievement gap" between white and non-white students. The strategies systemic reformers have chosen to address this gap have, for the most part, carefully sidestepped issues of race and culture, preferring to emphasize purportedly "race blind" measures like high stakes tests and "exemplary" teaching methods. At the same time, researchers investigating cultural effects on learning continue to pursue useful approaches to the problem of minority student achievement. Their work has received little regard from systemic reformers. Neglect of a broad, deep, and rapidly growing knowledge base on the relationship between cultural identity and schooling can be regarded as a signature failure of urban school reform.

In 1986 Ogbu and Matute-Bianchi summarized the then-current state of thinking around language, culture, and school performance:

In the United States language minorities . . . are among the minorities that experience *persistent disproportionate* school failure. (italics in orginal) There are many competing explanations of the school failure, ranging from genetic deficiency to institutional discrimination. Since the early 1970s some social scientists have, however, increasingly emphasized the role of language and cultural differences. . . . Many appear to have concluded that a major part of the problem lies in the cultural and language discontinuities between the minorities and the schools (an institution reflecting the culture and language of the dominant group in society).

They then went on to say, "Public policy has, as a result, moved more or less in the same direction, generating bilingual and bicultural education as "solutions" to the problem of minority school failure."[37]

At about the same time, Heath identified both a gap and a bias in the existing research. She pointed out that "educators know relatively little" about how language minority children learn to use language and that it was "not possible to generalize" to these children from existing studies "reporting the language learning of mainstream middle-class first-born children, either interacting at home with their parents or in a laboratory with props provided by researchers." The bias caused by this gap in the research arises because "behind language arts curricula in schools stands an image of a 'natural' path of development . . . for all children" based on studies with only mainstream children. Because the "sociocultural, religious, and socioeconomic contexts" of minority learners "often differ markedly" from "mainstream patterns that dominate the thinking of school . . . personnel," there is often a mismatch between "exemplary" curriculum and instruction and the learning needs of non-mainstream groups.[38]

Since the 1980s many things have changed. Urban schools have grown increasingly diverse and typically now contain a majority of non-mainstream learners. Heath and other researchers, including those cited in the conclusions to the previous chapter, have produced a growing body of knowledge on socio-cultural causes of minority school failure. Despite our growing knowledge (or perhaps because of it), public policy and attitudes have done an about-face and are moving rapidly away from supporting culturally relevant solutions to minority underachievement. As California's Proposition 227 attests, states continue to espouse the goal of equal educational opportunity, but religiously avoid culturally based approaches to teaching and learning, preferring to define equity as "one-size fits all" in terms of curricula, pedagogy, and testing. In the new century, the *knowledge gap* identified by Heath has been significantly narrowed, but the *bias* has been enshrined as public policy.

In short, we now possess many of the tools necessary to mount an intelligent attack on the achievement gap, with more on the way. But corporate-influenced reform plans see little value in these tools, perhaps because using them would require both government and the private sector to acknowledge past and current inequities regarding minorities and the poor. School committees rarely address such issues by choice. Most frequently, as in Boston, a legal case followed by a court order forces action after the situation has already reached crisis proportions.

Let me offer an example of the current "race-and-culture-blind" policy. Systemic reformers who regularly call for pedagogical and curricular change based on "best practice" research have consistently ignored research on the learning patterns of non-mainstream students. Instead, school system after school system has mandated literacy programs based on the same fallacy that Heath identified in 1986—that there is a single, "natural" path to language acquisition and it is the one used by middle-class, English-speaking, native-born students. What is worse, these misguided curricular initiatives have then been linked to high-stakes, standardized tests which reinforce with a vengeance the same message: the mainstream way is the only way, and if you differ from it you will be penalized.

Boston's policy approach in this area is similar to that of many cities. The school department's reform plan sets as an explicit goal, "to improve teaching and learning to enable all students to achieve high standards of performance." In support of this goal, the superintendent and school committee have jointly named as one of their priorities, to "close the achievement gap among racial groups by SY2003."[39] Yet in a city whose schools have been riven by racial controversy since the nineteen century and which has grown increasingly diverse, the "exemplary methods" adopted for closing the gap take little or no account of the part racial and cultural factors play in schooling.

Much of this stance has been forced on the city by the state's insistence on using the MCAS test as the sole requirement for graduation. As things stood in the 2000-2001 school year, up to 2/3 of Boston's high school students were in danger of not graduating under this requirement. That percentage represents 2/3 of those who choose to stay in school and take the test, after many students have already dropped out. Researchers studying 1999 MCAS results found that in Boston, 85 percent of Latino tenth graders failed the math and 70 percent failed the science tests and projected that only 15 percent of Boston's Latino students were on track to graduate in 2003. They linked the results to patterns of course enrollment in math and science courses necessary to pass the exam.[40]

Criticism of MCAS is mounting. Parent and teachers groups, as well as many urban school committees in Massachusetts, are actively campaigning to do away with MCAS as the sole criterion for graduation. Susan Goldberger, a Senior Research Fellow of a national reform program that works closely with urban schools, argues that,

For MCAS proponents, higher academic standards, combined with sanctions for not meeting them, is the way to improve urban schools. But the poor performance of urban high schools is not primarily a result of setting standards too low. Rather, low standards are often the consequence of trying to serve a dizzying array of student needs.

(In) the freshman class of a typical Boston high school. . . . Of the first-time ninth-graders, one third are chronic absentees on the verge of dropping out. Among those who attend regularly, a large percentage are immigrants with limited English proficiency and students with some type of learning disability or remedial need . . . raising standards will do nothing to reach the large proportion of students who are disengaged from learning, whether because of past failure, frequent moves, or some other reason.[41]

Even the president of Harcourt Educational Measurement, the Texas firm that holds the $71 million contract to develop and administer the MCAS, has recommended that "no single test be used for high-stakes purposes" and that tests "should be supplemented with other kinds of indicators."[42]

This situation is not unique to Boston or to Massachusetts, and it can hardly be described as a success for "color-blind" reform policies. The most widely known test of this type is the Texas Academic Assessment System (TAAS), instituted in 1990-91, which under the Bush presidency may become the model for a national testing program. By the late 1990s TAAS was being touted as the driving force behind a "Texas miracle" in education that had reduced dropout rates and raised performance for all, including minority students, by introducing tough new accountability measures.

Long-term studies of the "Texas miracle" have now provided detailed evidence that the student performance gains claimed by Texas reformers are largely illusory, that teaching methods and curricula have significantly

narrowed due to TAAS, and that there is a hidden story of damage to
minority populations, particularly Hispanic students, caused by the TAAS
initiative.

A research team from the RAND Corporation compared TAAS data to
Texas student performance on national measures such as the NAEP test,
and found discrepancies between performance gains as measured by TAAS
and by NAEP scores. Apparently, Texas students had succeeded at becoming better takers of the TAAS exam, but had achieved few gains that carried over into other areas, including non-TAAS tests. According to the
RAND team,

The stark differences between the stories told by NAEP and TAAS are especially striking when it comes to the gap in average scores between whites and students of color.
According to the NAEP results, that gap in Texas is not only very large but increasing slightly. According to TAAS scores, the gap is much smaller and decreasing greatly.
Many schools are devoting a great deal of class time to highly specific TAAS preparation. While this preparation may improve TAAS scores, it may not help students
develop necessary reading and math skills. Schools with relatively large percentages
of minority and poor students may be doing this more than other schools. We raise
serious questions about the validity of those gains, and caution against the danger
of making decisions to sanction or reward students, teachers and schools on the basis
of test scores that may be inflated or misleading.[43]

A second researcher, Walt Haney, found that "The passing scores on
TAAS tests were arbitrary and discriminatory. Analyses comparing TAAS
reading, writing and math scores with one another and with relevant high
school grades raise doubts about the reliability and validity of TAAS
scores." He also cites "missing students and other mirages in Texas enrollment statistics that profoundly affect both reported dropout statistics and
test scores."

Contrary to "Texas miracle" claims, Haney found that,

Only 50 percent of minority students in Texas have been progressing from grade
nine to high school graduation since the initiation of the TAAS testing program.
Since about 1982, the rates at which black and Hispanic students are required to
repeat grade nine have climbed steadily, such that by the late 1990s, nearly 30
percent of black and Hispanic students were "failing" grade nine. Cumulative rates
of grade retention in Texas are almost twice as high for black and Hispanic students as for white students. . . . The numbers of students taking the grade ten tests
who were classified as "in special education" and hence not counted in schools'
accountability ratings nearly doubled between 1994 and 1998. A substantial portion of the apparent increases in TAAS pass rates in the 1990s are due to such ex-
clusions. In the opinion of educators in Texas, schools are devoting a huge amount
of time and energy preparing students specifically for TAAS, and emphasis on TAAS
is hurting more than helping teaching and learning in Texas schools, particularly

with at-risk students, and TAAS contributes to retention in grade and dropping out.[44]

Urban reformers may feel that, given the stormy history of urban schools and the part courts have played for almost fifty years, adding racial and cultural issues to the already complex reform process would be counter-productive. What is needed, in this view, is not more but less emphasis on this contentious subject, a return to the true issues of schooling—good teaching, rigorous curricula, accountability. To understand why this "color-blind" argument is fallacious, we need to look briefly at the current status of the concept of race itself, then relate it to current trends in schooling, particularly standardized testing. An essential point to understand as we proceed is that language is a primary aspect of culture, and both tests and instruction leading to tests are not "neutral" but culturally laden and language-imbedded.

### Race as a Cultural, Not a Biological, Reality

Language differences are part of a larger pattern of cultural difference, including race, ethnicity, class, and other factors, that has become increasingly complex in both schools and society. This is true whether we are talking about speakers of a major language such as Spanish or Mandarin, a creole such as Haitian or Cape Verdean, or Ebonics or another form of non-standard English.

Racial differences have long been seen as rooted in biological fact, but over the past decade or so views on what constitutes race have been rapidly shifting. In the 2000 Census, for the first time, the U.S. Government acknowledged biracialism as a possible identity for Americans. In genetic research, DNA-based studies have suggested that there is so little difference in the makeup of various "races" that race is no longer supportable as a scientific or biological category.

In the words of one writer, researchers "have been undermining the wide-spread belief that groups of people differ genetically in character, temperament, or intelligence. . . . They have revealed the folly of attributing group behavioral differences to biology rather than culture."[45] Robert W. Sussman, a biological anthropologist, refers to recent work by colleague Alan Templeton,

The folk concept of race in America is so ingrained as being biologically based and scientific that it is difficult to make people see otherwise. We live on the one-drop racial division—if you have one drop of black or Native American blood, you are considered black or Native American, but that doesn't cover one's physical characteristics. Templeton's paper shows that if we were forced to divide people into groups using biological traits, we'd be in real trouble. Simple divisions are next to impossible to make scientifically, yet we have developed simplistic ways of dividing people socially.[46]

Templeton himself says, "Humans are one of the most genetically homogenous species we know of. There's lots of genetic variation in humanity, but it's basically at the individual level. The between-population variation is very, very minor."[47] Humans demonstrate wide differences in pigmentation, facial structure, hair texture, and other physical characteristics commonly associated with race, but these differences can be as large within so-called races as they are between them.

This is not to say that racial distinctions do not exist. They are real and have a strong effect on human behavior. But race is a cultural, not a biological, entity and is therefore created by mutable social belief systems, not by an immutable genetic order.

So regularly have we altered our official definitions of race, points out economist Carolyn Shaw Bell, that statistical comparisons of racial figures over time are inherently unreliable. In the early days of the national census, which began in 1790, "enumerators" who visited households made their own determinations of race based on observation. By the 1850s,

Census takers were instructed to write white, black, mulatto, quadroon, octoroon, Chinese, Japanese, or Indian. "black" was used to describe people who had three-fourths or more of black blood; mulatto, three-eighths to five-eighths of black blood; quadroon, one-fourth of black blood; and octoroon, one-eighth or any trace of black blood. Thirty years later, they were obliged to label people of mixed white and black blood as "Negro," no matter how small the percentage of black blood. . . . Not until 1960 did people start defining their own identity, . . . the term "black" was substituted for Negro.[48]

The medical and scientific research communities are also seriously questioning the usefulness of current racial categories. For instance, after studying "how well the cancer research programs at the National Institutes of Health (NIH) address the needs of ethnic minorities and the medically underserved," the Institute of Medicine (IOM) recommended that NIH move "away from the emphasis on fundamental biological differences among 'racial' groups to an appreciation of the range of cultural and behavioral attitudes, beliefs, lifestyle patterns . . . and other factors that may affect cancer risk."[49] Even the Office of Management and Budget, which creates and defines racial categories for federal agencies, makes clear that its categories "represent a social-political construct."[50]

### The Racial/Cultural Experience Gap

It makes no sense to talk about the achievement gap in schools without acknowledging the realities of race outside of school. Such a discussion is difficult, because in mainstream discourse these realities have been obscured and denied for years, and only recently has it begun to become legitimate to even raise such issues. Reform plans typically call for "community outreach" and "parent involvement" at the school level, but treat racial and cultural issues that are important to minority communities and parents as if they have no legitimate place in central office policy development.

In any race- and culture-sensitive area, the views of white and minority communities often diverge sharply, as the O.J. Simpson trial famously demonstrated. This is due to a logical but difficult fact: as long as Americans' life experiences diverge sharply along racial lines, opinions will too, because experience shapes opinion. Any conversation, including our national conversation about schools, that does not begin by acknowledging this experience gap risks irrelevance or failure.

Major mainstream institutions outside education, including conservative religious organizations, are recognizing this. Harvard chaplain Peter Gomes, himself an African American, celebrates the fact that,

In the summer of 1995, one hundred and thirty-two years after the Emancipation Proclamation, one hundred and thirty years after the end of the Civil War, and twenty-seven years after the death of Martin Luther King, Jr., at their annual meeting the Southern Baptist Convention, America's largest Protestant denomination, apologized for the role it had played in the justification of slavery and in the maintenance of a culture of racism in the United States.[51]

In March, 1999 the New York *Times* reported this story,

The mention of mass graves brings to mind the genocidal wars that have bloodied Bosnia, Rwanda and Central America. But at its meeting last week, a state commission in Oklahoma discussed its search for mass burials along the Arkansas River in downtown Tulsa and elsewhere in the city. The panel, the Tulsa Race Riot Commission, was created by the state legislature in 1997 to investigate violence that swept the city in 1921. In less than one day, rioting whites killed perhaps as many as 200 to 300 black citizens, burned more than 1,000 residences and razed one of the most prosperous business districts in the Southwest. The exact casualty figures and property losses were obscured in a cover-up that kept the riot out of polite conversation and school history textbooks for nearly half a century.[52]

In addition to owning up to past wrongs, there is also a greater openness in the larger society to acknowledging previously taboo multigroup identifications and exploring the dynamics of race not just between black and white, but within non-mainstream groups. The young Haitian-American novelist Edwige Danticat tells of a reader who approached her at a book signing in Miami:

Before I could sign, he whispered, "Would you please write 'From one AHA to another?' I stopped to ask him what he meant. . . . He said, "Well, AHA, spelled

A-H-A, is an acronym for African American-Haitian. That's what I am. That's what you are." . . . He proceeded to tell me that this was a new way for young Haitians who had been in the United States for a while to define themselves, partly to combat all the negative labels they are bombarded with, among them "boat people" and "the AIDS people."[53]

Veronica Chambers writes on culture for Newsweek magazine and has published books for young adult readers. Issues of cultural and racial identity were constant concerns for Chambers during her school years, and remain so today:

I was born in Panama to black Panamanian parents. My father's parents came from Costa Rica and Jamaica. My mother's family came from Martinique. I left Panama when I was two years old, we lived in England for three years, and I came to the United States when I was five. Having dark skin and growing up in Brooklyn in the 70s meant that I was black—period. . . . As a black woman in America, my Latina identity is murkier than my mother's. Without a Spanish last name or my mother's fluent Spanish . . . I've often felt isolated from the Latin community. Latinos can be as racist as anybody else: there are pecking orders and hierarchies that favor blue-eyed blonde rubios over negritas like me. Sometimes, I feel that I put up with enough racism from white Americans, why should I turn to white Latinos for a second share?[54]

Marta Cruz-Jansen, a university faculty member exploring racism's effects on black Latino women or *Latinegras*, recalls negative cultural messages from her own early schooling:

When I was in third grade, in Puerto Rico, I wanted to be the Virgin Mary for the community Christmas celebration. A teacher promptly informed me that the mother of Christ could not be black. A girl with blonde hair and blue eyes was selected for the role, and I was given the role of a shepherd. In middle school, also in Puerto Rico, I played a house servant for a school play. Only children of black heritage played the slaves and servants. A white student with a painted face portrayed the only significant black character . . . I learned then that non-white persons could not be anyone or anything representative of the nation's greatness but could only serve as servants and slaves to the great white leaders.[55]

Cruz-Janzen, voicing a view held by a number of anthropologists,[56] argues that Latino cultures are stratified by race in a way that is more complex, but no better for blacks, than the bipolar black/white dichotomy of the United States. Some countries such as Mexico have adopted an official stance of *mestizaje*, or race-mixing, that emphasizes the European and indigenous elements of the culture while ignoring the African. In other countries *blanqueamiento* (whitening) or *mejorando la raza* (improving the race) is seen as a social goal: "These policies promote the improvement of the race through intermarriage with whites, increased white European immigration, and, at times, the outright elimination of black and indigenous groups."[57] Only French- and Creole-speaking Haiti, a nation founded on an uprising of black slaves against European masters where 95 percent of the population is of African descent, has at times in its history promoted an official policy of negritud, or affirmation of black identity.

Why is this important for urban school reform in the United States? Immigrant and minority students must construct a cultural and racial identity not just within the mainstream social order, but within the non-mainstream social order of their families and ethnic communities. If students have spent a significant amount of time in their home countries before arriving in the United States, or if they move back and forth regularly between the mainland and their birth land as do many students from Mexico, Puerto Rico, the Dominican Republic, and Haiti, the changing cultural messages they must sort out can be a substantial obstacle to learning. Reform strategies that treat these learners as if they were mainstream, English-speaking, and middle class offer them no entry point and little support, making an already difficult task even harder.

## THREE SOURCES OF CULTURAL LEARNING STRATEGIES

Reform planners have access to three sources of high quality ideas and strategies for meeting the needs of their culturally diverse student populations: culturally responsive teachers and principals within their own school systems, culturally based administrative professionals, such as bilingual education and ELL specialists, and socio-culturally oriented academic researchers. Unfortunately, if one were to rank-order groups who lack credibility with systemic reformers, these three might well top the list.

Much of reform proceeds from the premise that teachers are the problem and outside thinkers the solution to current school failures, so the notion of practitioners as knowledge-makers is hard for policymakers to swallow. Bilingual, ELL, and desegregation-related professionals, who often have a wealth of knowledge about culturally relevant teaching methods, are prophets without honor in their own school systems, and often have a place at the decision making table only because court decisions require them to be there. Academic researchers, whose gifts are welcomed when they come wrapped as teacher-proof, exemplary programs or off-the-shelf staff development models, are shunned when their contribution is to raise thorny questions about racial and cultural bias or provide support for community groups who oppose some aspect of systemic reform. If we are sincere about raising achievement for culturally diverse populations, the contributions of these three groups must be taken seriously even, or perhaps especially, when they run counter to prevailing reform philosophies.

### The Contributions of Culturally Responsive Practitioners

Within any large urban system certain practitioners are recognized by their colleagues as particularly thoughtful and knowledgeable in the area of cultural diversity. Many culturally responsive practitioners have written of their experiences, so their approaches and strategies are accessible to anyone who makes the effort to seek them out. Often, the starting point for these practitioners has been to question their own assumptions about culturally different learners, a stance which policymakers almost never take.

In Boston, elementary teacher Carol Miller has recorded one such exploration in her essay "No longer 'too White': Using multicultural literature to promote academic achievement and cultural understanding."[58] High school teacher Eileen Shakespear examined the racial dimensions of her role as a white, female teacher of black, adolescent males and reported her findings in "What I'd tell a White gal: What my black male students taught me about race and schooling."[59] A racially mixed group of Boston teacher-researchers of my acquaintance has been meeting for three years to gather data on and try to understand their greatest concern, the low performance of African American males in their classrooms. They have undertaken this project not with the support of the school system, but outside it, because they feel that their discussions raise difficult questions that the reform-obsessed school department does not wish to acknowledge.

Other teachers in Boston are equally adept and committed, I cite these examples only because they are well known to me, as are similar examples in Philadelphia, Chicago, San Francisco, Oakland, and other cities. The point is not to praise a few exceptional teachers, but to demonstrate that classroom-based knowledge about culturally relevant teaching can be found in any city if you look for it.

Equally important, culturally relevant practitioner-researchers understand that the development of successful approaches starts with a look inward, at their own beliefs and assumptions. This is followed by a reaching outward, to students and parents whose lives are significantly different than their own, to colleagues of different cultural and racial groups, and to a community of co-inquirers—Lisa Delpit, Gloria Ladsen Billings, Jim Cummins, and Sonia Nieto[60] come immediately to mind—represented in the growing literature in this area. The achievements and attitudes of these practitioners "raise the bar" for advocates of systemic change—can reformers be as open and honest about this difficult issue as those whom they are trying to reform?

### Specialists Within the School Department with Culturally Relevant Knowledge

Cambridge, MA is known worldwide as the home of two great universities, Harvard and M.I.T. Its public school system is an urban mixture of town and gown that includes working-class white ethnic and African American populations as well as recent immigrants who speak Spanish, Haitian, Korean, and many other languages. Several years ago the bilingual education department, under the leadership of director Mary Cazabon, created Amigos, a citywide, two-way, K-8, English-Spanish bilingual program. Amigos was designed to meet desegregation goals by dividing the English-speaking seats between white and African American students, and to meet second-language needs by providing academic instruction in two languages for Spanish-speakers, who make up half of Amigos pupils. Quantitative analysis of long-term data conducted by Cazabon and others has documented the program's success in achieving both its academic and interpersonal goals.[61] By the time they reach high school, Amigos students score higher than non-Amigos students on both English and Spanish language tests, and they hold a positive attitude towards languages and cultures other than their own. Cambridge is now developing similar programs for Haitian speakers and Korean speakers, and demand is high for seats in all three programs. Cazabon stresses, however, that creating such programs "demands a paradigm shift in the typical way that school systems view and treat language minority students" and sustaining them requires "a fragile balance of power relationships between and among students, teachers, parents, community and school administration."[62]

Similar multipurpose programming can be created with the input of ELL, Desegregation, and other specialists. The Eastern Massachusetts Initiative (EMI), an antiracism professional development course for teachers, has been in place for over a decade in 10 suburban towns surrounding Boston. The towns all participate in METCO, a voluntary, urban-suburban desegregation program, and minority student achievement is a high priority. EMI is supported at the highest levels, by Superintendents and school committees, and research conducted by Blake and by Martin suggests that the course has made measurable changes in white teachers' knowledge, attitudes, and classroom practices.[63]

These examples show that top-level leadership can regard diversity positively and make use of professionals who are already on board or readily available to address specific local needs. When the need for culturally relevant teaching is taken seriously at the policy level, school systems can create win-win solutions that improve academic achievement, build respect for difference, and appeal to diverse parent interests while helping the system to comply with equity-based court mandates. Nationally, there has been a great deal of movement in this area since the College Board released a series of reports on minority achievement in 1999. The Council of Great City Schools, the National Urban League, and the Minority School Achievement Network (a coalition of 15 suburban and small city districts), are all working on aspects of this problem. Edmund W. Gordon, co-chair of the College

Board task force on the issue, reports that "We are finding a much higher degree of tolerance for discussion than we experienced five-to-10 years ago."[64] These are hopeful signs.

## Powerful Concepts from Research and Theory

One of the characteristics of the people and programs mentioned above is familiarity with the ideas of researchers and practitioners exploring culturally, linguistically, or racially relevant teaching and learning. Cultural factors have strong effects on teachers, students, and parents, and we need to learn more about these effects if we are to teach today's students successfully. In the notes to the last chapter I listed a few important sources in this area. Here I will offer two examples of recent academic work that introduces powerful conceptual tools for thinking about issues that are central to urban schooling and urban reform.

### James Gee's Definition of Literacy as Command of Secondary Discourse

As a result of the near-elimination of bilingual programs and sheltered ELL support in many states, more and more second-language learners are showing up in regular education classrooms. Mainstream teachers usually have little experience dealing with the challenges presented by ELL students, particularly in terms of reading, writing, speaking, and listening. Since these skills are required across the curriculum—on social studies essay exams, to solve math word problems—both teacher and student may feel mounting frustration and failure. School systems—or publishers who have sold a basal reader series to a school system—sometimes provide staff development to support a prescribed reading method used with both native English and ELL students, but such training cannot adequately equip teachers for the instructional challenges they face.

In contrast, many teachers have felt a sense of liberation when exposed to Gee's explanation of discourse as an "'identity kit' that comes complete with the appropriate costume and instructions on how to act and talk so as to take on a particular role that others will recognize." For Gee, literacy is composed of "primary discourse," which is an "oral mode" or our way of "using our native language in face-to-face communication with intimates" and "secondary discourses," which "crucially involve social institutions beyond the family" and "require one to communicate with non-intimates."[65]

Using this discourse-based framework, Gee defines literacy as "control of secondary uses of language (i.e., uses of language in secondary discourses)." This means that "there are as many applications of the word literacy as there are secondary discourses," including "dominant literacy," which is control of the dominant or mainstream discourse patterns.

When students come from homes where the primary discourse patterns are close to the patterns of dominant literacy, they enter school with an inherent advantage over students whose primary discourse is widely divergent from the dominant pattern. When teachers can begin to see student literacy in terms of primary and secondary discourses rather than "right" or "wrong" language, new possibilities open for pedagogy and curriculum, possibilities that can build bridges between home and school and between students' oral language and the skills needed for academic success.

Both Delpit and Bartolomé have extended and qualified Gee's insights in important ways, Delpit in "The Politics of Teaching Literate Discourse,"[66] Bartolomé in *The Misteaching of Academic Discourses*.[67]

### Theresa Perry's Argument for a Specifically African American Educational Epistemology

In critiquing past attempts to explain African American school performance, Perry argues that most writers, including Ogbu, "focus disproportionately on failure." Perry attempts to turn traditional assumptions on their heads, arguing that "if one considers the long and persistent denial and limiting of educational opportunity to African Americans, from slavery to the present," what requires explanation is how so many African Americans have excelled and particularly how they have "succeeded in producing a leadership and intellectual class."[68]

Perry's central thesis can be briefly recounted as an example of a strong counter-view to prevailing, "race-blind" reform thinking. She argues that there is a specifically African American educational epistemology that "links schooling to citizenship, leadership, and racial uplift," and that most current efforts to improve African American student achievement fail because they impose an epistemology of "whiteness" that forces students to choose between school success and their own communities and identities. She cites studies establishing "a strong relationship between racial identity and achievement" and contends that,

In order for African American children to succeed in school, they have to negotiate membership in three different communities: membership in a race discriminated group; membership in mainstream society; and membership in a cultural group in opposition to which "whiteness" has been constructed. Membership in these groups is not inherently contradictory—but often is.

When district policies, teaching strategies, and curricula help African American students to negotiate these identities and to pursue "citizenship, leadership, and racial uplift," they promote success. When they do not, they promote disengagement, resistance, and failure.

## SCHOOL CULTURE AND LEADERSHIP MODELS

"Today . . ." Robert Evans reminds us, "the need to change school culture has become axiomatic," fostering both "sophisticated analysis" and "glib prescription." At bottom, though, "changing organizational culture is far, far more difficult that analyzing it," a fact which engenders frustration among reformers who hold "unrealistic expectations borne of a misunderstanding of culture."[69]

In general, *school culture* refers to "patterns of meaning or activity (norms, values, beliefs, relationships, rituals, traditions, myths, etc.) shared in varying degrees by members of a school community."[70] Over the past thirty years varying approaches have been taken to studying it.

In *The Culture of the School and the Problem of Change*[71] Seymour Sarason focused attention on the relationship between culture and reform. He studied schools as systems of relationship among individuals, including power relationships between principals and teachers, and teacher burnout as a product of isolation, boredom and routine.[72] More recent approaches have used techniques drawn from management studies, particularly organizational analysis. Sergiovanni counsels, "the power of leadership is derived from building a unique school culture . . . that promotes and sustains a given school's conception of success . . ."[73] Senge's Fifth Discipline[74] guides are so popular that a Fifth Discipline resource book of almost 600 pages has now been created for "educators, parents, and everyone who cares about education."[75]

Overall, school culture studies strongly support two conclusions: that "shared patterns of meaning and activity" significantly affect teaching and learning, and that to create change school leaders, particularly principals, must influence school culture. It therefore makes sense to approach school culture by examining the effects systemic reform has had on the relationship between culture and the principal's role.

Reform policy gurus, far from the classroom, typically feel an affinity for the systems-based, business-oriented approaches of organizational analysis over the people-centered approach favored by Sarason. Unfortunately, designs for organizational change authored at a secure distance from schools often make it harder, not easier, for school-level leaders to create authentic change. Principals are called on to be budget managers, public relations specialists, inspirational leaders, and organizational strategists, all for a salary only marginally larger than that of a senior teacher and with job security that approaches that of corporate "temp" workers. Let me offer two examples.

First, under systemic reform the principal's primary role has ostensibly been transformed from "manager of the status quo" to "leader of the change and definer of the culture." But no blueprint has been provided for how this new role is to be performed. Instead, central offices have frequently provided only mandates and threats: mandates to "go forth and create change," threats that if change is not forthcoming, and fast, principals will be removed.

Second, principals' responsibilities have practically doubled, as a new set of reform-driven, change-oriented tasks has been laid over the previous set of management-oriented, hierarchical tasks. Layers of responsibility and accountability have been added, but none have been taken away. The result? Principals face a new set of demands with no blueprint for addressing them, their workload has substantially increased and their job security has all but disappeared. This scenario is being touted as the "management response" that will transform failing schools.

David De Ruosi, an energetic, successful administrator in an urban middle school just outside Boston, talked to me about the unrelenting effort it takes to stay on top of his responsibilities:

I find myself questioning my ability to complete a job that at times seems to be overwhelming. I'm in an environment that involves high-stakes testing, ever-increasing accountability, and expanded boundaries, including the participation of many types of stakeholders such as parents, community groups, and school councils. I must not only survive, but also produce positive results. Just managing a building is no longer good enough. Many of my principal colleagues would echo the words of management writer James Champy, "Nothing is simple. Whatever you do is not enough. Everything is in question. Everyone must change."[76]

The justification given for these changes is often that schools should be more accountable, should adopt the bottom-line management tactics that govern business. In fact, the conviction that educators have much to learn from management chiefs continues to be a core belief of many educational policymakers. This is hardly surprising since local school committee members and appointees to state boards of education are often successful business people.

Too often, the adoption of corporate culture as a model for school culture has been completely uncritical. The president of Continental Airlines, hailed for bringing the company "from worst to first," stresses empowerment of workers and "a very deep respect for people" as keys to success.[77] Other airline CEO's advise slash-and-burn budget cutting and widespread layoffs. What lessons can usefully be taken from a corporate world that is itself in such disagreement? If we take corporate America seriously as a model for change, rather than as an amulet or totem, corporate organizational analysis raises more questions than it answers. What is required, old-style or new-style management, or a combination of both? How do you "manage for change" in a reform environment that is itself constantly changing? How do you value people in a systems-based approach?

Such problems are compounded because, though the application of organizational analysis to educational settings has been widespread, it has often been superficial. When policymakers embrace the aura surrounding management studies rather than its complex substance, confusion follows. When applying the work of Argyris, Senge, or Sergiovanni, most school systems have given little attention to these authors' inclusion of a caution- ary counter-literature that questions easy categorizations and guru-like pre- scriptions.

A classic locus for this counter-literature, Mintzberg's "The Manager's Job: Folklore and Fact," condenses findings from studies on many types of managers, including educational leaders. Addressing "the basic question: What do managers do?" Mintzberg concludes there is still a basic ignorance on this question which results in "the inability of our large public organi- zations to come to grips with some of their most serious policy problems."[78] He contrasts myths of the classical view of management with facts from research about what managers actually do, facts which will have a familiar ring to school administrators.

Managers are not "reflective, systematic" planners; rather their work is characterized by "an unrelenting pace," and their actions by "brevity, variety, and discontinuity." They much prefer action to reflection. Because of this, information that is informal, verbal and immediately accessible (par- ticularly "gossip, hearsay, and speculation") is much more valued than documents or formal management information systems. Overall, rather than being scientific or professional, managers' techniques are intuitive, insight- ful, and "locked deep inside their brains."[79]

If we ask "What do principals do?" under reform, we find exactly the policy conundrum Mintzberg identifies. Reform has given principals more power, but has also limited and undermined that power. It has created stan- dards of accountability, but also increased vulnerability. Reform plans pro- mulgate maxims about *what* principals should strive to achieve, but offer little useful guidance for *how* to go about achieving it.

In a K-12, statewide study with national relevance, Portin looked at Washington principals and assistant principals after five years of mandated reform. He found them to be both "committed" and "overloaded." "Fun- damental shifts" had occurred in the principal's role, making it "more com- plex and onerous " with "'layer-upon-layer' of devolved responsibility." Increased complexity was accompanied by limitations on their capacity to do the job, resulting in decreased morale for both principals and schools.

Portin found administrators highly supportive of reform, but struggling to balance administrative/management tasks such as evaluation of teach- ers and preparation of budgets with instructional leadership tasks such as curriculum oversight and professional development, all while learning a new set of reform-related tasks which included chairing school site councils, "marketing" their schools to the community, improving relationships with parents, and forming partnerships with business. Significantly, factors which characterize urban school culture, such as linguistic, racial, and economic diversity and increased numbers of special needs students, greatly increased the complexity of leadership roles and were areas in which principals felt they needed more preparation. Overall, Portin found the work involved in running a school was becoming "more intricate, diverse, and nettlesome" under reform and "new means of understanding principal roles, combined with clear understanding by policymakers" were critical if school leaders are to be effective.[80]

According to Gerald Tirozzi, executive director of the National Association of Secondary School Principals, "While the teacher shortage has been clearly recognized, there has been near silence on the lack of qualified candidates applying for the principalship." The position has "accumulated increased responsibilities without the incentives needed to attract high quality candidates." Half the districts in the country are having trouble filling positions because "the principal's job has become more complex and demanding," "principal training, support, and professional development are largely inadequate," and "states lack a coherent vision and system for developing and retaining high quality principals."[81] Vincent Ferrandino, Tirozzi's counterpart at the elementary level, points out that during the reform-dominated decade 1988 to 1998, the elementary principal attrition rate stood at 42 percent. In the current decade it is projected to rise, perhaps to as high as 60 percent. Contributing factors include "inadequate compensation," "job-related stress," and "not enough hours in the school day for a conscientious principal to fulfill the many responsibilities."[82]

Given this scenario it is not surprising that burnout-related problems among urban principals are increasing and qualified new applicants are decreasing. Many school systems give lip service to the maxims of experts like Sergiovanni, but few provide conditions that enable principals to play the culture-building role associated with success. This was brought home to me dramatically when I talked to Wes Manaday, a well-trained, energetic, first-time principal appointed in 1997 under the first wave of Boston's systemic reform. In four years, Manaday had "turned around" the John Eliot, a 220-student elementary school in Boston's historic North End. I wanted to learn more about the Eliot because, to use a metaphor from earlier in this chapter, it is a station where many powerful trains cross.

In 2000–2001 its student body was 40 percent African American, 25 percent Hispanic, 25 percent white, and 10 percent Asian. There were twenty-two full and part-time teachers and twenty support staff. The high ratio of adults to children was largely due to the fact that 37 percent of the students were special needs and an additional percentage were Limited English Proficient, requiring many paraprofessionals and part-time specialists. The rapidly gentrifying neighborhood was made up, Manaday told me, of "half old Italian immigrant families and half upwardly mobile, predominantly white professionals with children below school age."

When Manaday and I talked in the spring of 2001, I was interested in his perspective on the school change process. I began with the question, "How did you become principal?":

I accidentally stumbled on the job when I worked with the school as a comprehensive school planning specialist in 1996. The principal was on her way to accepting another position and I put in an application, was interviewed by the school-based management team and then by the superintendent, and they offered me the job. I had some second thoughts about accepting, knowing that the school culture was really fractured. I would be the third principal in two years, there was no instructional focus, and no alignment with the superintendent's six mandated components of school reform.[83]

The reputation it had was that all these children were bused in from outside the neighborhood and they were the leftovers from the Boston Public Schools, because a lot of the students were in Special Education or had social and emotional problems. The school had a 43 percent Special Needs population and the number was rising as I stepped into the building. There was a schism between the regular and special education teachers and there didn't seem to be any teamwork or collaboration. There was a lot of duplication and vying for resources that created so much animosity that some teachers weren't talking to one another.

There were also many LEP (Limited English Proficient) students who were at level one on the Stanford 9 Test, the failure level. There were no safety nets really in place for these students. On paper, a certain teacher was responsible for servicing these students, but as far as direct services there weren't any. A lot of the LEP students had been transitioned out of bilingual programs and placed in regular education classrooms and the regular education. Teachers felt that SPED was getting much more of the resources, they were getting a paraprofessional with 12 children in their classrooms, so there was a lot of friction that there was more money in SPED than there was in regular education. I think what saved the school the last year before I began as principal was that the business partner gave the school an exorbitant amount of money. The partner asked the school to make a wish list and the teachers in regular education made this huge wish list equipment, curriculum resources, manipulatives, computers, library books—and the business partner met all of those wishes.

The teachers were very leery of change. I was their third principal in two years and the superintendent had only been in place for a year and a half. My first week as principal I walked through the building and one of the teachers who had been teaching for forty-three years was very, very cordial and welcomed me, but she took me aside and said, "You know, I hope you're not making any sweeping changes in this school because we just can't go through more changes." She mentioned that she had been teaching longer than I had been alive, and I was a little taken aback that she had the boldness to tell me this, but then she became one of my strongest allies that very first year. At that point I knew there was a lot of work ahead of me, that this was a very fractured school. My predecessor had written the comprehensive school plan, which is a change plan for reform, on her own in her office and didn't involve anyone else. But she did go around when she was done to have the teachers sign off on her plan. There was no ownership of the plan, so I knew that I needed to build community and I knew that it would take at least three years to do so. One of the theorists I'd read in one of my principalship courses that came to mind was Sergiovanni, "real change can only come as a result of the commitments of both the minds and hearts of the total school community, teachers, parents, students, administrators, and school board. Reform should be based on careful identification of deeply and commonly held values."

Very slowly, change began to happen. My first and biggest goal was to be a principal, a leader, that they could trust. I had to build trust amongst the staff, yet I also needed to know, in the terminology of Bolman and Deal, what the different cultural frameworks were in the building in terms of structure, human resources, symbolism, and most of all politics. Who were the ones that I should solicit as allies, to help me reform the school? How could I build relationships, build trust, let them know that I was in there to effect changes not by coming in to evaluate, observe, and terminate people, but to build on the strengths of the teachers that were in the building.

In the second year, support was what was needed. Coming in and supporting teachers to get the professional development they needed, the resources they needed to put in place the things we were trying to do. Like in Maslow's hierarchy of needs, if you take care of the lower end, people feel like they've been nurtured. The third year was the pressure, like OK you've met some of these goals, now it's time to look at some higher goals on which you can work on. And so the support and the pressure needed to go hand in hand. So there was first the support, then pressure. And I did have a couple of teachers that I pressured to leave.

Now that I'm finishing my fourth year there are some significant changes in the student test scores and this is a direct result of changing the culture of the school. The teachers now are collegial with one another, they work in teams, they have conversations that are actually child-centered. They're sharing teaching strategies and they're also helping each other by peer tutoring one another or peer evaluating one another. In the first year that fourth graders took the MCAS (Massachusetts Comprehensive Assessment System) tests, our school was second from the bottom in the whole school system. The second year we did a little bit better, but not much better, and in the third year we were one of thirty-four schools in Boston identified as meeting or exceeding the state goals for improvement in reading and math scores. So if you looked at the comparison of school ranking, we were number fifty-five as opposed to second from the bottom of about 130 schools overall and about ninety elementary schools.

In Massachusetts, Special Education and LEP students take the test too—they're not exempt—and that was one of the big issues as to why our scores were low. We had a Parent Night in March, 2000 and 350 people including school age and less than school age parents from the neighborhood attended the meeting. And a parent raised a very important question. He was a lawyer and his wife was a lawyer, and their son was entering kindergarten, and he said, "Well your school was my third choice, why would I want my son to come to your school if your scores are so low?" And I took the mike and said "Because we have a 42 percent Special Needs population, we have forty-eight children that took the MCAS test and of

208 Policy Versus Reality

those 48 children, 28 were identified with special needs, another seventeen were Limited English Proficient, the remaining three were in regular education. And scores from our school are just compared straight against a school that may have no LEP students and 10 percent special needs students. And what the newspapers don't report and the rank ordering doesn't show is what the population of the school or the students are. The Boston Globe doesn't show whether the school has a huge bilingual or LEP or SPED population, it just rank orders the school. So people have a field day with the rank ordering. We do everything we can to move the children from one level to the next level, with the resources we have at hand, we do everything that is humanly possible."

A big change from four years ago is that now the parents from the neighborhood are embracing the school. There's a lot more parental involvement, and a lot more community involvement. We've been invited to participate with the other elementary school in the neighborhood, a parochial school, in different events—bringing in a speaker on drugs, having a joint literacy fair, inviting their teachers over to our computer lab.

Presently there is a 50-50 policy in the BPS. 50 percent of the seats are reserved for children that are outside of the neighborhood and 50 percent of the seats are reserved for neighborhood children. The idea of a "walk-to" school was the initiative of the mayor. One of the major changes in the school is that when I took it on as a principal, 90 percent of the children were bused in from outside of the neighborhood. Now in grades K, 1, 2, and 3 we have a 50-50 split between neighborhood children and bused children, which is a significant change. We now have a waiting list in grades K, 1, 2, and 3. We disaggregated the data and the ones on the wait list are predominantly children from the neighborhood. The school has gone from being underchosen to having a wait list, and now the parents have gone before the school committee and met with the superintendent asking that the school be extended to grade eight.

You have two different sets of parents from the neighborhood, the old time Italian families, and they're happy with how the school is going, and the parents who are very educated, more recently arrived in the neighborhood, and they come with a sense of entitlement. If they ask me to do something, they expect it to be done, because they are now at the same educational level as my staff and I am. I now have interns from Massachusetts General Hospital, who are going to be there two or three years, wanting to bring their children into my building, and they've come in and questioned the different instructional practices, which I've never had before. Now we have parents that want behavior logs, that want follow-up on more challenging kinds of work, that want to know what the reading lists are for each grade and how they can support their children at home.

The thing I'm proudest of is that we've completely changed the school culture, we've built a community. The teachers and the staff feel that we're like a family, that we take care of each other and that we make sure that we hold each other accountable, and when we do fight, there's a big blow-up and then we come back together again and we move on.

The very, very important thing that I've learned is to take a look at the political framework of the school. In Boston a lot of the decisions are made on politically sensitive grounds. I had never ever imagined that I would always have to be very politically astute in the decisions that I have to make. Even though the system's reform plan says that principal's decisions should be child-centered and instructionally focused, I really needed to look at the political ramifications of every decision. I've learned that within every culture there's a political framework that a principal really needs to be aware of, because if you don't operate within those frameworks, you're doomed. The thing that has helped me most is having some political allies, people that would steer me out of minefields, and to have a school leadership team that was also very politically astute.

But changing the school has had a lot of costs for me personally. I've worked more than 70 hours a week for the past four years. I've put my doctoral work on hold for the past two and a half years. I've had less time with family and friends and less of a social life. I've also landed in the hospital a couple of times and my doctor feels that my health problems are directly related to the stress levels that I was experiencing. More recently I've broken out in acne, which is also stress-related, so you can see it there too. I'm pretty sure I won't be here as principal next year.

## TWO INSIDER/OUTSIDERS TALK ABOUT THE "CULTURE OF REFORM"

As the new status quo for urban schools, systemic reform has generated its own "shared organization of ideas" that includes the convictions that:

- urban schools are failing badly and need major intervention and greater accountability;
- state-mandated curricula and high-stakes tests, by "raising the bar," can ensure accountability and close the minority/white achievement gap;
- corporate managers are often better qualified than experienced educators to serve as superintendents and corporate management techniques can provide effective solutions to school problems; and
- most teachers lack the skills and motivation to make schools better, so the involvement of skilled "insider/outsiders" is needed to jump-start change in entrenched school cultures.

These beliefs can be seen coalescing into a "reform culture" when, as is now common, urban school systems turn to "intermediary organizations" for assistance in developing reform policy and implementing it:

Representing a coalition of interests supporting reform, the intermediary organization lives at the boundaries of the educational system, neither "of" the system nor wholly outside it. It enjoys the license—at least on a temporary basis—to cross the organizational boundaries dividing the various parties whose actions affect children in schools, and to serve as the catalyst for some kind of change.[84]

Intermediary organizations like the Annenberg Challenge, Success for All, James Comer's School Development Program, and many others typically employ "insider/outsiders" in a variety of roles—consultants, coaches, in-service providers, project managers, evaluators, and more. In this section we will take a look at the culture of reform through the eyes of two unique "insider/outsiders," Tom Hsu and Pamela Trefler. Each has worked extensively with reforming schools in Boston, and each has earned credibility in both the corporate arena and the urban classroom.

Tom Hsu, the CEO of his own multi-million dollar software and textbook company, has been a content-area coach in math and science for teachers in Boston and many other school systems. Trefler, a former investment banker, heads her own Boston-based foundation, which since 1995 has given more than $15 million to aid education in Boston. Trefler herself has taken an active role in both teaching and school-level restructuring processes.

In my conversations with them, neither Hsu nor Trefler used their corporate experience as a platform to indict teachers. On the contrary, when they viewed their experience in urban classrooms through a corporate lens, they identified reform culture's lack of support for teachers, lack of understanding of the way schools actually work, Byzantine budgetary systems, and unsophisticated implementation of mandated change as important causes of the continued failure of urban schools.

## Tom Hsu

Tom Hsu is a teacher, engineer, curriculum designer, and corporate CEO who since 1995 has served as a math/science consultant and coach for over 10,000 teachers from fifty states. He is in no doubt about the need for improved math/science instruction and greater accountability, and sees content-knowledge coaching as an important role for insider/outsiders, because "knowledge in the physical sciences—physics, chemistry, and mathematics—is particularly weak among teachers. Nationwide 88 percent of science teachers have either biology as a background or no science at all."

But his experience in schools has convinced him that it's the system, not the teachers, that most needs to be fixed:

I left the classroom because I was no longer able to change the system from the inside and, in my opinion, the system's broke pretty badly and we're shortchanging kids and teachers, because we're forcing very good people to do a poor job. There's nothing worse you can do to someone's spirit than to force them to do a bad job, because then not only do you get a bad job but you break the person. And in many cases that's what we're doing to teachers.

Applying his corporate experience to his school change issues, Hsu drew these conclusions:

A lot of the teachers we work with are not well supported by the system. Basically the way teachers work in a lot of big urban systems is, the door closes and that's their kingdom and they have to make do with whatever they have. If you compare it to the business world, a typical business manager can handle seven to twelve direct reports, where the average teacher handles 150. And not only that, but they get randomly changed on them, sometimes weekly. The "employees"—the students— didn't choose to be there. You can't cut their pay, you can't fire them. You don't have much leverage over them, in some sense. And so you have to wheedle and cajole and somehow get the students to buy into their own learning process, to take responsibility for why they're there. And you have very few resources for it. The typical business person would consider this an impossible situation. I'm being held accountable to achieve a goal that's definitely important, however, I'm given ab- solutely no authority to make any decisions regarding achieving that goal.

And so one of our roles is to just help the teacher cope and believe in them- selves and believe that there are people there to help them and they can go ahead and take risks. They don't have to be afraid all the time that they're not "covering the material." Nobody covers the material. I've never seen a teacher cover more than 60 percent of the "curriculum." And the better teachers cover less because they're more concerned that kids learn than that they "cover the material."

## Pamela Trefler

Pamela Trefler is an "insider/outsider" with a unique perspective. The Trefler Foundation funds multiple reform efforts in Boston and is the second largest contributor to Boston's Annenberg Challenge. But Trefler is much more than a funder. She is a certified teacher with a Master's Degree in Education from Harvard, she is enrolled in the Leadership in Urban Schools Doctoral Program at the University of Massachusetts Boston, and she teaches English two days per week at Dorchester High School, one of the schools where she funds reform. Trefler's work is an example of "venture philanthropy" or "new philanthropy," a type of giving that began in the 1990s as a result of the vast individual wealth spawned by the high tech boom.

New foundations express the social visions of their relatively young cre- ators, who prefer hands-on involvement with projects, give for the long term (five years or more), and apply to their giving the same principles that made them successful in business.[85] In 1997 a *Harvard Business Review* article urged traditional foundations to heed these new models of giving by invest- ing in the organizational needs of their non-profit clients.[86]

Trefler described her foundation and its goals to me in these terms:

The Trefler Foundation is a private family foundation founded by my husband and myself in 1996. We differ very significantly from traditional foundations and par- ticularly from foundations in Boston in that we tend to give very large grants but very few grants, and we give them over a long period of time. Plus, for every school or nonprofit that the Foundation funds in any major way, someone at the Foundation works either on site at the school or very closely with the nonprofit. A condition of our doing a large grant with a nonprofit is that we take a seat on the board. So every employee at the Foundation from the President all the way to the receptionist spends some amount of time working on projects we fund.

Our focus is almost exclusively on education, and our particular area of interest is high school restructuring—How do you take a high school and structure it so that it works for the students it has, not the students that someone else has. That's what we have spent most of the last four years attempting to do by donating reasonably significant sums of money to capture public interest and bring resources in to the schools and by actually working in the schools. Our ultimate goal, which is kind of a big one, is to find a way to restructure urban high schools in such a way that all students in the United States get an equal and excellent education.

When we enter a school, our first goal is to improve communication between the administration and the faculty so that the right hand and the left hand aren't doing two different things. The next thing that we do is look at the school and see what resources are available that are being underutilized, to try to figure out how to get the school to think about a non-profit lets say, that might be available and needed but not being used. How do you get the school to automatically think about, "Oh, we need this service, we know this nonprofit, we can call on them." And then thirdly, as we get to know the school, we look at how the school is actually structured. By structure I mean, how do the kids travel during the day? Are they in clusters, are they in small learning communities, or are they grouped by grade? Do groups of students travel together for one year, for three years? We ask the question, how is this school structured and is that structure working for the student population of the school?

Trefler gained national attention in 1998 when she announced what was believed to be the largest single gift ever made to a public school, a million-dollar contribution to Boston's Dorchester High School. At the time the school was the city's worst in terms of test results, violence, dropout rates, and students' reluctance to choose it. Trefler had student-taught there several years earlier and wanted to do something that would be a catalyst for turning the school around. Since her gift, Dorchester has been on an upward trajectory. Trefler is the first to point out that the school's progress has been due to a collaborative effort led by Headmaster Robert Belle and involving the teaching staff, faculty and students from the University of Massachusetts Boston, and other contributors. But the impact of Trefler's gift on creating these collaborations, as well as her personal involvement, have been crucial:

I personally take a very active role in the things that we fund. We gave a million dollar grant to Dorchester High School here in Boston and during the first two years of the grant I co-taught in the ninth grade one to two days a week. I personally sat on the steering committee, I attended Instructional Leadership Team meetings, and I also sit on the board of the academy of public service, which is a Small Learning Community within the school. I have a long-standing relationship with the school and many of the faculty because I student-taught there seven year ago. Everyone at the foundation mentors a student from Dorchester High School. I don't think we're really perceived as outsiders, we're perceived as part of the team.

Being in a classroom on a regular basis has given Trefler a perspective on change similar to the one expressed by Tom Hsu:

The minute you step into a classroom as a teacher the rest of the world ceases to exist. Thirty-three pairs of eyes attached to 33 students look at you. There are probably over a thousand other people in the building but during that class all that really exists are you and the students in the room.

This feeling is very difficult to describe to someone who has never done it. Everyone talks about the fact that teachers work in "isolation" from their peers, and they do. It is actually more than that—for four to five hours a day you have complete responsibility for the students sitting in your classroom. At the end of the day, your success or failure as a teacher will be measured on how well those students perform on standardized tests, grades, attendance and other criteria that the teacher has little, if any, control over.

I spent only five hours a week in the classroom this year, yet every hour I am in the classroom, I wonder, What on earth are all these policymakers, educational experts, and people in the Department of Education (both State and Federal) thinking about? The average urban high school teacher has a student ability span in her classroom of up to ten years. It is not unusual to have students who are illiterate in the same room with students performing at the college level.

The powers that be have decided that "better" teachers and additional professional development will solve the performance problems in the school and allow all students (or at least the vast majority) to be brought up to grade level. Contrary to what we read and are told, most of the teachers I know are very open to trying new methods of teaching in their classrooms. The problem is they are not given any support to try these new methods with a realistic chance for success.

Take a very simple concept —students working in groups. In many cases, it can work quite well. The problem is that introducing the group concept and getting it to work takes time and more than one adult in the classroom. Most teachers have neither. If you spend two weeks teaching students to work in groups and getting them comfortable with each other, that is two weeks you are behind in some curriculum introduced by someone who has certainly never been in your classroom and probably never taught a class anywhere. Without another adult or two to help you might not be successful, and you have lost two or more weeks and your performance will be criticized.

This does not take into consideration the wear and tear on the teacher who is trying to introduce a new way of doing things while coping with classroom management problems, crises of the various students, unexpected fire alarms, lost books, no supplies and so on. While teachers are willing to try new things, it is not hard to understand why many never come to fruition.

In all the time I have spent teaching, no one has ever asked me, or most other teachers, what they need to be more successful. Certainly no one with any authority to make large changes has ever asked with any real intention of doing anything about it. If you take the time to ask a group of experienced teachers, the first thing they ask for is smaller class size. They will forgo books, supplies, heat, clean class-rooms, professional development, a desk for themselves, computers, and anything else you can think of for class sizes of twenty or less.

Since I wear many hats, I am often invited to meetings where school reform is discussed by people who do not work in the classroom. I cannot recall ever having a teacher present at one of these meetings. Usually we have business leaders, edu-cational experts, the Mayor, people from the BPS administration, everyone except teachers. Almost invariably the discussion winds its way to teachers and why they are not doing their job. Somewhere during this discussion, I raise my hand and say "I'm a teacher and I find your discussion uninformed at best and leaning toward teacher bashing at worst." The silence is always deafening.

Trefler's regular presence in schools gives her a critical perspective on the system-level culture of reform:

In Boston there's a lot of *talk* about reform. As a matter of fact when you talk about education K through 12, *all* people talk about is school reform and how we are going to "fix" the schools by reforming them, but there is an enormous discon-nect between the talking and the doing, the implementation. I think that the cul-ture of reform in Boston is based almost exclusively on theory. There are a lot of theories about how to change schools, about how to reform schools, but at the ad-ministrative level no one has really taken a long hard look at where theory and practice come together. I think that what we've done in Boston, particularly at the high school level, is created a culture of change that's not been very successful and that unless the thinking changes, I don't think has a lot of hope of bringing suc-cess across the board.

At the state level, I don't think that curriculum and testing mandates have had much impact on really changing urban schools. Those are mandates from outside, where real change takes place inside the school building. Most teachers do the least amount of work possible around those mandated changes if they don't see value in them, and very often they don't, because one of the problems is, those changes are mandated by somebody who doesn't spend any time in the school, and it may seem like a good idea, it may sound like a good idea, but in reality it may be a bad idea or just an idea that doesn't bring any benefit.

I asked Trefler what specific strategies from the private sector she found effective for creating change in urban schools. She named three:

I think there are three big things: the concept of leverage, the ability to create stra-tegic partnerships, and skill in analyzing budgets. When I was an investment banker I put together a $100 million deal involving a large telecommunications company. My company put in no money but had great significance in making the deal come together. As CEO of a non-profit foundation I've consciously looked at giving as deal-making, such as putting together a package using leverage, not just a one-to-one donor/donee relationship as in traditional philanthropy. We have given out a number of million-dollar grants because one million is a "magic number" publicity-wise. We realize that, over four years, $250,000 per year will not make a big dent in the school. But it takes on value far beyond it size.

You can see this clearly at Dorchester High School. When the idea of putting together an effort to restructure Dorchester first occurred to me, I realized that we did not have the expertise, manpower or financial resources for such a massive initiative. Strategic partnerships were a logical way to bring in additional expertise and manpower at a relatively low cost. Our financial contribution would be the first step in the process and we would need to make this an amount large enough to allow us to "buy" an adequate amount of leverage. This leverage would allow us to increase our rate of return on our investment, similar to what is done in institutional financing all over the world.

The first thing we needed was a partner that was a large, well-respected university that we could work with and that understood urban education. There was only one logical choice—University of Massachusetts at Boston. What I envisioned was access to the Graduate School of Education's faculty—and eventual involvement by other members of the University. What I did not anticipate was the decision to use Dorchester as a professional development site for the Graduate School of Education which further enhanced the amount of leverage the partnership with the University brought to the table.

We have used the same leveraging strategies in each of the schools in which we are involved. We have used our $1 million donation to facilitate the involvement of individuals and institutions who contribute services whose value far exceeds any compensation they receive from the grants.

The tactics I've just described are not much different than what is used in the for-profit community on a routine basis. We simply adjusted them to fit the entity we are now trying to serve. What has transpired, however, that I did not anticipate and is, I think, different from what is typically seen in corporate America is the benefit each organization has seen from the leveraging effect of these efforts. The non- profits have all been able to leverage their increased visibility into larger and more grant money from other funding sources. The School Department has some tangible success and models of high school restructuring to point to and the Mayor now has a model of high school reform in his city.

I concluded my conversation with Pam Trefler by asking her to talk about an often-overlooked aspect of reform, the system-level budget process:

I spent about the first 18 years of my career as an investment banker, and a lot of my thinking tends to revolve around numbers and the way they work. When I was in graduate school at Harvard I had an opportunity to take a very hard look at the Boston Public Schools budget. It's actually presented as a line-item budget, which makes it very lengthy and almost impossible to figure out where money is actually spent. I'm not in any way implying that money is being spent in places where it's not supposed to be spent, but I think that the system uses a way of budgeting that makes it almost impossible to figure out how efficiently funds are being used and to figure out how much money goes to central administration and how much ultimately trickles down to the students.

In the analysis that I did, it seemed that a lot of money was going towards things that were nonstandard or non-school-based. I think that the current budget of $600 M plus probably is in the range of being adequate, if not overly generous, but certainly adequate to make some of the changes that we'd like to, if it were just used in a more intelligent, sophisticated, and efficient manner. But we've set up a system that makes it almost impossible to figure out where it really goes.

If I think about the system's budget from the perspective of a Boston high school headmaster, using the kind of "money in/money out" format that's basic to running a business, here are some of the questions that should be starting points for creating a useful, school-based budget:

- Money In. What is my school's overall receipt from the BPS central office, money that comes through the city budget? How is the dollar amount calculated? It's generally in terms of some kind of dollars per student formula, with different allocations for SPED and Bilingual, but what else is included? What funding is the school receiving under Title I and other state and government sources? What are the encumbrances (pre-existing commitments) on this money? Is my school receiving any other type of funding from the BPS, city, state, or federal government? If so, for what and why? How much discretionary money do I have as headmaster and where does it come from?

- Money Out. What charges must the school pay back to the BPS, charges that are assessed by central office and over which the school has no control? What are those charges for? I would expect to find heat and lights, transportation, janitorial services, salaries, maintenance, and a host of other things. Undoubtedly there is some overhead for central administration, the trick would be to figure out how much. Then you'd have to think about personnel. What is the school's staffing pattern and how much of it is dictated by state law and union mandates? What expenditures are in the budget that the school has decided upon and what is the purpose of those expenditures? What other expenses are incurred by the school that are paid for either voluntarily or involuntarily and what goods or services do these funds provide? How much money is left for books and supplies? What services does the school actually receive from BPS and how much of some of the services it pay for does it really need?

If the school were able to answer these basic questions, it could put together a budget that looked like a business. Then the school could think about eliminating things it is obligated to pay for but does not want or use, and adding things it would rather have. Having this financial autonomy would begin to make a reality out of reform slogans like school-based decision making and site-based management, whereas under the current process they're mostly unreal.

## CONCLUSIONS ABOUT CULTURE AND REFORM

In this chapter I argued for the importance of cultural analyses to our understanding of urban reform, and explored three types of cultural influence on schools: ethnic and race-based influence, the demands of "school culture," and the effects of a system-level "culture of reform." I used the analogy of the train station and train wrecks to describe the ways these three cultures can interact, ignore, or collide with each other at the school level.

I began by arguing that race is a cultural, not a biological phenomenon. This is important because it places racial attitudes and behaviors in the realm of mutable cultural realities rather than immutable, genetic ones. I then argued that purportedly race-blind reform policies are not race-blind at all, and in fact do significant harm to urban school students. Standardization is not the same as equity, and when curricula, teaching strategies, and tests treat the dominant cultural style as a "natural" learning style, non-mainstream learners are seriously disadvantaged. As evidence in both Massachusetts and Texas shows, cultural and racial differences do not go away because those in power act like they are not there. When poorly designed and culturally biased high-stakes tests make children disappear from school, the children don't also disappear from society. They are on the streets, in the courts, in emergency rooms, on the unemployment line, at drug treatment centers, in low-wage, dead-end jobs.

Fortunately, we are beginning to better understand the part cultural difference plays in student achievement and to develop innovative strategies and concepts for addressing it. Unfortunately, most of this knowledge has been ruled out of bounds by current reform policies. If urban reform is to reach the next stage, we must find ways to marry the current emphasis on higher standards and innovation with realistic analyses of cultural difference and successful techniques for reaching a wide range of learners.

In discussing school culture I emphasized the narrow way organizational analysis techniques have been adapted to schooling, causing school departments to issue sets of goals and prescriptive formulas for principals without any corresponding understanding of what the principal's new role under reform actually looks like. This has resulted in a worsening shortage of qualified principals nationwide. Wes Manaday's story largely speaks for itself: a new, energetic principal has been successful, and is leaving the job after four years because of health, political, and burnout factors. Clearly, the implication here is that the principalship as constructed under reform is the kind of job that only sometimes attracts, and even less often holds, the kinds of candidates we need to manage the complex changes that schools are experiencing.

The insider/outsider section continues the theme of corporate influences on reform. Tom Hsu and Pam Trefler are private sector successes with an abiding interest in schooling. Each voices the conviction that it is not the teachers and administrators of urban education who need fixing, but the system-generated culture of reform itself. They point out the futility of mandating systemwide change without also creating the school-level conditions which are prerequisites for lasting change to occur. These include support for teachers in word and deed; the willing involvement of those who are to be changed; an adequate resource base; a positive working relationship between a school's administration and its faculty; and careful, caring implementation that involves school-based personnel, central office staff, and outside agencies in a long-term pursuit of shared goals.

Hsu and Trefler prove that corporate influences and opinions are far from monolithic, that there can be many different readings of what the private sector's lessons for education actually are. Trefler particularly identifies the use of leverage as a powerful concept for reform and calls for school departments to follow the private sector in developing simplified, useful models of budgeting to replace the current Byzantine arrangements.

In sum, reform is more complicated than many people think. If the factory model from the start of the twentieth century isn't appropriate for schooling in the twenty-first, neither is the corporate model from the twentieth century's end. As Fullan puts it, "The old way of managing change, appropriate in more stable times, does not work anymore."[87]

Private sector models don't transfer easily to education, and the corporate culture should be just one of many sources, not the definitive source, from which we draw ideas to make schools better. If we must look to business, we should forego the current uncritical embrace of "pop" management strategies and look at the whole range of lessons business teaches, some of which contradict each other. In particular, we can learn about accountability for middle and upper management.

In education as well as business, blaming the workers (teachers and principals) and the clients (students and parents) for every failure is not a viable long-term strategy for success. Good budget management in education means good management of people, because most of the budget is in personnel. A school system where much of the teaching staff is demoralized and principals come and go like temp workers is a school system where the budget is being mismanaged, and that is not a failure that can be laid at the door of teachers and principals.

At bottom, the use of corporate strategies may arise from the same impulses that leads school systems to turn to exemplary programs. Top leadership doesn't want to deal directly with racial and cultural differences because of fears the system will go out of control—a not unreasonable fear in light of recent educational history. The public and the school committee want a panacea, a quick fix to justify increased investment of tax dollars and effort. So the school department turns to outside ideas that will transfer the responsibility to some other group of people, some other system of thinking, than the local one which appears to many to be, in Oakland Superintendent Dennis Chaconas' words, "operating in a permanent crisis mode, unable to move beyond day-to-day survival to address the fundamental structural and cultural issues creating the crises."[88]

Relying on outside experts and programs hinders as well as helps the development of local educators and schools, whose labor and goodwill hold the keys to long-term success. Again turning to Fullan, "you need to develop local capacity for showing an interest in, deciding on and incorporating good ideas into practice. . . . Ultimately going to scale does not mean the spread of *ad hoc* proven programs; it means developing the capacity of the system . . . to manage and integrate the complexity of choices and innovations that abound."[89]

Among these choices and innovations are powerful analytic tools and teaching strategies based in racial and cultural analysis of schools. As nonmainstream students comprise a higher and higher proportion of all public school students, these tools and strategies become more widely applicable.

A mind-set that excludes such strategies from consideration because they are too "dangerous" or "political" cuts itself off from a major source of solutions to the problems of urban education.

If it is to succeed, urban reform must admit that current practices are not "race-blind" and begin to utilize the solutions that racial and cultural analysis has to offer. If such strategies are intelligently integrated with existing professional development and restructuring efforts, we will have taken a major step in addressing the real range of needs of urban students, not just the narrow range of technical pedagogical improvements currently sanctioned by mainstream authors of reform.

## NOTES

1. Sonia Nieto, *Affirming Diversity*, 2nd ed. (New York: Longman, 1996): 110.

2. Theresa Perry, "How Racism Affects African American School Achievement" keynote address, Amherst College, 31 March 2001.

3. Cigdem Kagitcibasi, *Family and Human Development Across Cultures* (Mahwah, NJ: Lawrence Earlbaum, 1996): 9.

4. *The American Heritage Dictionary of the English Language*, 4th ed., s. v. "culture."

5. Robert A. Le Vine, "Properties of Culture: An Ethnographic View," in *Culture Theory: Essays on Mind, Self, and Emotion*, eds. Richard A. Shweder and Robert A. Le Vine (New York: Cambridge University Press, 1984): 67.

6. Ibid.

7. George Kaplan, "Friends, Foes, and Noncombatants: Notes on Public Education's Pressure Groups," *Phi Delta Kappan* 82, 3 (2000): K4.

8. W.E.B. Du Bois, "The Souls of Black Folk," in *The Norton Anthology of African American Literature*, eds. Henry Louis Gates, Jr. and Nellie Y. McKay (New York: W. W. Norton, 1997): 615.

9. *The African Meeting House in Boston: A Source Book* (Boston: Museum of Afro-American History, 1988).

10. Thomas H. O'Connor, *The Boston Irish: A Political History* (Boston: Northeastern University, 1995): 44–8.

11. Thomas H. O'Connor, *Boston Catholics* (Boston: Northeastern University, 1998): 64.

12. O'Connor (1998): 138.

13. Boston Public Schools, "BPS at a Glance/Facts and Figures," <*http://www.boston.k12.ma.us/*> (9 June 2001).

14. United States Commission on Civil Rights, *Desegregating the Boston Public Schools: A Crisis in Civic Responsibility* (Washington, DC: U.S. Government Printing Office, 1975).

15. Ronald F. Formisano, *Boston Against Busing: Race, Class, and Ethnicity in the 1960s and 1970s* (Chapel Hill: University of North Carolina, 1991).

16. Ibid.

17. Dick Lehr and Gerard O'Neill, *Black Mass* (New York: Public Affairs, 2000): 6.

18. J. Anthony Lukas, *Common Ground: A Turbulent Decade in the Lives of Three American Families* (New York: Knopf, 1985).

19. O'Connor (1998): 305.

20. Boston Public Schools, "BPS at a Glance/Facts and Figures," *<http://www.boston.k12.ma.us/>* (9 June 2001).

21. Ibid.

22. Ibid.

23. E. Hornor, ed., *Massachusetts Municipal Profiles, 1996–97* (Palo Alto, CA: Information Publications, 1996).

24. Boston Public Schools, "BPS at a Glance/Facts and Figures," *<http://www.boston.k12.ma.us/>* (27 October 2001).

25. *Boston Public Schools Demographic Profile* (Boston: Boston School Department, 1997).

26. *Community Needs Profile* (Boston: Massachusetts Family Literacy Consortium, 1996).

27. *Demographic Profile*, 2.

28. Boston Public Schools, "BPS at a Glance/Facts and Figures," *<http://www.boston.k12.ma.us/>* (9 June 2001).

29. Boston Public Schools, Department of Bilingual Education, June 2001.

30. Boston Public Schools, "BPS at a Glance/Facts and Figures," *<http://www.boston.k12.ma.us/>* (28 October 2001).

31. Ibid.

32. Thomas Payzant, "A Letter from Superintendent Thomas Payzant," *Focus*, Vol. II, School Year 1999–2000, 1.

33. Boston Public Schools web site, *<http://www.boston.k12.ma.us/>* (9 June 2001).

34. Ibid.

35. R. Duran, "Term of Payzant Pact Protested," *Boston Globe*, 26 June 2001, B5.

36. Joan Vennochi, "Boston Is Nickel and Diming Students on Books, Supplies," *Boston Globe*, 26 June 2001, A15.

37. John U. Ogbu and Maria Eugenia Matute-Bianchi, "Understanding Sociocultural Factors: Knowledge, Identity, and School Adjustment," in *Beyond Language: Social and Cultural Factors in Schooling Language Minority Students* (Los Angeles: California State University, 1986): 73.

38. Shirley Brice Heath, "Sociocultural Contexts of Language Development," in *Beyond Language: Social and Cultural Factors in Schooling Language Minority Students* (Los Angeles: California State University, 1986): 144.

39. Boston Public Schools, "Policies and Priorities to Support Student Achievement," *<http://www.boston.k12.ma.us/>* (28 October 2001).

40. "Why are Latino students failing the MCAS?" *For the Record. . . .* Newsletter of the Ph.D. Program in Public Policy at the University of Massachusetts at Boston (spring 2001): 1.

41. Susan Goldberger, "Erasable Fallacies of Education 'Reform': MCAS is Founded on Misconceptions about What Makes a Successful Student," *Boston Globe*, 9 July 2000, F3.

42. Ed Hayward, "MCAS Words Spark Furor," *Boston Herald*, 23 May 2001, 1.

43. Stephen P. Klein, Laura S. Hamilton, Daniel F. McCaffrey, Brian M. Stecher, "What Do Test Scores in Texas Tell Us?" *Education Policy Analysis Archives* 8, 49 (2000).

44. Walt Haney, "The Myth of the Texas Miracle in Education," *Education Policy Analysis Archives* 8, 41 (2000).

45. Steve Olson, "The Genetic Archaeology of Race," *The Atlantic Monthly* 287, 4 (2001).

46. "Genetically Speaking, Race Doesn't Exist in Humans, Researcher Says," *Science Daily*, <http://www.sciencedaily.com/releases/1998/10/981008051724.htm> (9 October 1998); Alan R. Templeton, "Human Races: A Genetic and Evolutionary Perspective," *American Anthropologist* 100, 3 (1998): 632–50.

47. "Genetically Speaking," 1998.

48. Carolyn Shaw Bell, "As Rules Change, So Do Counts, " *Boston Globe,* 26 June 2001, D4.

49. Gerald M. Oppenheimer, "Paradigm Lost: Race, Ethnicity, and the Search for a New Population Taxonomy," *American Journal of Public Health* 91 (2001): 1049.

50. Ibid.

51. Peter J. Gomes, *The Good Book: Reading the Bible with Mind and Heart* (New York: William Morrow, 1966): 84.

52. Brent Staples, "Searching for Graves—and Justice—in Tulsa," *New York Times,* 20 March 1999, A14.

53. Edwidge Danticat, "AHA!," in *Becoming American: Personal Essays by First Generation Immigrant Women,* ed. Meri Nana-Ama Danquah (New York: Hyperion, 2001): 39.

54. Veronica Chambers, "Secret Latina at Large," in *Becoming American: Personal Essays by First Generation Immigrant Women,* ed. Meri Nana-Ama Danquah (New York: Hyperion, 2001): 21.

55. Marta I. Cruz-Janzen, *Madre Patria (Mother Nation): Latino Identity and Reflections of Blackness,* Occasional Paper No. 47, William Monroe Trotter Institute (Boston: University of Massachusetts Boston, 2001): 2.

56. See, for example, Marisol de la Cadena, "Reconstructing Race: Racism, Culture, and *Mestizaje* in Latin America"; Norman Whitten and Rachel Carr, "Contesting the Images of Oppression: Indigenous Views of Blackness in the Americas," in *NACLA Report on the Americas* XXXIV, 6 (2001).

57. Cruz-Janzen, 9.

58. Carol Miller, "No Longer 'Too White': Using Multicultural Literature to Promote Academic Achievement and Cultural Understanding," in *Cityscapes: Eight Views from the Urban Classroom,* eds. Art Peterson, Joe Check, Miriam Ylvisaker (Berkeley: National Writing Project, 1996).

59. Eileen Shakespear, "What I'd Tell a White Gal: What My Black Male Students Taught Me About Race and Schooling," in Sarah Warshauer Freedman, Elizabeth Radin Simons, Julie Shalhope Kalnin, Alex Casareno, and the M-CLASS teams, *Inside City Schools: Investigating Literacy in Multicultural Classrooms* (New York: Teachers College Press, 1999): 77–89.

60. Lisa Delpit, *Other People's Children: Cultural Conflict in the Classroom* (New York: The New Press, 1995); Gloria Ladson-Billings, *The Dreamkeepers: Successful Teachers of African American Children* (San Francisco: Jossey-Bass, 1994);

Jim Cummins, *Negotiating Identities: Education for Empowerment in a Diverse Society* (Ontario, CA: California Association for Bilingual Education, 1996); Sonia Nieto, *Affirming Diversity: The Sociopolitical Context of Multicultural Education* (New York: Longman, 1992).

61. Mary Cazabon, *The Use of Students' Self-reporting in the Evaluation of the Amigos Two-way Language Immersion Program* (Ed. D. diss, University of Massachusetts Boston, 2000); Mary Cazabon, E. Nicoladis, & Wallace E. Lambert, *Becoming Bilingual in the Amigos Two-way Immersion Program* (Santa Cruz, CA: National Center for Research on Cultural Diversity and Second Language Acquisition, 1998); Mary Cazabon, Wallace Lambert, & G. Hall, *Two-way Bilingual Education: A Progress Report on the Amigos Program* (Santa Cruz, CA: National Center for Research on Cultural Diversity and Second Language Acquisition, 1993).

62. Cazabon (2000), 150.

63. Carroll Blake, "Transformation of Teachers' Thinking in Suburban Schools through Antiracism Education" (Ed. D. diss., University of Massachusetts Boston, 2001); Paula Martin, "The Effect of Antiracism Education on Racial Identity Development and White Privilege Awareness in White Teachers" (Ed. D. diss., University of Massachusetts Boston, 2001).

64. Robert C. Johnston and Debra Viadero, "Unmet Promise: Raising Minority Achievement," *Education Week*, 15 (March 2000): 1.

65. James Gee, "What is Literacy," in *Rewriting Literacy: Culture and the Discourse of the Other*, eds. Candace Mitchell and Kathleen Weiler (Westport: Bergin and Garvey, 1994).

66. Lisa Delpit, "The Politics of Teaching Literate Discourse, in *Other People's Children* (New York: The New Press, 1995).

67. Lilia I. Bartolomé, *The Misteaching of Academic Discourses: The Politics of Language in the Classroom* (Boulder: Westview Press, 1998).

68. Theresa Perry, *Toward a Theory of African American School Achievement* (Boston: Wheelock College, 1993).

69. Robert Evans, "The Culture of Resistance," *The Jossey-Bass Reader on School Reform* (San Francisco: Jossey-Bass, 2001): 511.

70. Educational Resources Information Clearinghouse (ERIC) Thesaurus, s. v. "school culture."

71. Seymour Sarason, *The Culture of the School and the Problem of Change* (Boston: Allyn and Bacon, 1971).

72. Sarason, 195–210.

73. Thomas. J. Sergiovanni, *The Principalship: A Reflective Practice Perspective*, 3rd edition (Boston: Allyn and Bacon, 1995): 88.

74. Peter Senge, *The Fifth Discipline: The Art and Practice of the Learning Organization* (New York: Doubleday, 1994).

75. Peter Senge, Nelda Cambron-McCabe, Timothy Lucas, Bryan Smith, Janis Dutton, Art Kleiner, *Schools That Learn: A Fifth Discipline Fieldbook for Educators, Parents, and Everyone Who Cares about Education* (New York: Doubleday, 2000).

76. James Champy, *Reengineering Management* (New York: Harper, 1995).

77. Matthew Brelis, "I've Got the Trust." *Boston Sunday Globe*, 3 June 2001, E1, E5.

78. Henry Mintzberg, "The Manager's Job: Folklore and Fact," *Harvard Busi-*

*ness Review*, reprint 90210 (Cambridge: Harvard Business School, 1990): 3.

79. Mintzberg, 6–7.

80. Bradley S. Portin, "Compounding Roles: A Study of Washington's Principals," *International Journal of Educational Research* 29 (1998): 335–46.

81. Gerald N. Tirozzi, "The Artistry of Leadership: The Evolving Role of the Secondary School Principal," *Phi Delta Kappan* 82 (2001): 434–39.

82. Vincent L. Ferrandino, "Challenges for 21st-century Elementary School Principals," *Phi Delta Kappan* 82 (2001): 440–42.

83. Vision and mission, instructional focus, looking at student work, alignment of resources with budget, community outreach, professional development for staff and principal.

84. Barbara Cervone and Joseph P. McDonald, *Preliminary Reflections on the Annenberg Challenge* (Annenberg Challenge: Brown University, 1999).

85. Jonathan Lerner, "Philanthropy Made Modern," *Hemispheres* (November 1999): 48–52.

86. Christine Letts, William Ryan, and Allen Grossman, "Virtuous Capital: What Foundations Can Learn from Venture Capitalists," *Harvard Business Review* 75, 2 (1997): 36–44.

87. Michael Fullan, *Change Forces: The Sequel* (Philadelphia: Falmer Press, 1999): 3.

88. Dennis Chaconas, "Superintendent's Report," Oakland, CA Board of Education Meeting, January 10, 2001.

89. Fullan (1999): 74.

# Selected Bibliography

Ackerman, Richard, Patricia Maslin-Ostrowski, and Charles Christensen. "Case Stories: Telling Tales About School." *Educational Leadership* 53, no. 6 (1996): 21–23.

Anderson, Gary L. "Toward Authentic Participation: Deconstructing the Discourses of Participatory Reforms in Education." *American Educational Research Journal* 35 (1998): 571–603.

Applebee, Arthur. *Contexts for Learning to Write: Studies of Secondary School Instruction.* Norwood, NJ: Ablex Publishing, 1984.

Batton, Barbara and Linda Vereline. *Literacy Practices at C. E. S. 28 and C. J. H. S. 117.* New York: Institute for Literacy Studies, 1997.

Berliner, David and Bruce Biddle. *The Manufactured Crisis: Myths, Fraud, and the Attack on America's Public Schools.* Reading, MA: Addison-Wesley, 1995.

Carini, Patricia F. *Observation and Description: An Alternative Methodology for the Investigation of Human Phenomena.* Grand Forks, ND: University of North Dakota Press, 1975.

Calhoun, Emily F. *How to Use Action Research in the Self-renewing School.* Alexandria, VA: Association for Supervision and Curriculum Development, 1994.

Check, Joe. (1997) "Teacher Research as Powerful Professional Development." *The Harvard Education Letter* XIII, no. 3 (1997): 6–8.

Chenoweth Tom. "Emerging National Models of Schooling for At-risk Students." *International Journal of Educational Reform* 1, no. 3 (1992): 255–69.

Collier, Virginia P. "Age and Rate of Acquisition of Second Language for Academic Purposes." *TESOL Quarterly 21,* (1987): 617–41.

Cremin, Lawrence A. *Popular Education and Its Discontents,* New York: Harper and Row, 1990.

Cummins, Jim. *Negotiating Identities: Education for Empowerment in a Diverse Society.* Ontario, CA: California Association for Bilingual Education, 1996.

Elmore, Richard. "Getting to Scale with Good Educational Practice." *Harvard Educational Review* 66, no. 1 (1996): 1–26

Elmore, Richard and Milbrey McLaughlin. *Steady Work: Policy, Practice, and the Reform of American Education.* Santa Monica: Rand, 1988.

Fullan, Michael. "Turning Systemic Thinking on Its Head." *Phi Delta Kappan* 77, no. 6 (1996): 420–23.

Graham, Patricia A. "Battleships and Schools." *Daedalus* 124, no. 4 (1995): 43–46.

Haney, Walt. "The Myth of the Texas Miracle in Education." *Education Policy Analysis Archives* 8, no. 41 (2000).

Hoffman, James. "When Bad Things Happen to Good Ideas in Literacy Education: Professional Dilemmas, Personal Decisions, and Political Traps." *The Reading Teacher* 52, no. 2 (1998): 102–11.

McDonald, Joseph P. *Redesigning School: Lessons for the 21st Century.* San Francisco: Jossey-Bass, 1996.

McEntee, Grace Hall. "Diving with Whales: Five Reasons for Practitioners to Write for Publication." *The Quarterly of the National Writing Project* 20, no. 4 (1998): 21–26.

McLaughlin, Milbrey. "The Rand Change Agent Study Revisited: Macro Perspectives and Micro Realities." *Educational Researcher* 19, no. 9 (1990): 11–16.

Miller, Edward. "Idealists and Cynics: The Micropolitics of Systemic School Reform." *The Harvard Education Letter* XII, no. 4 (1996): 1–3.

Muncey, Donna and Patrick McQuillan. "Preliminary Findings from a Five-year Study of the Coalition of Essential Schools." *Phi Delta Kappan* 74 (1993): 486–89.

National Commission on Excellence in Education. *A Nation at Risk: the Imperatives for Educational Reform.* Washington, DC: U.S. Department of Education, 1983.

O'Connor, Thomas H. *Boston Catholics.* Boston: Northeastern University, 1998.

O'Connor, Thomas H. *The Boston Irish: A Political History.* Boston: Northeastern University, 1995.

Oppenheimer, Gerald M. "Paradigm Lost: Race, Ethnicity, and the Search for a New Population Taxonomy." *American Journal of Public Health* 91 (2001): 1049–52.

Perry, Theresa. *Toward a Theory of African American School Achievement.* Boston: Wheelock College, 1993.

Sarason, Seymour. *The Culture of the School and the Problem of Change.* Boston: Allyn and Bacon, 1971.

Senge, Peter. *The Fifth Discipline: The Art and Practice of the Learning Organization.* New York: Doubleday, 1994.

Sergiovanni, Thomas. J. *The Principalship: A Reflective Practice Perspective*, 3rd edition. Boston: Allyn and Bacon, 1995.

# Index

**About the Author**

JOSEPH W. CHECK is Associate Professor of Educational Leadership,
University of Massachusetts, Boston.